IN A DIFFER

CRICKET'S
NORTH – SOUTH
DIVIDE

JIM CARNEGIE

IN A DIFFERENT LEAGUE

CRICKET'S
NORTH – SOUTH
DIVIDE

Matador
5 Weir Road
Kibworth Beauchamp
Leicester LE8 0LQ, UK
Tel: (+44) 116 279 2299
Fax: (+44) 116 279 2277
Email: books@troubador.co.uk
Web: www.troubador.co.uk/matador

ISBN 978 1848761 636

British Library Cataloguing in Publication Data.
A catalogue record for this book is available from the British Library.

Typeset in 11pt Palatino by Troubador Publishing Ltd, Leicester, UK
Printed and bound in Great Britain by TJ International Ltd, Padstow, Cornwall

Matador is an imprint of Troubador Publishing Ltd

To my long suffering wife, Marg:
Sorry, my love, but I will retire one day.

INTRODUCTION

The north-south divide is based on the perception that southerners are largely privileged pansies while northerners are deprived and hard-nosed. If, therefore, one had to guess where the first piped water supply ran from in 1230, most would rightly plump for Paddington to Westminster rather than Bury to Burnley, leaving Lancastrians to wash in the Manchester Ship Canal. Londoners have Kensington Gardens to sunbathe in. Mancunians can get wet strolling around Boggart Hole Clough.

Cricket is no different. The first practice nets in 1839 weren't to be found in Salford but in Eton. The setting for the first boundaries in 1866 overlooked the game between Batley and Ramsbottom for Eton versus Harrow. The Paupers School in Oldham missed out on the first recorded team photo. Eton didn't. The first recorded cricket club, founded in 1744, curiously wasn't Moss Side CC but London CC, 230 miles to the south. Surprise, surprise, the first inter-school match involved Eton and Westminster, presumably so that the players could have a shower from the now 566 year old piped water supply which was still on its way to Wakefield.

The north was even beaten to the punch regarding first use of blazers as sports wear in 1838. This time, however, it wasn't by any silver-spooned public school kids but, yes, you've guessed it, the Mexican Cricket Union. (Mexico, of course, borders the southern United States.)

Nevertheless, soft southern batsmen were, by now, protected by pads introduced by Oxford's H.Daubeney whose father certainly wasn't a coal miner from Barnsley.Their wicket-keepers even had the luxury of gloves to keep their hands soft and fluffy from 1848, the same year northerners were more concerned with the introduction of the circular cork life belt for saving lives in the North Sea.

Although London housed the first recorded club, cricket must have been so civilised and none too competitive in and around the capital. Indeed, even though the rules weren't written until 1744, this did not prevent Middlesex and Kent playing the first 'official' match 25 years beforehand.

No rules presumably provided much scope for spontaneity:

'How many balls left in the over, umpire?'

'As many as you feel like bowling.'

'Is he out?'

'How should I know? Let's have a vote on it.'

It took the nowse of Yorkshiremen to sort out the inaugural organised cup competition in 1883. Heckmondwicke CC, none of whose members were Old (or Young) Etonians, lifted the trophy administered by the Heavy Woollen District League. I doubt if the league had a knitting section and it definitely wasn't twinned with the Windsor and District League.

Southern clubs had obviously faffed about playing friendlies for 139 years and encouraged Page Bros. of Surrey to put poncey rubber grips on bats in 1880. The north, by contrast, had introduced silverware to fight over and had prompted Hamlet Nicholson of Rochdale to patent more manly items by way of the first composition ball. Severe bruising was now far more likely.

In keeping with its dour image, even runs were harder to come by up north in the 18ᵗʰ and 19ᵗʰ centuries. If you wanted to boost you average, a trip down to Norfolk was a must. W.Ward was glad he did in 1820. He wielded his 4lb.2oz.bat to good effect there to make the first recorded double hundred and set the tone for the next 180 years. The consensus amongst pundits remains that bowlers in East Anglia are as venomous as grass snakes; a ton in Norwich equates to about 15 in Wigan.

But these are merely snippets and only a truly 'displaced' veteran can genuinely make an unbiased judgement on cricket's north-south divide. That narrows it down to two. Edward Barratt was professional for Lonsight in 1870, a club I played against in the Lancashire and Cheshire League a few years later. He was born in Stockton-on-Tees but somehow got chosen to represent the South against the North. I can only assume the selectors thought he was from Stockwell. This displacement didn't hold him back. His 10 for 43 for the Players versus Australia in 1878 earned him £5 and the match ball.

Born and raised in London, playing cricket up to the age of 23 solely in the south-east, I was as southern as the majority of Manchester United supporters. Moving up to Leeds to attend Teacher Training College and staying on to do missionary work there for six years called this into question. I began to understand the rules of rugby league and suddenly realised that the M1 extends beyond Hertfordshire.

Coming to Manchester in 1976 and staying put means I have spent over 60% of my life nearer 'Bratfud' than 'Bracknawl.' As a result, nowadays I support Lancashire as well as Middlesex. (Better safe than Surrey.) This has caused me to reflect on whether or not A.Crook was an appropriate name for Lightning's Australian all-rounder. Less obviously, was it worth the Crusaders signing Ed Smith when they already had Ed Joyce? I believe it was. Everyone knows that two Eds are better than one.

Southern or northern? I say 'aye' as well as 'yeah.' I've played in Barrow-in-Furness (a cul-de-sac off the M6) and in Weston-super-Mare. (The 'super' remains a mystery to me.) I now drink dark mild instead of Watney's Red Barrel but prefer jellied eels to black pudding (just). My accent is so screwed up that, to my chagrin, I am often mistaken for a bloody Aussie. Like the Young Cricketer of the Year 2005 who answers to Sam Northeast, despite being born in Kent, I am 'displaced.'

Having played competitively for 50 years and still counting (particularly on the sixth ball of the over), I've tasted the relative highs and absolute lows of timed club cricket in the south and league cricket in the north. They are as different as the Waugh twins, Steve and Evelyn. I couldn't say in which part of the country the standard is, or was, higher. The divide is definitely not as big as that of the £1 million homes. In 2004, there were 124 of them in the north-west and Yorkshire. In the south-east there were 3616. Both halves first met in 1836 and it henceforth came to be regarded as 'the greatest match of the season.' In 1937 the two clashed to celebrate the MCC's 150th anniversary. I wasn't selected for either side. The south won by six wickets, probably because they could afford better bats with grips and had practised in Eton's nets.

In a roundabout way, I have Baden Powell to thank for assisting me in being able to make this comparison. As a nine year old cub, I was told to run round a freezing church hall 'making a noise like a motorbike.' My friends, Harley and Davidson, took to it like ducks to water. I quickly ran out of petrol, only to be informed that our next entertaining activity involved tying knots in string while hopping in a straight line.

Not wishing to indulge in an early form of tests for drunk drivers, I decided to curtail wiggling my woggle. My dybbing and dobbing days were over.

In its place I would take up rock climbing, gymnastics or cricket. As I've always been scared of heights and believed crampons to be pieces of bread found in posh soup, rock climbing looked like a non-starter. This was confirmed when Yellow Pages indicated a distinct lack of qualified Sherpas in the Kilburn area. Being as stiff as a corpse, the only roll I could manage was a ham one. Lords was only 10 minutes away on the 159 bus. The Alps weren't. Cricket it was and has been ever since.

Why haven't I stopped? Quite simply, it's better than going shopping with the wife. Some athletes peak young; Joy Foster represented her country at table tennis aged eight. Even though I started playing cricket so long ago that I used those batting gloves with rubber pimples now on show in the Museum of Ancient History, I still live in hope. A friend, 'Hard Nut' – his initials are GBH - had to wait until he was 52 before scoring his first ton.

What's more, sad as it sounds, I remain convinced that a well-timed shot through the covers is more pleasurable than a bad jump. (Is that what is meant by sex drive?) I believe Harold Pinter was of similar persuasion, although I expect he expressed his feelings far more eloquently.

Now that I have set out my 'displaced' and 'veteran' credentials, I feel qualified to present a balanced view of the north-south divide. The characters I have met, the tales I've heard and the contrasting approach to events on and off the field make it more like a gaping chasm, as the forthcoming pages will show.

This isn't to say that nothing is similar. Most club cricketers either side of Spaghetti Junction are easy to spot; we've developed long, floppy ears and buck teeth due to the amount of bloody salad we get for tea on match days. Salad is not food. Salad comes with the food. We also break out in an allergic rash at the mere sight of angel cake or swiss roll for the same reason.

Anyone fully involved in the game will have heard an abundance of stories concerning professional cricketers. Some are true. Some are embellished. Some are funny. Plenty do the rounds. The same tale can be attributed to Ian Botham in the West Country, to Fred Trueman in Yorkshire, to Brian Statham in Lancashire, to Mike Gatting in the Home Counties or to Mel Whittle in Crompton. ('Who's Ian Botham?' I hear you ask.)

Before starting with my own yarns, I'll kick off with this trio of comments attributed to a recently retired, ex-public school England International. A former army officer from a well-heeled family (yes, he's a southerner), this relative of a famous writer was asked, as is the custom, by a customs officer:

'Did you pack this case yourself, sir?'

'God forbid!' he replied. Then, upon arriving in Australia, he was asked if he had a criminal record. This time he quipped: 'Oh, I didn't know you still needed one to get in this country.' Finally, when pinned against the wall by an aggrieved team-mate, our ex-paratrooper came out with: 'Oh, fisticuffs. I've never tried it but I'll give it a go!'

There always has been, and always will be, humour to be found wherever this great game is played. In my humble attempts to give credence to this, my intention is to throw up a few stories of my own. Anything attributed to anyone in this book is as near verbatim (southern for a likely story) as an ageing cricketer with fading senses can put it (making me ideal umpire material). I must, however, confess that I do subscribe to the Einstein (Albert, not Frank) school of thought which maintains:

'If the facts don't fit the theory, change the facts.'

My wife thinks I'm dateless and some dates may be as inaccurate as my throwing, which, pinching a David Pleastism, has always been 'as straight as a nut.' Where surnames have been omitted it is solely for self-protection. After all, a smack on the nose can lead to a loss of blood. As Christopher Martin-Jenkins stated:

'There is nothing as imprecise as a cricketer's memory.'

At least, I think it was him. I'd alter it so that it reads:

'There is nothing as imprecise as a cricketer's batting average.'

It's similar to a fisherman exaggerating the size of the sprat he has landed in an attempt to convince sceptics (everyone else), that sitting around endlessly cultivating rheumatoid arthritis is enjoyable. Instead of turning three inches into three feet (wishful thinking), batsmen tend to turn 20.01 into 'nearly 30.'

I confess to being intrigued by nicknames. My favourites amongst county players are 'Picca' for Graham Dilley, 'January' for David Sales and 'Human' for Paul Romains. My constant use of them is again meant to protect my physical well being. If anyone feels I've taken a cheap shot at them, it will come as no surprise to those who know me well. I've always been cheap. Please note, I no longer live where you think I do.

My obsession for tinkering with names is also displayed via the 'food for thought' sections at the end of each chapter. I find this to be an almost justifiable means of putting off doing household chores. Why get a bad back painting skirting boards when you can considerer such posers as did Roger Twose of Warwickshire ever run threes or is county colleague Jonathan Trott interested in quick singles? Instead of wrenching your shoulders out of their sockets scraping mould off the bathroom ceiling, why not consider how well did England's Bob Barber cut, who is West Indian Michael Holding and is South African Clive Rice a pudding?

He isn't. When Nottinghamshire were dismissed by Kent for 143 in 1981, Clive made 105 not out. Did this help him to settle in his adopted county or did the fact that the nearest thing to a jungle being Sherwood Forest make him feel as displaced as a Londoner trespassing in Leeds and Manchester without a phrase book or voice coach?

Chapter 1

FROM LONDON TO LANCASHIRE VIA LEEDS

How can a 'cockney' make a balanced assessment on differences between club cricket in Ascot and Rotherham? On the face of it, it's as likely as Geraint Jones becoming the next Alan Knott. My case rests on the fact that, in terms of time spent playing 'God's own game,' I now regard myself as a northerner. I've played in the Bradford League for Lidget Green, in the Central Lancashire League for Middleton, and in the Lancashire County League (formerly the Lancashire and Cheshire League) for Thornham, for 35 years. (20 years longer than I swanned around playing in the bottom half of the country.) The trouble is, whenever I get hit on a fleshy bit I still pronounce 'bastard' with an r in the middle. As a Mancunian friend stated upon learning I was a Londoner:

'Oh, I didn't realise you were from down there. I just thought you were posh.' (For posh, read 'displaced.')

In the introduction, I intimated that southerners are privileged. They certainly are when it comes to the weather. Mancunians and Tykes are disadvantaged on two counts. As well as being hampered by having to turn out in flippers and overcoats, they also have to endure those annoyingly blinkered forecasts from the BBC. Since 1878, a Fish called Michael and Jack Charlton's niece have kidded the nation that it would be 'fine' on Saturday. What they really mean is only bad light might stop play at Lords or the Oval. Never mind that every game in Yorkshire, Lancashire, Cumbria, Northumberland and Durham would be washed out without a ball being bowled.

Nowadays, to get an inkling of when it will chuck it down, I'm reduced to sneaking downstairs early, well, earlyish, on a Saturday morning to phone the 0898 number for the local forecast. It has to be done clandestinely to avoid getting both barrels from the trouble and strife:

'Why do you need to know when it's going to rain? It makes no difference. If it's going to rain, it's going to rain. It won't change anything.'

What she doesn't appreciate is our need for pre-match preparation time. Should we take our wellies to mop up in, sun cream or thermals? Will it be a four sweater day, or just the usual three? If the game is curtailed or doesn't even start, we'll need extra beer money and a supply of 50ps for the pool table. We need to know.

It's like the Spanish Inquisition when the telephone bill arrives. My 'better half' – I'm an ordinary 6ft2, she's a classy 3ft1 – scrutinises the bill more closely than I study Test scorecards or the juicy bits in the Sunday Sport. When first interrogated about the plethora of 'dodgy numbers,' the best I could come up with was that if it wasn't her, it must have been our teenage son phoning a sex chat line. Sorry son. Your mother is disappointed in you. You'll go blind.

My impression is that it does rain more in Blackburn than in Blackheath. It doesn't, however, seem to matter half as much. A water-logged pitch in Wandsworth or Ashford is no more than a green top in Unsworth or Ashton. Up here, everyone merely mops up and gets on with it.

It definitely used to be the case with my two London clubs, the Old Quintinians at Chiswick and Evershed at Boston Manor, that even a dark cloud on the morning of a game meant 'rained off.' In 1966, it was so cloudy that of the 23 proposed Sunday fixtures, the Old Qs played only 11. In 1968 we had as many as 16 games cancelled. The use of saw dust may well have been authorised from 1788 but it remained classified information in the capital for nearly 200 years.

As such, I had virtually no experience of playing on soft wickets until I went into the Bradford League in 1974. To make up for it, in that season I experienced nothing else. In both white and red rose country, it's rare to find a featherbed outside of Rumbelow's.

I recall asking Dukinfield's (even the name conjures up wetness) opening bowler, the round-headed 'Cromwell,' how their square plays when it's hard:

'I've no idea. I've only played here 12 years,' he duly confessed in a cavalier manner.

It was 1973 when I last played in the metropolis. At that time, league cricket there was the exception rather than the rule. The vast majority of club games were timed, 'friendly' fixtures - two concepts totally alien to cricketers who battle under the Roses banner. On either side of the Pennines a friendly fixture qualifies as an oxymoron. It's on a par with a 'cultured Australian,' a 'good humoured fast bowler' or a 'generous Yorkshireman.' Come to think of it, I can recall being called a 'poxey moron' by a Tyke opening bowler at Saltaire after I'd deftly snicked him through the slips. I soon learnt that there is no point in playing in any fashion other than as if your life depends once you've got as far north as Derbyshire.

Our games in the south started at 2.30 and finished at 7.30, although it was often an early finish with the Old Qs. Tea could last anything from 30 to 50 minutes. Proceedings were unrushed and civil. Since neither they nor Evershed were in leagues, the annual fixture list had to be earned. This was done by being up to scratch on and off the field. Evershed had no problem. Boston Manor was a beautiful ground with excellent facilities. It had a superb playing area, relatively decent beer (for London), hot showers, two big sight screens, enough capable cricketers to field three XIs and sufficient funds to provide a new ball for every game.

Not so with the Old Boys. The ground was communal. The wickets were good but were wasted on us. The beer was like the showers – weak and tepid. We all thought a sight screen was something you went to an optician for. The nearest thing we came to having one was whenever a white car drove past the ground. We had just the one team, just. Occasionally, we had as many as 11 players. A victory was as likely as giving birth to quadruplets (600,000-1). Our ineptitude was written in the stars. Our home ground was in Chiswick, the venue for the only game of cricket which reputedly ended 0-0. As traditionalists, we merely did our best not to break with convention each time we batted.

Being Old Boys, and everybody was either very old or very young, Chelsea we were not. We had enough cash to toss up with but the balls weren't even the right shape, never mind new. The same one was used so many times that I've squeezed harder marshmallows. Professionals complain about balls going soft after 30 overs. Try using the same one for 30 games.

'Migraine' (more of him later) informed us that the Essex bowlers struggled as Yorkshire's Holmes and Sutcliffe put on 555 for the first wicket in 1932. They didn't know they were born. We could go for weeks without getting anyone out. Our sole claim to fame was that our home ground was spitting distance from the country's oldest brewery. This explains why the beer after games tasted as though it had been standing for 250 years.

Whereas Evershed sought to win each game, the Old Qs main objective was to turn up more or less on time, at the right place, with at least nine pulses. It was character-forming and infinitely better than tying knots or pretending to be a 750cc Norton.

As Churchill (not the dog) rightly stated:

'Success is going from failure to failure without losing enthusiasm.'

New Zealand went 27 years without winning a Test. Derbyshire lost every game in 1920. Northants didn't win a single county game for four years. The Old Quintinians were similarly enthusiastic.

Turn up we did. Win we rarely did, but unlike Mahasashtra's opponents, Kathiawar, in India in 1948, we never gave up. They deprived B.Nimballkar of a possible world record score (nine short of Bradman's 452) by refusing to take the field after lunch. It's not clear whether it was due to indigestion or indignation.

Poor performances didn't dampen our ardour even though it did become 'arder and 'arder to get 11 bodies out of either the Senior Citizens Rest Home or the Nursery each week. On one infamous Saturday in 1967 we were reduced to turning out with seven. It gave us the chance to be magnificent. It appeared, on first count, that there were as many as eight of us. This included our very own wrinkly, 'Bob Hopeless,' which meant seven pulses, but eight bodies did mean we could have a 3-3 field. We were then devastated to learn that our star man,

'Copperbottom' (real name Nicholas) had voted with his feet.

The opposition, Melrose, were far less choosey. They arrived with a full compliment, plus their own crowd. They looked on disdainfully as our twelfth hour deserter informed our hapless, or more precisely, hopeless, vice-captain Bob that he was like the milk. He was off. There was no point in him telling our skipper, Jack. He was even more ancient than Bob and would have merely pulled up his tartan blanket and gone back to sleep in his deck chair.

'Copperbottom' was leaving us to go and watch Grandstand. (At least he hadn't sold out on us to go to Woolworths.) Acutely aware of our number, his upbeat parting shot was:

'Yul Brynner did it, so can you.'

Consequently, like the glabrous actor and his six mates, we steeled ourselves to do battle against seemingly insurmountable odds. One thing in our favour was that at least we didn't have to put up with having Robert Vaughan on our side.

Before anyone starts thinking I'm building up to one of the great victories of all time, I feel obliged to mention two things. Firstly, this was the Old Qs. Secondly, we had Bob and Jack. Bob was a hindrance. 'Jack of no trades' wasn't even that good. Despite being small, scruffy and liking Weetabix with hot milk, Jack could not keep wicket. He couldn't actually keep anything, but he was our leader ... by default:

'I'll do it if nobody else wants to.'

That was tantamount to a landslide victory.

A pessimist by nature, Jack even looked both ways when crossing a one-way street and was in the RAC as well as the AA.

'You can't be too careful,' exclaimed the man who believed an optimist was someone who tested eyes.

As a cricketer, by his own admission, he was worse than useless. He regularly joked that his surname was completely inappropriate. He was called Handy. The only handy thing about him was that he was one of just three members in the side with a car. Jack was as gifted as fellow southerner, Christopher Biggins. The portly actor took up cricket after having been labelled 'too heavy to be a good gymnast.' His school report indicated that the change was ineffective:

'Quite keen on cricket but no great performer. (3rdXI scorer.)'

On the plus side, Christopher would have been an automatic choice for the Old Qs, while Jack did let anyone borrow his headgear to field in. Bearing in mind his lack of ability, as the negative vibes rubbed off on the wearer, it became a 'handicap' in two senses. This, in turn, was about as many as Jack had remaining of the five he inherited at birth.

This left us, in real terms, with five players, or maybe only three since our opener 'Mars' might as well have been on another planet and Stan Hind had, once again, turned up legless. Yet all was not lost. Spotting 'Copperbottom' riding off into the smog, Melrose elevated our number to nine by giving us 50% of their crowd. They turned out to be our two best players.

Our opponents informed us that they had won the toss and would bat first. (No coin was involved but Jack was none the wiser.) They proceeded to smash our already battered ball all over Chiswick. This was hardly surprising as we were so short of bowlers that even I had to turn my arm over, or more precisely, round. Now, even as a teenager I never had the highest of arm actions. I'd have been far more at home in 1835 when the round arm action was legalised.

Melrose then bowled us out for next to nothing (or it might even have been nothing) and went home. We never saw them again but did try to sign their two spectators on loan deals. Predictably, Sam Allardyce got in first.

We might have fared better if we'd been playing another of our regular opponents. The Diplomatic Service would have sympathised with our plight:

'Don't worry. It could happen to anyone. Grandstand is a most enjoyable programme. We'll lend you our fastest bowler and our best batsman for a nine a-side. Do you want to bowl or bat first? You can bowl with our new ball and our number three can't play spin.'

With one gap to fill in the following year's fixture list, we feared the worst after a game at University Vandals. We had turned up with a young but relatively decent side (11 pulses). The dressing room was, therefore, more crowded than usual. It also hummed considerably before the game. This was not because we were musically-minded. It was rather that eight of us had rushed to the ground 'fresh' from playing Sunday morning football. There had been no time to use 'Lifebouy' and under-arm deodorant was considered to be an iffy item for a sportsman in those days. Better 'whiffy' than 'iffy.' We'd just about had time for a hasty liquid lunch. We were now ready to swap crossbars for cross bats and tackles for tickles.

Unusually, we competed well. 'Zorro,' the flashing blade, a window cleaner, made a painful 40. Painful, not because he often got hit but because it hurt watching him grind out his runs. In no way did he chasten the attack. 'Grant,' our full time student, did. He scythed a quick 30, ignoring any advice proffered in coaching manuals. 'Biro,' a writer, whose real name is Parker – 'Biro' is only his pen name – then took four wickets with some devastating 'bog-roll' bowling. In layman's terms, he picked up all the crap at the end. He was normally as much use as ostrich wings or the Swiss Navy but today was different. Only 'Zorro's' brother, 'Zero,' didn't contribute. He got his customary duck and again proved as effective as a fart in a hurricane.

All that remained to guarantee retaining the fixture was a sociable couple of hours in the bar. This was usually our forte. My one concern was that 'Bungalow' (nothing upstairs) might show us up in such elevated company. Apart from thinking a leg-cutter was a blunt lady-shave, 'Bungalow' firmly believed that Beethoven wrote loud music because he was deaf.

I needn't have worried. 'Bungalow' wasn't staying. He and 'Sri' (cockney rhyming slang) had loads of homework to do. 'Nancy boy,' who wasn't from France but did sleep on a camp bed, also came out:

'I'm not staying. My tea's in the oven.' (This was preferable to it being in the dog.) 'It's shepherd's pie.'

Off he minced. Unfortunately, 'Sri' and 'Nancy' were two of our three car owners on the day. Jack wasn't playing. He'd gone to a First World War veteran's reunion but ended up in Dundee instead of Dunkurque.

Never mind. There were still three of us left to socialise with the opposition:

'What do you want, Borussia?' I asked.

'Borussia' was really called Robin. He had been forced to answer to this nickname because of his fielding. He displayed a total inability to bend his back to stop the ball. Hence, 'glass back' which soon became 'Borussia' from that German outfit, Borussia Munchen Glassback:

'Oh, I'm not staying either. I'm off for a quick dump and then I'm going home to watch Sunday Night at the London Palladium. Norman Wisdom's on.'

Our third and final means of transport was jeopardising our chances by leaving us to watch the man who was to comedy what Derek Pringle was to cricket. What next?

Buses home were as frequent as runs from Glamorgan's Ossie Wheatley. (12 ducks in 13 innings.) This was why I'd been reliant on Robin. The bad-tempered 'Fitz' and I had no choice. We'd have to be ready to go as soon as Robin had finished wiping his bum. Luckily, he must have taken Playboy into the loo with him. We managed to sink a couple of pints with their skipper, 'Digger,' an Australian with a degree in archaeology, before I conjured up a speculative:

'See you next season,' as I spotted Robin – did that make me a twitcher? – looking very smug after his dump.

Prior to setting off in his three wheeler (beggars can't be choosers), we got the response we desired. Despite being 'Vandals,' they didn't kick us into touch. Being one to bear a grudge, I did hope 'Sri' got nought for his homework, 'Nancy's' pie was cold and Norman wasn't funny. At least one of those three was a sure bet.

Every now and again (twice), the Old Qs encountered teams even we weren't bothered about playing again. Although, nowadays, I struggle to remember what I had for breakfast this morning, I can still vividly recall walking out to the middle with the captain of a proper Old Boy's side, despite it being 40 years ago. I had the coin but he was the tosser. Before I had any chance of one-upmanship, this gnome got in first with a masterful:

'I've just been reading about myself in the local rag.'

In hindsight, I wish I'd asked him if he'd been found guilty. Without me being able to think of a suitable put-down, he produced a well-thumbed newspaper cutting. He thrust it under my nose, which is not a difficult since my beak is the same size as Richard Hadlee's. (Big noses run in our family!) As with the billiards player of a byegone age, Henry Lewis, it could double as a cue. The little bighead (was that a battle?) pointed to the section which was heavily underlined in pen. He'd scored 72 in his previous innings and relived every run with me. I couldn't counter. All I'd done was drop another catch and play an innings as exciting as stripping unco-operative wallpaper.

I didn't applaude. I was far more concerned with whether or not our missing player was 'doing a US' and turning up late or had stayed at home to watch Liberace on tele. (For younger readers, Liberace was the 60s answer to Jools Holland, plus sequins. Even back then, he'd have had no reservations about using under-arm deodorant.) Despite my distraction, I did manage a sneering:

'You won't do that well today, Lester.'

That was the first name that came into my head as I looked down at him, so to speak. My thinking here wasn't that this supercilious short-arse didn't have another decent innings in him. It was more that he'd won the toss and invited us to bat. Our batting was as reliable as the long-range weather forecast so the opportunity for an opponent to score 70 plus simply would not occur.

Incidentally, he was called Ray. I found this a most appropriate name for someone who thought the sun shone out of his own backside. I also concluded that he was an acupuncturist or a porn star. Both have a close connection with the word 'prick.'

Nor were we too enamoured by Queensbury. They certainly didn't play by the rules. At that time and level, 150 was considered a safe total batting first. Protocol dictated a target of around four an over. Queensbury Francis Chichestered past 200 before eventually calling it a day at 230 for 5. Half that total would have been enough, even if we'd been allowed 'three bat handles' on the fall of each wicket. (If you're unsure, ask an old person.)

Obviously concerned, they graciously left us about 23 overs. This meant we'd have to average 10 an over to win. Ha! None of us could remember an occasion when we'd achieved that off even one over. To spur us on, 'Matt' (his wife walked all over him) recalled that Kent made 219 for 2 from 23 overs to beat Gloucester in 1937 so why couldn't we follow suit? I'll restrict my reasons to just two. Kent were good and every Queensbury bowler was over seven years of age.

It was a dilemma which fell to our captain, old Ernie (old Jack's predecessor) to solve. He was so-called because his name was Ernie and he'd been around longer than sand, not because he owned out-of-date premium bonds. Ernie used all of his experience to devise a cunning plan:

'Don't go for them.'

Brilliant. Dot balls were greeted with loud cheers and our total of 63 for 4 was deemed to be a triumph. Queensbury, like Melrose, disappeared from our list but somehow, we did manage to hold on to the lion's share of our fixtures each season, which was more than we did to our catches. Over the years, we even found three or four teams as weak, or twice, weaker, than us.

St. Nicholas Old Boys stumbled into this category in the 1960s. They were so poor that we thought it was Christmas when we played them. Most of their players couldn't even bat an eyelid, whilst in the field they hardly pulled out all the stops. They were as well prepared as the fire station in Sussex which burnt down in 2006. It wasn't fitted with either a smoke detector or a fire alarm.

Back then, anyone scoring 50 or taking five wickets in a game bought a jug. In other words, you were made to pay for your success. Years later, I discovered that in the north the reverse is true. Such achievements are rewarded through collections. I wonder what befell John Wisden when he bowled all 10 North batsmen in the North v South 1850 fixture at Lords. More of such differences later. Returning to that quaint custom of buying a jug; it wasn't the jug you bought, it was the beer to fill it up.

Unsurprisingly, that didn't cost any of us very much. Alternatively, it did mean we could get merry on the cheap after most (mis-) matches. That especially suited our man with short arms and deep pockets, 'Bill.' (We don't think he ever paid one.) He is as tight as Dolly Parton in a 'B' cup.

Amazingly, we managed to fill our fixture list without much hassle. If you did have a blank date, which, unless we look like Brad Pitt, most of us have, all was not lost. There was a central bureau who arranged matches for you. All you had to do was put aside a whole morning to dial their number a couple of thousand times and state your playing strength. This was a distinct misnomer in our case.

There were three categories – 'strong,' 'medium' and 'weak.' Since there was no 'verging on the infirm,' we plumped for the latter. We weren't proud. Some clubs were. Two, both based in north-west London, made up their own fourth category – 'very strong.' I had visions of Tarzan opening the batting, wielding a 6lb. bat, and Geoff Capes trotting in to open the bowling. Strangely, our paths never crossed. If they had, the result might have been similar to when Dera Ismail Khan – that's a team not just one bloke – lost to Pakistan Railways by an innings and 851. (910 for 6 dec. played 32 all out and 27 all out; a case of all the points going one way.)

To be fair to one of them, Hampstead has always been a prestigious club. In 1886, AE Stoddart did scrape 485 for them against Stoics. Hopefully, the opposition 'bore their suffering impassively.' Hampstead did win the National Club

Championship in 1969 so 'weak' wasn't an option. Did they expect to win it, being better than strong? I bet the team who won it in 1992 did. They were called Optimists:

'It's not looking good, skip. We're 12 for 7 and there's only 1 over to go.'

'Don't panic. We'll be fine!'

The central bureau did throw us and Ranji together for an epic encounter. We travelled to Southgate by bus – all of our car owners were competing in the London to Brighton Vintage Car Rally – full of curiosity. Were we mistaken? Should we actually be going to Southall? How would we counter a team of wristy stroke makers and wily spinners?

They all turned out to be Jewish. Why not call darts and snooker sports? You might as well label Shahid Afridi cautious, Greg Chappell cheerful, Tony Greig an Englishman or Evershed's 'Alexander,' who considered himself a 'great' bowler, intelligent. We convinced him that 'Save the whale' was the slogan used by 'Weight watchers Anonymous' and that bare back riding was doing so with no shirt on.

Match of the Day it wasn't. Our clash was as exciting as Formula One motor racing on the radio. We'd found a second side who were worse than us, yet this brought with it a major concern. I'm not referring here to my worries about a future Prime Minister. It was just that the lack of talent on view was so glaring that we could have got into the Guinness Book of Records. What if we emulated that infamous game between two prepatory schools which ended with a hockey-like score of 1-0? All out for 1 and you win. I needn't have worried. Both sets of bowlers sent down so many long hops that even the aforementioned Ossie Wheatley would have emulated a Stain Devil and got off the mark.

As well as Ranji, there were other team names which

stirred my imagination. Would there be confusion when we played Seven Sports? There wasn't. They didn't turn up. Perhaps they were playing bowls or tennis somewhere else. Would the teas be over-cooked at Chard? They weren't. It was bloody salad. Could we expect only polite enquiries for lbw from Bath Civil Service? If only. What a shower. They shouted for everything. Could Crazy Horse be in the Indian Gymkhana side? He wasn't. They were a bunch of cowboys. When we turned up at Gorran might they had already left? No. They were more reliable than Seven Sports. Would the opposition turnout in pinks instead of whites when we faced Old Gaytonians and Hurlingham Oddfellows? Only one did. His wife had washed his shirt on hot along with her red knickers.

As with lift attendants, we had our ups and downs, but I cherish every minute of my time with the Old Qs. We were as likely to achieve success as the hitchhiker I spotted sitting by the A5103 in Moss Side in 2006. He was holding up a sign. Where was he trying to hitch to? Wythenshawe? Oswaldtwistle? Not a bit of it. Bombay! (He couldn't spell Mumbai.) Failure is relative and we couldn't fail to fail with the relative ineptitude of our team.

To back up the array of talent already described, 'Long Hop' bowled little else and gave more substance to his nick-name by driving from West London to Aberdeen after a game to attend a stag night, which, unsurprisingly, had finished by the time he arrived.

'Nipper' had an annoying habit of pinching team-mates' nipples. He tried to extend his range to females but made the wrong choice with 'Perky's' wife, 'Pinky.' She kicked him in the cods and warned him that a repeat performance would result in him never needing to wear a box again. It was no coincidence that 'Nipper' fielded at backward point and was our slow left armer. Even though his right arm was quicker on the uptake, we were able to kid him that Hare Krishna and Taj Mahal opened the bowling for Ranji. He was, in fact, so numb that every time he took a single it was considered a dummy run.

'Flash' Gordon wasn't much brighter. Gordon bought his clothes from Carnaby Street and only dealt in designer gear. Even his cricket shirt was made-to-measure. Everything had to be the real deal. He went off Derbyshire's Bud Hill because Bud showed early promise but then failed to blossom. He assumed that 'unisex' was what university students got up to on Friday nights but wasn't impressed because they were only undergraduates.

Less naive was 'Lincoln' Green. 'Lincoln' saw the funny side in everything. During a club outing to Lords to watch Middlesex play Derbyshire in 1967, he spotted England's Fred Rumsey coming out of the nets. 'Lincoln' approached him and with a completely straight face, asked:

'Alf, could you please explain how you found the time to play 1st class cricket and also guide England to their World Cup Final success against Germany?'

Fred thought briefly and came back with:

'It's not difficult. It's no different from you organising your time so that you can watch cricket and sign on as well.'

'Lincoln' was in the Territorial Army. Before each game, he automatically hit us with:

'Has anyone spotted my camouflage trousers? I put them down over there but I can't see them.'

Familiarity supposedly breeds contempt but none of us was mature enough to breed.

'Migraine' got his name because he could be more irritating than a mere headache. He was our answer to Leslie Welch (the

'Memory Man'), 'Stato's' precursor. 'Migraine,' however, never blotted his copybook as Leslie did. Leslie put his title in jeopardy by telephoning a club he'd appeared in to ask whether he'd left his coat there. 'Migraine' was less forgetful. He began most sentences with:

'Did you know …?'

Of course, we didn't, so he told us. It could be as fascinating as Richie Benaud if you were in the mood. If not, it was as uplifting as 'Bloers' droning on ad infinitum.

But for 'Migraine' none of us would have known that in the 'Victory Match' of May 1945 between England and Australia at Lords, Australia's number seven, for the record, was Sergeant Pepper. As keen as mustard (that's a compliment and a condiment) on cricket trivia, he was equally besotted with his wife, Gabriel:

'My wife's an angel,' he told 'Matt.'

'Matt' was unimpressed:

'I wish mine was, but she's still alive,' he sighed and harped on about his lack of runs, which had resulted from him cracking a mirror merely by looking at it.

At times, 'Migraine's' innocent divulgences caused unintended friction. For instance, when he let it slip that Ted Alletson of Nottinghamshire scored 189 from 51 balls (slogger) in 1911 batting at nine, it prompted our lazy number nine, 'Dr. Doolittle,' to pipe up with:

'I hope you're not expecting anything like that from me. There's more chance of old Jack running a single or Bob hitting one off the square.'

Similarly, we learned that Guppy or Gubby Allen took 10 for 40 for Middlesex against Lancashire in 1929. Impressive enough in itself, but Gubby wasn't there for the start. Now we could see the link with the Old Qs. Grubby (he hadn't had time for a wash) arrived late because he worked at Debenhams on Saturday mornings. Our young opening bowler, 'Spotted Dick,' looked flustered. Acne-ridden Richard had a Saturday morning milk-round and felt 'Migraine' was trying to make him look a bit of a pudding.

Last, and by every means least, came 'Garibaldi. The follically-challenged Gareth really took the biscuit. Blessed with hollow legs, he was our best drinker. This was a plus when socialising in the bar after games but a minus for 'Garibaldi's' brain cell. Amongst his misconceptions were that an aphrodisiac was the hairstyle currently sported by the West Indian Tourists and that a flipper was a smart-arsed dolphin. He failed every exam he ever took. He even had trouble passing water and believes 'Bird Line' is a speed-dating agency.

We did boob though, when we tried to convince him Barbara Windsor was the Queen Mother. He was obviously keeping abreast with developments within the Royal Family and retorted with one of his own. He told our stand-in captain, 'Birdseye':

'Skip, I hereby declare that one is full of rubbish.'

After five seasons of unpredictability (who would make me laugh most, how many players would we have this week, who would 'Migraine' undermine next time, who was on at the Palladium), I moved on.

My sister Maureen, who I call 'Maur,' due to her demanding nature, had a boyfriend who thought trigonometry meant having three wives. 'Trig' heard I'd once owned my own bat. He was so impressed that he invited me to play for 'his club,' Evershed at Boston Manor in West London. He didn't own the place but did sell it to me as a cricket club where I'd see 'a more serious form of the game.'

Did this mean that nobody at Evershed would have

laughed their rocks off when Old Qs stalwart Max went base over apex as he moved to try to take an easy catch to actually win us a game off the very last ball? Max couldn't bowl jaffas or hit a ball with sufficient venom to call 'wait.' He now showed us that he couldn't even remain vertical. Following this involuntary piece of gymnastics, he was renamed 'Olga,' after Ronnie's wife.

I'd gone as far as I could go with the Old Qs (away to Bognor). I was ready to be 'serious.' Games now always started on time, with 22 sportsmen under the age of 70. Players didn't have to umpire as well as play. What was written in the scorebook was no longer a work of fiction. Scores of 200 plus weren't restricted to Queensbury. Some of our players were gifted enough to have to buy jugs. Nobody rushed home to watch Norman Wisdom and Ranji weren't on our fixture list.

With a team of talented cricketers, we played to win and often did, but we still had a giggle. 'Mark' from Staines and '007' from Basildon were fine players and both were easily influenced. 'Mark's' hero was Denis Compton and he was desperate to be like him. Unfortunately, he couldn't play the sweep like Denis could so he contented himself with daubing his hair with Brylcreem and running out a couple of team-mates every week.

'007' had a bond with the esteemed William Clarke. Back in 1837, Clarke married a widow who owned the Trent Bridge Inn. He then turned the neighbouring field he now possessed into his very own cricket ground. (The clue's in the name.) Well played William. Your own ground and bar in one fell swoop. The move served him well. In 1855 he took an incredible 476 wickets and any jugs he bought would have been at cost price. Incidentally, this tally was 10 times the amount achieved by all three of the Evershed Clarkes in 1970 and that includes those taken in the nets, in their dreams and in the back garden.

'007' couldn't match that either, although he also married a rich widow, Mary Le Bone. Like David Beckham years after, he had to endure taunts that he'd married above his station. He didn't care that Mary had a hold over him –usually a full nelson- and made him wear a collar and tie (plus trousers) on match days. He was so easy-going that this left him neither shaken nor stirred.

Mentioning ideas above one's station, the parents of Derbyshire's GO Dawkes were perhaps guilty of the same. He hadn't a prayer of living up to those initials, despite taking three catches in three balls from Les Jackson in 1958.

Evershed was popular enough to run three XIs and only had one member who wasn't easy to get on with. 'Noah' actually believed that Noah was married to Joanne of Arc. He has recently been rechristened 'Ratner.' This is purely because he is so full of crap. He could 'field anywhere,' 'take any attack apart,' 'bowl offers, leggers, inners, outers, uppers, downers.' This was as near to the truth as when a dentist tells you it won't hurt, an estate agent says you can trust her, a builder promises he'll be there tomorrow or an umpire boasts that he doesn't give front foot lbws.

A new fixture list provided the opportunity to toy with more names. Would Kew keep us waiting? Would Collie Smith be playing for Barking? How did Turnham Green do that? Were High Wycombe a team of pot smokers? Would we have to clear the ground of sheep when we played at BAA? Surely we'd have a good chance of beating the Naval Cadets as they'd probably be all at sea, particularly since their opening bowler's Christian name was Caspian. Would Wellington be sponsored by Boots and was there any mileage in turning up to play Invincibles? 'Noah' couldn't see the point but did think they were called 'Invisibles.' Finally, did Olinda, led by Surrey's Roger Harman, have a sister club called Ocarol, led by Neil Sedaka?

Instead of competing against the likes of St.Nicholas Old Boys, I was now with a club who entered the Cricketer National Knockout Cup. The words 'sublime' and 'ridiculous' spring to mind, as does a third round game at Highgate in 1971. We were Canada. They were Australia. By that, I don't mean our team was full of lumberjacks whose main function was to protect the USA from ice while theirs was made up of convicts who appealed for everything. I'm merely intimating that we weren't expected to win. That said, who would have predicted that Eton would beat 'The World' in Naples in 1820?

We posted a decent score (which the organiser received nine days later, despite it being 1st class) and were still in with a fighting chance with one over to go. Our skipper was normally keen on maintaining the status quo but this time 'Francis Rossi' wasn't sure whether or not to change things. He called Vic, who was good at rubbing chests but little else, and I together for a conflab. (Southern for: 'I don't know what to do so I'll pretend to discuss it and then blame you if things go wrong.')

'Francis' sought a volunteer. We both obliged. I volunteered Vic. He volunteered me. I must have looked more panic-strickened. Vic hadn't been expecting a bowl. He hadn't, therefore, held back at tea. He'd scoffed four Penguins. This caused him to waddle, rather than run, in to bowl.

Highgate required 12 to win. They managed only six from Vic's first five balls. He was set to be crowned our very own Billy Whizz. Our illustrious opponents still needed a very unlikely six runs from the last ball of the game:

'Everyone out,' cried 'Francis.'

I considered asking about arbitration but didn't fancy being called a scab. Anyway, it didn't even matter if I dropped a catch as long as I didn't palm it over the boundary (again). Seconds later the ball was sailing out of the ground and Vic was being labelled our very own Billy Bunter.

I felt as distraught as Michael Vaughan when England amassed the second highest ever (as was) international one-day score of 391 for 4, give or take a bye or a catch, against Bangladesh in June 2005. He contributed an 8 ball duck.

The following year, we travelled to Ashford in Kent in the same competition. Or it might have been to Ashford in Middlesex the previous year in the FA Cup. (Just to bear out Christopher Martin-Jenkins' observation.) They must have had links with Mexico as they all wore club blazers and so were undoubtedly a long way from classing themselves as 'weak.' Their opening bowler had something in common with Casanova and Mao Tse Tung. He wasn't horny or Chinese but he, too, was a librarian. He certainly stamped his authority on the game with his pacey in-duckers. Even so, he couldn't book them a place in the next round. Vic didn't bowl the final, or any other, over and we won comfortably.

Chesham were also very worthy opponents. Their side in the early 70s contained a couple of Buckinghamshire's XI which beat Glamorgan in the Gillette Cup. One of them, Fred Harris, opened the bowling. Although he bowled a good line and length (whatever that means), the main problem Fred created was the noise he made. He didn't grunt like a bulimic tennis player. He did, however, rattle. He wasn't popping a cocktail of pills to lower blood, peer or tyre pressure. The background music was caused by him running up to bowl with his pockets full of coins. Did this make Fred a change bowler?

If moving from Chiswick to Boston Manor was a culture shock, it was six levels on the Richter scale lower than my next move. I'd have cheerfully stayed at Evershed for the rest of my playing days but the Teacher Training College I attended was 230 miles away and the 159 bus only went as far as West Hampstead.

Coming from the sedate form of timed cricket in the Home Counties to league cricket in Yorkshire is like comparing wrestling to American football. It's as if you've intended to procure a water pistol but have ended up with a water canon. Ostensibly, they are of similar stock. In reality, one is a harmless bit of fun whereas the other can be nasty.

When you are involved in league cricket there's no necessity for anyone to be nice to you. Teams don't have to socialise to retain fixtures. Jugs in Yorkshire are solely for ogling at. Up to now, sledging had been reserved for when it snowed. Virtually all batsmen in club cricket in the south walked when they nicked it. Bumpers were restricted to cars and a beamer was a person who smiled a lot.

Welcome to the 1st division of the Bradford League. It was 1974. My formative years in London would be as significant as a teardrop in the Pacific. To quote George Orwell:

'Sport is war minus the shooting.'

George had seemingly watched some contests in West Yorkshire. I soon discovered each match was like Celtic versus Rangers, minus the niceties.

My debut for Lidget Green was at Undercliffe. I mistakenly tried to break the ice by enquiring:

'Who are, the Shadows?'

Understandably, no one laughed. I immediately realised it was akin to being at home with my northern wife:

'Speak only when you're spoken to, you smart arse southerner.'

I also noticed that a few local rules applied in the top half of the country. You could be given out caught even if the ball had bounced a couple of times, especially if the incident occurred on the umpire's blind side. Since most octogenarians seem to be cursed with two blind sides, chances of surviving any appeals were like Twiggy ... slim.

In Bradford, instead of the southern softies' customary:

'Nice shot mate,' for a well-executed stroke off the sweet spot, it was now:

'You spawny twat!'

I naively took this to be a compliment until I noticed the accompanying hand gesture. A smile was seen as a sign of dubious sexuality and even one's social circle was likely to be a vicious one. I felt as out of place as Bryan Sewell on stage at Gipton Working Mens' Club in downtown Leeds, trying to sing 'On Ilkley Moor bar t'at' late on a Friday night.

The 1974 season was memorable if only for a game against Bingley and because I got more threats of violence than runs. Most of these arose whenever I opened my mouth. Cockneys/Aussies are as popular as diptheria in West Yorkshire. I quickly learned that I was much safer trying to sound like Ray Illingworth rather than Ray East or Ray Lindwall when I called, appealed or cried.

The Bingley match, like 'Chesty' Morgan, stood out for two reasons. Firstly, it didn't rain. Secondly, it culminated in the daftest piece of cricket I've ever witnessed. Lidget Green got 202. Bingley were 200 for 8 with one ball to go. A swish and a miss resulted in the ball going through to our keeper, Alec, who, tragically, was not of the smart variety. Every single person on the ground, bar one, was aware that Bingley could have the one bye they were scampering for and victory was still ours. Alec was the 'bar one.' Despite the single having been completed, Alec took a wild shy at the stumps. He missed by a distance and the Bingley boys went through for two overthrows and a win. It goes without saying that Alec never came close to winning a coconut at a fairground, although he did pass his accountancy exams.

Somehow, I survived the season and escaped to Lancashire. From 1975 to 1982, I played for Middleton in the mighty Central Lancashire League. Big crowds, big names, big fast bowlers and big collections were on offer. I didn't score enough half-centuries to move into a higher tax bracket but did get a collection under false pretences. It was a rain-affected cup game at Rochdale on a Sunday in 1980ish.

We were struggling at 82 for 6 chasing about 175. It was very dark when I edged a two to move on to exactly 50, according to the scoreboard. As is the custom, team-mates went round the considerable crowd as the umpires called it a day, or more appropriately, a night. I don't know how much they collected but it had already stood a couple of rounds before our scorer, 'Ludwig,' who once came out with the classic:

'Isn't that one of Beethoven's sinatras?' pointed out that I only had 49.

The rules called for a 6.30 resumption on as many mid-week evenings as it took to complete the match. Rochdale isn't far from Manchester and it rained for the next five days. We then paddled our way through two weekend league games before preparing to try again. Five more wet days meant I'd been on 49 for a fortnight, which was slow going even for me. The following Saturday was fine for our fixture with Stockport. I pulled a fetlock whilst batting and had to retire hurt. Two days later we travelled back to Rochdale for the twelfth time. I was praying for rain since I could barely stand, never mind pretend to move my feet.

Rain it didn't. I couldn't have a runner, as my injury had

occurred prior to the start of play. I decided to deal solely in boundaries.13 fours and I'd reach my ton. First ball up was a full toss. I missed it and was 'adjudged' lbw, still 13 fours shy of 100.

Three weeks later, to counter withdrawal symptoms, we returned to Rochdale for the league fixture.This time I scraped a few more than 50 but didn't fare too well in monetary terms. The consensus was succinctly summed up by a local:

'You'll get nowt for 'im today, lads. We've got memories like elephants 'ere y'know.'

After eight years in the firing line, I stopped firing blanks myself so that my daughter Jenny was born. This prompted a transfer demand from my wife to the slightly less dangerous Lancashire and Cheshire League for a nominal fee (nine pence) to play for Thornham. I've remained there up to the time of writing and am still wheeled out to play whenever my iron lung is in good working order. One reason why I've stayed so long is that everyone has always been, on the face of it, so nice to my wife. For years, she was greeted with a friendly:

'Hi ya, hun.'

Only recently have I discovered that people weren't actually being pleasant. They simply thought she was from East Germany. When I explained she was local, it became 'dear.' Fair enough, until it transpired that the consensus was she had expensive tastes. Worse still, the term of apparent endearment for another player's wife, 'Manyana' (she's called Tamara) is 'love' because she's useless at tennis.

In the 600 plus games I've played for Thornham, I'm struggling select one to highlight here. I could go for any of the matches in 1987 when we won the 1st division title but I'll opt for a 2nd XI game at Glossop in 2003. It was one of only two tied games I've ever featured in. This is curious enough in itself but is made more singular by the fact that during my innings I was responsible for running one short. Oops! Ironically, in the other one, it was my batting partner who did so. Bad enough, but not as daft as Dave Bright's gaff in 2008.

Dave failed to match his surname for Thornham 3rds. He clubbed the ball towards the boundary and set off for either a leisurely two or a frantic three. He opted for the former. He strolled there and back only to be run out for a duck. The silly sod ran one short on the first trip. He then surpassed this by being narrowly run out coming back for the second, giving a new meaning to the term 'a double short.'

The Lancashire and Cheshire League provided more puzzlers. Would there be any seats at Stand? Did any Sikhs play for Hyde? More worryingly, would our female scorer be safe at Darcy Lever? Equally, what was I doing playing in a league in which the chairman's name was Crook, the best scorer was called Fidler and the top umpires were Cheetham and Bent?

At any rate, one thing will never change. Be it in the 60s, 70s or now, in Wembley or Werneth, Sidcup or Saltaire, fast bowlers don't like batsmen.

Food for thought:
1. Why was Australia's Ian Quick a slow bowler and Somerset's Peter Bowler a batsman?
2. Did the crowd expect fireworks every time India's SB Bangar took the field?
3. Did G.Fitness of Queensland ever get injured and has Hampshire's Jonathon Ayling's health worsened with time?
4. When the Tyke league bowler, Jennings Tune took 10 wickets for 0 runs in 1922, was it music to his captain's ears?

Chapter 2

FAST BOWLERS (SOUTH)

Most of us who are under the delusion of being batsmen aren't too keen on facing fast bowlers. In fact, unless we've been goalkeepers in a previous life and are, therefore, oblivious to pain, fear or danger, we tend to have a certain trepidation when up against these psychopaths. I need do no more to prove my point than to ask any batsman which team he'd have preferred to have played for in the 1841 fixture at Lords between 'A Slow Bowler's XI' and a 'Fast Bowler's XI'? Off the top of my head, I can only think of Robin Smith and 'daft Les' who'd opt for the former.

Fuller Pilch certainly wouldn't have. Representing Gentlemen against Players (South v North?) in 1837, he was given out 'hat knocked on wicket.' Perhaps he was Fuller Beer at the time.

My own phobia began soon after leaving the Cubs. During my primary school days in Kilburn we only played one cricket match. That wasn't because it was like a timeless Test. It was more that the one male teacher preferred to get home in time for Crackerjack.

For this historic game, more of which in chapter nine, only three pads were available. This was fine when we were fielding. Our wicket-keeper had an extra one to stuff wherever he wished. It was more disconcerting when we were batting, especially as the opposition only had two pads in total and none to lend. This meant just one pad each for the first three batsboys.

Our teacher, presumably an advanced coach, instructed us to put the pad on our front leg and pray. He omitted to be more specific. We all figured we had a 50-50 chance of getting it right. Some went for the right leg. Some went for the wrong leg. It wasn't a two-legged match. I guessed correctly but got rapped squarely on the back leg so I would have been better getting it wrong.

I might not have been hit if I hadn't convinced myself that the bowler was going to be too quick for me purely because he rubbed the ball on his short grey trousers, just like Middlesex's Alan Moss did. (Alan always wore grey shorts.) This made me easy prey.

Since I didn't seek counselling, my unease continued at secondary school. Any bowler with a run up of more than six paces caused my life to flash before me. I was always keen to know my fate straightaway. Before facing any bowler, I would always ask:

'Are you fast?'

If they were quick on the uptake, they'd immediately sense they'd already got the rabbit in their headlights. None said:

'I am now you smooth talking devil.'

Some nodded, a few growled and one revelled in his newfound position of eminence: 'You'll find none faster,' was a real choker.

It caused me to swallow my chewing gum. (Chewing was obligatory. Middlesex players did it so we had to do likewise.)

The strangest reply I received was:

'No, it's not Ramadan.'

I thought he said:

'No, I'm like Ramadhin,' and expected him to bowl spin with his cap on.

Such apprehension was hardly ideal for a 'promising' opening bat. (I kept promising to drop down the order.) I should explain that I only opened at under 12 level because I was the sole bat owner. Unless you went to Eton or Harrow, this was something of a rarity in the early 1960s. I hasten to add I possessed one only because my parents had used the money they'd saved for my cubs uniform a couple of years earlier to buy it as a birthday present. Even then, it was only a Gradidge size six. (I was still awaiting my growth spurt, unlike most opposing opening bowlers.)

Being one who is willing to share, I did let our team bully, 'Mac the Knife,' insist on using my blade. He didn't do it any harm. He tried to hit the ball so hard ('street cred') in the belief that you needed to burst the thing in order to score runs that he invariably missed it. He did fling the bat once after being dismissed for nought. A mallard cushioned its fall, thereby making it two ducks for the price of one. Big 'Mac' followed this up by punching the nearest person to him, our number seven, Ian Pinch. Did this make him a 'pinch hitter?'

A year later, and still opening, I was presented with the daunting prospect of facing the quickest u13 bowler on the planet – well, in St John's Wood, anyway. It was a local derby. It couldn't get more local. Quintin GS and Kynaston Comprehensive shared the same site. This made it easy for them to beat us up whenever they wanted to without having to travel far to do so.

The pre-match banter:

'We're gonna slaughter you, you Quintin queers,' didn't vex me.

They were just a bunch of ruffians. We would out-think them, I thought. As it turned out, the thought of facing 'Smiffy' did upset me, particularly in the bowel region. The battle scene was Canon's Park, near Stanmore. It was a good name for a ground where I would doubtless shoot my load.

The omens were not good. Their school was named after Sir JE Kynaston-Studd who had played for Middlesex and had been President of the MCC in 1930. Our founder was Quintin Hogg. It is said that Quint could have doubled as the heavy roller when it made its debut at Lords in 1870.

Kynaston didn't get many, so I could use plan A:

'Sir, as we haven't got many to chase, I'll let someone else open today.'

'No you won't. I want a 10 wicket win. Get out there and do your business.'

That's exactly what I was afraid of.

Plan B involved putting my fingers down my throat so that I heaved. I wasn't sick but nearly choked again. It would have to be plan C. I'd lock myself in the toilet until 'Smiffy' became tired. I couldn't. The toilet was already engaged. Our number three hadn't proposed to it, but he had got there before me. Plan D was to feign a migraine. However, I wasn't sure whether the word was 'migraine' or 'migrant' and didn't want to be labelled a gypsy.

Plan E was a last minute time-wasting tactic. I pretended I'd lost my plimsoles. (Southern for Dunlop Green Flash – paper-thin canvas tennis shoes called pumps in Sheffield.) It was to no avail. Our teacher, 'Neddy,' so named for his love of raw carrots rather than for being hung like a donkey, intervened. He trotted into the changing room. I was praying he had come to say I'd been timed out as H.Yadaz was in 1997 in Cuttuck or Cuttack or Cattuck or Catterick. No such luck.

He ascertained the cause of the delay – there were no flies on him – and found a solution. (We won't delve into that now, other than to say I had no aspirations of becoming a female East German sprinter.)

'Neddy' refused to be taken for a ride by a spineless child with five pathetic plans. He delved into a duffle bag:

'These will do,' he declared.

(I'd wished we had.) He threw me a pair of black elasticated pumps/plimsoles similar to those the girls wore for dancing lessons. If one of 'Smiffy's' express deliveries had hit me on the foot, these would have been as much use as a pacifist in a fight, Phil Tufnall batting in a 20/20 or Gareth Southgate in a penalty shoot-out.

In truth, there was no danger of that occurring. For it to have done, I'd have had to get behind the line. The only thing I'd be getting behind would be the square leg umpire. Short of fainting, I'd run out of plans. I chose not to pass out because I'd previously heard 'Mac' announce:

'Only fairies faint,' after a boy called 'Tinkerbell' had done so during assembly.

If I did likewise, I was worried 'Mac' would shove a Christmas tree up my backside.

With Radio 1 blaring out, I had no choice but to go out there and face the music. The fact that the DJ was playing 'Keep on Running' didn't go unnoticed. I nearly took his advice. My batting partner, 'RC,' the outside left in our soccer team, and I, always took it in turns to face the first ball. We were both cowards. Mercifully, it was his turn today.

When I eventually got to the middle – it does take a while when you take one step forward and then two back – he was at the non-striker's end. I showered abuse on him. He responded by upholding that his generous nature dictated that I deserved first crack. I'd have liked to have given him a crack. Instead, I went for bribery. I offered him some wine gums to take the first ball. He declined, saying that, like his latterday hero, Roger 'Juice' Harper, he was teetotal. He also confessed he'd wound 'Smiffy' up for me:

'I've told him you're going to smash him all over Canon's Park. If he's angry he'll be all over the place.'

So, probably, would I.

Not surprisingly, 'RC' never made it to Oxbridge or Camford to read psychology. 'Smiffy' had been kept waiting by a jumped-up grammar school nob who had the audacity to boast about taking him to the cleaners. Before he was let loose, he wished me luck:

'It'll be you who needs to go to the cleaners, brain box, to have that brown stain removed from the arse of your whites.'

'Middle please,' I croaked.

I'd considered asking for a 'miles outside leg' guard giving me less distance to back away to square leg. I chose not to, even though one person in Britain dies every 60 seconds. I did, however, chasten myself for leaving the Cubs prematurely and contemplated hitting my wicket before 'Smiffy' let rip.

'RC' then struck again. My ex-mate strolled down the wicket. He'd informed our adversary I'd give him some fudge if he got me out, adding that I wouldn't have to as he couldn't bowl for toffee. My sole consolation was that it was a Wednesday and first lesson on Thursday was physics. I would be happy to miss physics.

My newest enemy came charging in off a run-up longer than that needed by a Jumbo Jet to get airborne. He eventually arrived at the crease and hurled the ball in my direction. I nearly hurled myself. Before I could move, the ball thudded against my bat handle and flew over the slips for four. 'Smiffy' now had smoke coming out of his ears and I was still facing. 'RC' helped things along with:

'Nice shot, Jim. Smash him for another four. He's rubbish. I've seen quicker Skodas.'

This time I was more focused, despite the distraction of 'white lightning's' smoking ears. I managed to keep all parts of my bat, and more importantly, my body out of the way. I surprised even myself. I was genuinely unaware I could jump so far. Bowled second ball. Not a bad day's work, though; a scoring rate of 200, not a bruise in sight plus a whole tube of wine gums to myself.

Out of the loo came a flushed 'Mucker' Barnes, our number three. We called him thus because Michael had an uncanny knack of mucking up most things he attempted. He lasted half as long as I had. It's not easy batting with your eyes closed.

Numbers four to six fared little better. We were only saved from total humiliation because our tormentor got bored. He asked to come off for a 'blow' (not wave or job, just a plain rest). 'RC' amassed sufficient runs from the other Kynaston bowlers to sneak us an unlikely victory. He then caused a smile by asking 'Mucker' to fetch him some 'dehydrated' water. He was unable to find any, making it very much a 'fool's errand.'

As we grew older, 'Smiffy' became more interested in playing hockey, albeit tonsil hockey, with the local talent. He then lost all street cred when he was spotted walking along Finchley Road in his socks during a rain shower. He'd been sporting a brand new pair of Hush Puppies and took them off to put under his jacket to keep dry. I had wet myself over someone who wore, or worse still, wasn't wearing, suede shoes. From that day on, like Nottinghamshire's John Clay, his name became mud.

By the time I was 14, my size six (I'm still referring to my bat, despite a growth spurt) had become too small for me.

Without a replacement, I had no claim to continue opening the batting. Indeed, for a further three years or so, I questioned the sanity of those who did. Why would anyone in their right mind, who wished to keep it, want to be first in the firing line when the opening bowlers are at their fastest and that nasty ball is at its most destructive? Why not just take up kick boxing or cheer leading? (See chapter seven.)

My thinking had been coloured (black and blue) by the occasion when I was struck squarely in the 'Jacobs' (southern for knackers) as a boxless 12 year old. I hobbled off, doing a passable impression of Aled Jones before his balls had dropped. I tried not to cry. That said, I've never subscribed to the school of thought which prescribes not showing the bowler you're hurt. If it hurts, rub it. I admire heroes, yet I've as much chance of being one as Ryan Sidebottom has of doing an advert fot hair straighteners.

With my cods having been pushed up my throat so that I appeared to have three Adam's apples, I went back out at the fall of the seventh wicket. (You can't rush these things.) Predictably, self-preservation decreed that I did an impersonation of a toreador as the bowler let go of that awfully hard ball so that the stump was uprooted rather than my testicles.

They remained undisturbed, which was good in one way, for quite a while after this. This was partly because, between 14 and 17, I contentedly hid at number three behind 'RC' and the vertically challenged 'Pee-Wee.' (He'd been hit by a lift as a youngster and it had stunted his growth.) Being small enough to use my size six, he'd swapped it with me for a whole bag of wine gums and, as a bat owner, now qualified to open the innings.

They were spurred on by the unashamed offer of 'boot money' from 'Neddy.' He forked out half a crown (southern for a small fortune for teenagers in the 1960s) to any of us who made 50 in a schools match. We'd have preferred him to buy a jug. Sadly, he didn't drink.

My maiden 50 came against Archbishop Tennyson – his robe and mitre must have hampered his bowling. I was now able to purchase some second-hand / second-feet footwear from our would-be actor 'Oscar' for half a crown, hence 'boot money.' Thanks 'Neddy.'

With my plates now adequately protected, it was time to become a man. I'd take over the opening berth from 'Pee-Wee,' who was now a jockey. Consequently, I stepped forward when the school 1stXI captain, who was called Les, despite being heterosexual, as confirmed by a six-four vote from the players, pleaded:

'Who wants to be number one?'

I thought he was referring to having a hit record. Actually, I didn't put one foot in front of the other. Everyone else took one step back. Before I'd caught on, my name was in the scorebook just above that of 'RC'.

Les was no bowler yet was aware of the anxiety pace bowlers can cause. We didn't have one but he was the next best thing. As the opposition's opening batsmen walked out to the middle, Les paced out his run up. It was longer than the runway at Florida airport. He would then sprint to the crease with a face like a constipated bulldog with worms and release a mock delivery, following right through to the stumps at the other end. This was a psychological masterstroke. The pity of it all was that Les had all the sense of direction of Christopher Columbus on an off day with the control and co-ordination of Oliver Reed on an on day.

Following his trial lift off, Les would toss the ball to our medium-pacer, 'Holland,' who was renowned for going Dutch on dates. 'Holland's' pies were accurate enough to hit any batsman in the nether-lands, but he was to fast bowling what many believe Little and Large are to comedy, a breach of the Trades Descriptions Act. Nevertheless, as a consequence of Les's antics, he regularly picked up early wickets.

Being back in the front line didn't prove too scary until we played William Ellis GS in 1965. William wasn't there himself but AJ Suffling was. Bloody hell! I was 15 and, if I stuck my tongue out, could easily be mistaken for a zip. He was the oldest looking sixth former I'd ever seen. He would have had trouble enrolling for an 18 to 30 holiday. 'AJ' was built like a concrete kasi. He put me in mind of Desperate Dan and made Vinnie Jones look cute and cuddly.

Worse still, he had a run-up as long as those of 'Smiffy' and Les combined and led the attack for MCC Schools. Preparing to face him, I was sweating so much I thought I'd gone through the male change at a world record early age. My stomach resembled a lepidopterist's delight. Les gave me and my new opening partner, 'Piers,' who spent most of his spare time at Lords, a few words of wisdom. Thankfully, they weren't of the Norman variety:

'Get right behind it.'

That would have been eminently sensible if he'd been talking about a brick wall. This 'sentence' gave me a dilemma. Les was 1st XI captain and the school's head boy – 'he who must be obeyed.' He also bought the first round in after the game. But this was pure folly.

Anyway, the immediate problem was 'Piers's.' 'RC' had pulled a muscle (he certainly couldn't pull a cricket ball), genuflexing and had cried off. He wasn't crying now. It was 'Piers's' turn to face the first ball and the team was in danger of becoming without match or equal, ie peerless. I'd forsaken the idea of feigning to lose a plimsole and had ensured I was already firmly entrenched at the non-striker's end. Through my binoculars, I could see this man-mountain walking back to his mark, sniffing out a further helping of raw meat.

A noble effort was required from 'Piers' to get us started. Not surprisingly, he wasn't up to it. He went one better than Cinderella. He missed the ball altogether. 0 for 1.

Why was he being replaced by 'Foetus,' our smallest, youngest player at number three? He normally came in at eight. It soon became clear. He was being prematurely pushed out onto the field by our usual number three, assisted by four, five, six and seven. 0 for 2 soon became 49 for 9.

Welcome to the fray, 'Skittles.' He didn't have an affinity for small, coloured sweets. He did, however, confess that ten pin bowling gave him a headache. As he trudged to the wicket, he looked decidedly pasty. By the time he'd avoided his first ball by performing a pike with double twist, I could honestly say I've seen more colour in a pint of milk. We didn't get to 50. None of us was surprised to subsequently learn that the protagonist later took up acting and was given the leading part in the re-make of 'King-Kong.'

During this period, troublesome fast bowlers on the club scene were, thankfully, like Graham Gooch's double, Lord Lucan, conspicuous by their absence. A notable exception was Mickey Dunne. Mickey 'Medium to Well' Dunne opened for the Hertfordshire side which reached the quarter final of the Gillette Cup in the 1970s. He was good enough and rapid enough to be selected for the full Minor Counties Representative XI. Inexplicably, I was asked to play for a Rickmansworth Club Invitation XI against Hertfordshire to commemorate something like the opening of the club's new toilets in 1968. Foolishly, I accepted and, as the youngest player on show, found myself being shovved in first.

The wicket was as docile as phosphorous out of water. Practically every delivery Mickey pummelled into it spat up towards my fragile frame intent on inflicting suffering. In an attempt to avoid bringing the cluster of short legs, plus a few long ones, into play, I initially opted to use my chest, stomach and shoulders rather than my bat. Being as well protected as a soft-back turtle, I soon came to regret this unsound decision. I've always bruised easily.

With the close-in fielders intimately close, bad light was a possible get out. So was trying to hit the ball. I wasn't scoring any runs, partly because the bloke at the other end wasn't for moving but principally because I'm not a giant. It was as enjoyable as an enema so I chose to surrender. Instead of another bruise, I decided to get bat on ball. I knew I had no chance of keeping any shot down as I wasn't standing on a step ladder. 'Limp along Leslie,' the shortest of the short legs, didn't have to move as I helpfully guided the next cherry into his enormous mits. The fact that he held on to it provided me with more relief than a whole crate of Settlers.

As Sod's Law would have it, Mickey pulled a muscle in his back four balls later. Our middle order gorged themselves on what remained of the attack which turned out to be no quicker than the QE2 doing a three point turn on a boating lake, leaving me with the Wasted Day Award.

Even when I moved down the District Line to Evershed, things remained relatively calm. This was mainly due to Evershed's tracks being so batsman-friendly that if a ball got above bail height there was an immediate inquest. No one had heard of helmets, arm guards, chest guards, mud guards or thigh pads in those days. Years earlier, the much-vaunted Percy Fender of Surrey and England only ever wore one batting glove. Softie. We played against a bloke from Hayes who must have come from up north; he didn't wear any.

Calm, that is, until the day, as a weedy 17 year old, I came face to face, or in some cases face to navel, with the might of Surrey Young Cricketers at Beckenham. I'd somehow scraped into the London Schools u19s. I'd borrowed a club bat for the trials but the selectors must have thought it was my own. They were sufficiently duped to have picked me, even though I didn't use it that well.

We travelled to the ground apprehensive in the knowledge that Dave Liston would be playing for Surrey. He was unquestionably quick enough to have a sleepless night over. Predictably, Dave answered to the name of 'Sonny.' This was by no means as a result of him being warm and pleasant. It was because he shared the same surname, and a similar mean streak, to the heavyweight boxer who could curdle milk merely by glaring at it. What we didn't know until we arrived was that his fellow opening bowler would be none other than Bob Willis, all 6ft12 of him. Even as a 19/25 year old, Bob was seriously speedy and not known for his love of batsmen or welcoming smile.

From being nervous about facing 'Sonny,' albeit without Cher, he had undoubtedly become very much the soft option. The difference between our 'Schools XI' and their 'Young Cricketers XI' wasn't too subtle. Boys go to school. Men can get away with being labelled 'young.' Still, at least I wasn't good enough to be batting in the top four. Thank goodness for mediocrity.

In the event, Bob and 'Sonny' each took so long to bowl an over, and it was timed cricket, that we managed to draw the game. I didn't have to face either of them.

The following season, armed with a new (full size) Warsop Hendren bat, (possibly one of the 1179 bats chiselled out of one giant willow tree felled in 1888) bought for me by an uncle who obviously didn't like me, I found myself opening for both London Schools and Evershed. I'd fallen for the 'one step back, one step forward,' routine again. All went reasonably well, thanks mainly to more placid wickets, until London's two day fixture against the West Indies Young Cricketers at Brentham. Come back Bob Willis!

The bush telegraph (more reliable than George W) had made it known they had a quartet of pace bowlers. Two were reckoned to be genuinely quick and the other two slipperier still.

In the previous game, they'd shot out a supposedly decent public school past and present XI for two less than the 26 New Zealand managed against England in 1955. Getting the runs looked as though it would be difficult in one sense yet oh so easy in another.

On the morning of the game, I woke to the welcoming sound of rain. I made my way across London, happy in the knowledge that fast bowlers don't like wet conditions. I revelled in the hope that we might now only have one innings each rather than two. (50% of that was to manifest itself.) Typically, by the time I arrived at Brentham the bloody sun was out.

At least, the uncovered wicket was fairly soft and the run-ups were wonderfully treacherous. The start was delayed. Our coach, Russ (Collins, not Conway), told us to greet their coach, Wes Hall, not the 45 seater, and socialise. My yellow streak drew me inextricably to their allegedly swiftest, nastiest fast bowler, Willie Bourne. (He later played for Warwickshire.) This prompted me to wonder will'e hit me on the head or in the nuts first? I was soon to wish he hadn't been Bourne.

Despite being by no means rich and the south's oldest newspaper deliverer, which made me a 'pauper boy,' I shelled out for a pint of pre-match orange juice for my new best friend. My cordial gesture was to cut no ice later, as Willie forgot his manners when we started after lunch.

I was the only one with a coin so had to captain the side. I tossed up and started as I meant to carry on. I lost. We were inserted. I opted for Les's line:

'Who wants to open?'

I enquired in a tone designed to make it sound a real honour. Stone silence. I knew an offer of wine gums wouldn't sway anyone so I lied that there was a pint for a volunteer. This was enough to persuade 'Mac,' who always seemed to wear a raincoat whatever the weather. The promise of alcohol always clouded his thinking.

I couldn't ask 'Mac' to take the first ball. I'd have to. How bad could it be? Willie was smiling. Perhaps he'd been appreciative of my generosity earlier. Instead of a gentle loosener as a pay-back, he slipped me a throat high beamer. I told Willie I'd already had my tonsils removed. He smiled briefly and then beamed no more. Instead, he dug between 99 and 101% of his deliveries in at my ribs. The longest known case of constipation is 102 days. I fell 14 weeks four days short of equalling that record

'Mac' soon capitulated to their 'umbrella' field but we did contrive to scrape a few runs here and there. I survived for a while, only to be dismissed by an amazing piece of fielding. I'd played forward to a rare non-short pitched delivery and said to myself:

'That's another one I've kept out.'

I was too previous. Richard Straker's left hand appeared from (very) short leg and all but removed the ball from the face of the bat. It really had to be seen to be believed. 'Olga' would have been floored by it.

For our second innings, 'Mac' had upped the anti. I couldn't afford to buy him the new house he demanded to open again. We cut cards for it. I convinced 'Magnus' ace was low. A 'mastermind' he was not. He had heard that the great Hanif Mohammed could bowl either right or left-handed and showed his admiration thus:

'I wish I was ambiguous like him.'

It wouldn't have mattered who had opened with me. We'd have still lost by an innings. They did the same to England u19s soon afterwards. I wasn't surprised since the West Indies attack also included a top-class left arm spinner. I justify including him in a chapter on fast bowlers since he was nearly as quick as our pacemen. His name was Boya Sahadeo and he cheated. He turned the ball both ways out of the back of his hand at a rate of knots with no discernable change of action. I was convinced that no one, not even their wicket keeper, David Murray, who later made a mint as a Test player, could read him.

I'd read how master spinner, 'Tich' Freeman used to hitch up his trousers before bowling his googly. (Tich the hitch.) Boya, too, must have had a signal. I soon spotted him pull on the cuff of his shirt sleeve prior to delivering his 'wrong un.' I quickly spread the word. He took seven for not very many. After the game, I mentioned my clever piece of detective work to the bowler, who replied:

'My shirt is too big. I have no signal.'

Hercule Poirot, I'm not.

More county u19 games brought more bowlers who hurried you up. Then along came Kent. They had the two England Schools opening bowlers, Messrs. Williamson and Graham–Brown (or is that three?). By chance, I overheard their coach reprimanding them with a scary statement of intent before the start:

'You both bowled beautifully last week but neither of you hurt anyone, did you?'

My instincts of self-preservation implored me to drop down the order with a migraine – I had now mastered the word - which would miraculously disappear once the pie-chuckers came on. Instead, I gleefully played second fiddle, well, fourth really, to my new-found partner, in the batting rather than petting sense, Dick. In no way did he bat like one. He smashed 150, mainly off their quicks, in our total of 292 for 3. The only things to get hurt were the ball and their bowling figures.

Not to be outdone, London did, occasionally, let loose its own demon 'strike' bowler. Saeed Hatteah was introduced to me as the 'Mad Hatteah.' I soon found out why. He possessed blistering pace. Sussex were unfortunate enough to face us at East Grinstead, which was hard and bouncy. Saeed felled their first four batsmen with some wicked short-pitched deliveries. It was like a re-run of watching Harold Larwood endearing himself to the Aussies 30 years earlier.

Being a caring sort of bloke, with obvious medical training, Saeed reassured us each time:

'He'll be OK. There's some blood but no broken bones.'

That's fine then. After the peace treaty was signed, he admitted he'd bowled 'fairly quickly' but only really let it rip when representing England Schools. True to his word, later in the1968 season, Saeed took four Combined Services wickets in five balls for MCC Schools at Lords. I wonder if he hit any soldiers in the privates.

Saeed wasn't quite as concerned about the batsmen's well-being as another London speed merchant. 'Black Beauty' was a bit of a dark horse with the ladies. In keeping with this, he never forgot his manners. After having rearranged Yorkshire's number one's features with a ball which kicked viciously, 'BB' was polite enough to ask him if he was alright before appealing for hit wicket. 'Yorky' had collapsed onto his stumps and was out (cold). I was soon to learn that northern quicks aren't as courteous.

Food for thought:

5.   Was Surrey's Peter May as unsure as team-mate Mike Willett?

6.   Is England's Stuart Broad in a band?

7.   When Rob Key of Kent drops a catch, is he rechristened Don by his colleagues?

8.   Was Kerry Packer ever an Irish docker?

Chapter 3

FAST BOWLERS (NORTH)

Due to a sheltered upbringing, big nose, wayward hair and teenage acne, my experience of even bounce and little deviation relates here to nothing more exciting than dry wickets. I'd batted on little else in the south so wasn't prepared for what was to come. From 1970-73, I played principally against other wing PE colleges and universities for Leeds Carnegie. Away games were fine. Home games were like Russian roulette. One of the top, if not the top (Loughborough would argue their case but they wore purple tracksuits) PE institutions in the country did not have a proper cricket square. We had to make do with the Acre. This was an undulating field, I guess about an acre in size, with the odd empty beer can, abandoned text book, tree, car, sun bather, passing lecturer, Frisbee thrower, courting couple and upset batter in situ.

The groundsman was a genius with roses but wouldn't get his lawn mower out for anyone. I had to cut the wicket. I worked on the premise that the less grass there was, the less bounce there would be. A process of error and error eventually persuaded me that no matter how much grass was left on the wicket it would still behave like a trampoline.

For variation, you'd get the occasional 'worm shagger' to

combat complacency. It was a fast bowler's paradise. As a batsman, options were limited. Instead of using a bat, you could arm yourself with two bargepoles for the balls that did bounce and a shovel for those which didn't. Even then, you needed to be aware of which trees and hillocks had fielders hiding behind them. We tried to play as many away games as we could.

I wonder what Lancashire's Andy Hayhurst made of the place 10 years later. He got a degree in Human Movement there. I bet he didn't use the groundsman as a case study.

One away fixture did cause a stir. It was down the road at Leeds University. Our heartbeats were sent racing by the appearance of Colin Lever. A 'mature' student – he treated our childish pranks with disdain – Colin was widely regarded as the best all-rounder in Minor Counties cricket in the 70s. He was easily good enough to have played at full county level, like his brother, Peter of Lancashire and England. This made him far too classy for us. Ironically, he only took two wickets. 'Coco' (the clown) at the other end bagged eight. We were all so relieved to get away from Colin's pace that we over-relaxed and paid the price.

1974 marked my first taste of league cricket. A friend, Keith Boden, an excellent opening bowler who had played for England Schools, coaxed me to join him at Lidget Green in the 1st division of the Bradford League. I should have anticipated it was going to be ultra-serious when I had to 'sign-on.' On the plus side, there would be no more 'Smiffy,' Suffling or Willis to haunt me. One was working in a shoe shop, one was appearing in the 'Incredible Hulk' and one was bowling out Australians.

In a league where it soon became apparent that even spin bowlers were hostile, I was happy to hide at number three. Our opening bats, 'Brent' Ford and 'Griffin' Parks, were the 'bee's knees.' Like Fred's aptly named niece, Abbie Titmuss, they were a fine pair to behold and, like the Americans, I rarely went in early.

'Brent' and 'Griffin' opened in every game of the season, except once – Lightcliffe away. Coincidentally, Lightcliffe had a rather brisk Pakistani Test bowler named Naseer Malik. Our leader, 'Brent,' always picked me up in Leeds and kindly took me to every game without problem, except once – Lightcliffe away. We always arrived at least three quarters of an hour before the start, except once. Correct. Despite having played at Lightcliffe several times before, 'Brent' inexplicably got lost. We arrived, via a tour of Huddersfield, 10 minutes before the start. We were so late that our vice captain, 'Nelson' – he always kept one eye on the clock – had to toss up.

We'd been inserted. 'Brent' benignly informed me he thought the time was right for me to open. I bet he did. All that rushing had seemingly left him ill-prepared to do so. Totally prepared myself, I got one that nipped back, testing my box and my rocks, from Malik first ball up, an appropriate term in the circumstances. As a consequence, my protector seemed to be playing a tune, making it a kind of juke box.

Since the second ball did the same, I had a stereophonic matching pair. I wanted the pain to disappear but was happy for the swelling to stay. Did I have the balls to get in line for a third time? I'd done so twice as long as Hitler could, but I'd run out. The next ball seamed away and feathered my outside edge. I then became a member of a most selective club in the league at that time. I walked. Notwithstanding that it was in the style of a newly circumcised, saddle-sore cowboy, I walked. For the record, 'Brent' was so traumatised by the journey that he was unable to bat until Malik came off near the end of the innings; a captain's prerogative.

Malik didn't play in the return match so I found myself in my usual spot. I only did one year in the Bradford League; missionary workers should never outstay their welcome. With it being the wettest summer I can remember, the wickets were always soft, except once. Consequently, I didn't face anyone quick, except …

In 1975 I crossed the Pennines to play in the Central Lancashire League for Middleton, the club which brought Basil d'Oliveira to this country as its professional in 1960. The CLL has always been one of the toughest leagues in England, with a plethora of big name professionals. The crowds were much bigger than in Yorkshire. This may be thanks to the water or purely that the Tykes were too tight-fisted to pay to watch.

As luck would have it, nearly every side had a top-notch opening bowler. A few early skirmishes made me realise it was best to deny ever having visited London, never mind having been born there. My accent, far from sounding cockney or Australian, needed to be considered 'refined Rochdale,' which is as much of an oxymoron as saying that Glamorgan became a 'first-class' county in 1921 or a wife telling her husband:

'This is a good time to go shopping.'

The next eight seasons turned out to be almost a 'Who's Who.' Joel Garner, Andy Roberts, Colin Croft, Franklyn Stephenson, Ehtesham-ud-Din, Geoff Lawson and Steven Jeffries all threatened my well-being during this time. (At the time of writing, four of the seven can claim to be in the top 12 all-time best career economy rates in Tests, with three in the top five.) Was it too late to learn how to do a flick-flack or to climb the Matterhorn?

Perish the thought, but should I feel moved to become complacent there were also plenty of other less well-known pace bowlers such as Duncan Carter, Junior Williams, Charles

Alleyne, Hartley Alleyne, Clem Thomson, all big, very big, West Indians. This lot, as well as a quartet of locals, the aforementioned Colin Lever and Mel Whittle, plus Kenny Stephens and Ian Gemmill, should all have carried a health warning. White men can't jump but they can bowl fast.

I'll start with the biggest. Joel 'Big Bird' Garner is 6ft8. As if that wasn't menacing enough, he has the longest arms known to man. This meant he was letting go from a height of 10 feet. Before embarking on an illustrious Test career which earned him 259 victims, he plied his trade for Littleborough. Their ground had one small and one large sightscreen. You can guess which one he dwarfed over when he bowled. (It would have been either but he went for the smaller one, just to turn a dog's chance into no chance at all.)

Joel could extract more bounce than a bra-less Pamela Anderson. Given the choice, I'd rather be suffocated than concussed any day. Back to the real world, Joel didn't take kindly to anyone hanging around for more than an over or two. Not many did.

I first faced him in 1977. He had just taken one of his 105 wickets (at 8.54 apiece) and seemed really fired up. We soon found out why. 'Basil,' who was obsessed with brushing his hair, was at the crease. He'd previously been on Surrey's books (as a cricketer, not as a librarian). He was a quality player with a wealth of experience and his own, expensive, full-size bat.

In an attempt to stop me shaking uncontrollably, he assured me he would face as much of 'Big Bird' as he could:

'What a great bloke,' I thought. (I've always been gullible.)

My mendacious batting partner got confused. He and the out-going man had crossed following a top edge to the keeper. 'Basil' then edged Joel's next ball straight to gully at speed. Ignoring the script, he screamed for me to run. (My call, I believe.) I got caught up in the frenzy and complied. Seemingly, one ball constituted the 'as much as he could.'

In a perverse way, I was looking forward, or upwards, to the challenge. I felt like Princess Margaret, although, not being as handsome as Keith Miller, I knew I couldn't have her, when she married Lord Snowdon. We both had a mountain to climb. Here I was face to knee – not even navel this time – with an incensed tearaway.

My captain, 'Basil,' had abandoned ship. It was up to me. What a shame the next delivery wouldn't be. We subsequently found out that Joel was feeling particularly pumped up due to a piece of opportunism from his skipper, 'Thirsty,' - he drinks a lot. Prior to kick off, Joel had been upset to learn that his weekly earnings had been taxed. He vented his anger on 'Thirsty,' who exploited the situation adeptly. He assured Joel that the only people he should be vexed with were those at the Inland Revenue and, coincidentally, Middleton's first four batsmen were all tax inspectors.

I now felt a similar sensation to the one I experienced on the way to play Ashton a month previously. I'd found myself on a road barely wide enough to drive down without removing the wing mirrors only to be confronted by a 'road narrows' sign and the sight of a huge tractor chugging towards me.

I kept telling myself to watch the ball as 'Big Bird' bounded in. It didn't help. My first glimpse of it did not come until after it had pitched and skimmed alongside a low-flying aircraft. Why hadn't I seen it? Was he too fast? He was quicker than 'Smiffy' but surely not so quick as to render the ball invisible.

Since Joel was like most postmen and didn't rush between deliveries, I had sufficient time to make two decisions. Firstly, should I sit down between each ball? More pertinently, what did I need to change in order for it not to degenerate into a spot the ball competition?

I opted to remain standing. Joel wasn't renowned for his sense of humour on the field. I also realised I hadn't seen the ball because I wasn't looking high enough. Forget the textbook. Keeping your head still didn't work. It was necessary to crick your neck and look to the heavens, ironically, as if seeking divine intervention. Only then did you have any chance of catching sight of the weapon flying out of hands as big as dinner plates.

Joel isn't a complicated man. He restricted himself to two deliveries – bouncers and yorkers.This meant both extremities were in danger. I did fail to get my size 12s out of the way of one yorker. Was I glad that I'd graduated from plimsoles for that one.

Middleton's 'Pat,' so called because he was the village postman and not because he put me in mind of cow muck, conjured up a novel idea for countering the threat of 'Big Bird.' 'Pat' had an uncanny knack of getting under the skin of most of the league's quickies. Bear in mind that this was 1978, so only motorcyclists and policemen wore helmets.

'Pat's' reasoning can only be described as flawed, and he nearly was. With an obvious death-wish, he contrived to 'track' Joel. His thinking was that if he stayed in his crease he'd get hit on the head. If he advanced down the wicket he'd 'only get hit on the body.' Strangely, the bat didn't seem to come into the equation. His preference for taking body blows was due to him being blessed with more natural padding than most. (Southern for he's a fat sod.)

True to his word, 'Pat' duly came down the track to meet his first delivery. The great fast bowler rubbed his eyes in disbelief as the ball disappeared into the willow wielder's floppy belly.

Joel displayed admirable restraint. He put up with this for fully two balls. 'Pat' had made the mistake of edging the second of these over the slips for a one bounce four. He then compounded the situation by announcing too loudly:

'First blood to me, old boy.'

Fancy mentioning blood. Unaccustomed to being clobbered all over the park, Joel countered. He grunted something incoherent and walked the 60 metres back to the sightscreen. This took him all of eight paces. He pushed the screen, with just one hand, from over to round the wicket and spun round. I thought he was going to start break-dancing. Instead, he began running and kept on running. I wet myself and I was already out. The ensuing delivery knocked a paralysed 'Pat's' middle stump clean out of the ground and almost out of the ground. Joel grunted again and pointed to the pavilion. No one ever tracked him again.

'Party,' who loves jelly, ice-cream and Punch and Judy shows, was next in. He could have been forgiven for appearing exhausted as well as petrified. He'd spent most of the previous day sawing down half a tree, situated behind the bowler's arm. (I did mention that this was 'serious' cricket.) He was convinced this would assist him in sighting 'Big Bird's' whirlwinds. He got it wrong on two counts. He was castled first ball and Joel bowled from the other end.

One CLL side did come up with a plan to minimise the Garner factor. Having bowled first, they bribed the groundsman to water the run-ups during the tea interval before he fled the country. To overcome this, Joel merely bowled round the wicket instead of over. Severely inconvenienced, he took 7 for 18 and nearly broke out in an uncontrollable smirk.

There was one bonus, just one, when playing against this

fabulous bowler. He could be relied upon to get wickets for both sides. He called in Braille. No Littleborough player had a clue what he was saying when he was batting. 'Yes', 'no' and 'wait' all came out in a baritone 'uuh.' They had to guess. The outcome was invariably a case of a run out waiting to happen.

Unfortunately, there were no such benefits when up against Royton's Colin Croft. Colin was good enough to have already taken 8 for 29 for the West Indies against Pakistan. Did he, therefore, need the added bonus of bowling on a pitch with a ridge? An army clairvoyant, (military medium) he was not. A small, fat, Welsh spin bowler, he was not. Bothered when he inflicted pain on you, he was not. Rapid, he was. 'Party' again can testify to this. The error-prone left-hander did choose to leave his saw at home this time but he still did something I hadn't been able to do in the Old Qs showers. He found himself in hot water.

The use of the wrong adjective to try to suck up to one of the premier fast bowlers of the era was about to cause a stir. As a ball whistled (they are very clever) past a surprised 'Party's' nose, he uttered:

'Bloody hell! You're swift.'

'Swift?' retorted an indignant Crofty, doubtless believing 'Party' was comparing him to a small bird rather than 'Big Bird.' 'Swift? I'ze the world's fastest bowler, man.'

Quite a claim, but he justified it next ball. It thudded against its target's inadequate chest. 'Party' spluttered, dropped his bat onto the stumps and staggered off, muttering:

'Could be, could be.'

Andy Roberts also brought terror to the league as Littleborough's professional in 1982. Good enough to get over 200 Test wickets, Andy didn't often bowl short. He just put the ball on a sixpence and looked bored. By now I was opening for

Middleton. (Blame my uncle.) I was trembling at the other end minding my own business when my partner, the vain but illiterate 'Varicose' misread the script. He hit Andy for a six. As something of an introvert, the legendary Antiguan had been bowling well within himself. Not any more. The next ball was a conservative 20 mph quicker. It all but dislocated 'Varicose's' shoulder. A knowing look from Andy, one of submission from 'Varicose,' first-aid on the shoulder and normal service was resumed.

Franklyn Stephenson played in the league for both Littleborough (who didn't go in for batting professionals) and Royton (ditto). Michael Atherton considers him to have been 'the master of the looping slower ball.' I only wish he'd opted to bowl more slower balls when we faced him. Franklyn is one of the nicest cricketers I've ever met (off the field). On it, he took no prisoners. Like page three models do, he regularly treated us to a good look at his bouncers. To compound the problem, they doubled as off cutters. To right-handers, it was 'chin music.' The erudite writer Neville Cardus would have considered them 'a danger to skull and thorax.' It was like facing a scud missile. There was no escape, not even if you were an accomplished limbo dancer like South African, Eddie Barlow.

Franklyn didn't only torment league cricketers. A few years later he was to do the double for Nottinghamshire and is one of only three county cricketers to score a century in both innings as well as take 10 wickets in the same match. As mentioned, he started at Littleborough. He then went to Royton, before moving on to Oldham, a schedule not to be found in any Thomson's holiday brochure. Although, in our first encounter, he did a Javeed's brother on me – Broke Miandad – my enduring memory of him was from another clash.

It was 1980. We were top of the league. Royton were second. Franklyn was steaming in. He 'did' my opening partner, 'Freddie,' a dreamer, who was convinced he would get a ton, early on with a chin splitter. Apart from having to retire hurt, the cut transformed his pristine white shirt into a replica Sunderland top. All I could think of saying to 'Freddie,' as he walked off for a blood transfusion, was a pathetic:

'You won't be shaving tomorrow, mate.'

Next in, and out, was 'Scoop.' 'Scoop' isn't a reporter, he simply likes ice-cream. You are what you eat and 'Scoop' melted, conveniently missing a straight one. He seemed to slip in a brown patch of his own making. (It wasn't chocolate sauce.)

'Scoop' was eventually replaced by 'Ringo.' 'Ringo' thinks he's a star but he took so long to get to the middle he was nearly timed out. He is left-handed so at least his chin appeared to be safe. His fingers weren't so fortunate. The middle two on his right hand had to be prised off the bat handle. Off he trudged, never to play the drums again.

Our professional, DS, normally batted at four. Not today. He'd mysteriously also slipped … down to five. As he joined me, he uttered these unforgettable words:

'You are playing Stephenson beautifully. You carry on taking him and I will slog the leg spinner.'

'My name's Billy, not Silly,' was my wasted response because all DS said was:

'It's not. You're called Jim.'

While gratified that he knew who I was, there was as much chance of me assisting DS in his plan as there was of the Old Qs ever having a twelfth man. I didn't quite go as far as 'Basil' by taking singles to gully but I did get our pro to take almost his fair share of the Barbadian's bombshells. This was mainly because my partner can't count to six without an abacus.

After the game, which we won, Franklyn, got a few icy stares from some of our spectators in the bar. I found myself standing next to him and, as we still had to play them away on their ridge, I decided to break the ice. I offered to buy him a drink. It was the best half of bitter I've ever bought. I faced Franklyn a further five times and he didn't bowl me a single bouncer. Before anyone sees this as a panacea, I must add that the pint of Guinness I bought Joel Garner was less efficacious. He had no hesitation in trying to behead me thereafter. Perhaps he prefers Murphy's.

Talking of decapitations leads me seamlessly on to the two Alleynes, Charles and Hartley. Both hail from Barbados. Both had a similar philosophy – don't pitch it up. Hartley's first game in England was for Rochdale against Middleton on a bitterly cold day for us, which made it positively arctic for him, in April 1980. Hartley wasn't in the best of moods with me prior to the start. He had stained his whites by sitting on some half-melted candy-covered chocolate sweets. I called him 'Smarty Pants.' He called me a 'Razclot.'

Before showing us how quickly he could bowl, he had a bat. His innings caused a smile or two – the calm before the storm. To begin with, he was bowled by a no-ball. Unwittingly, he walked off, only to be brought back. Soon after, he was caught on the boundary but didn't walk:

'What do you want, Hartley, jam on it? You're out, pal,' explained our bowler with terrible manners, 'Ivan.'

After tea, Hartley bowled quickly and short enough for us to have to continually bob and weave out of the way. We were like a load of 'jammy dodgers.' Indeed, he bowled well enough during the season to get a contract with Worcestershire the year after. As far as I know, he didn't kill anyone.

Charles might have done. No relation, he has such wide

shoulders that he has to come through doors sideways. Charles really did love to bowl bouncers. None of the umpires seemed to know what 'intimidatory' bowling meant and so he was never warned. I don't blame any of them for not confronting a beast who stands 6ft6 tall with the frame of an Olympic weightlifter (but not one of those fat ones).

Rumour had it that numbers weren't Charles' strong suit. Apart from forgetting how many short balls he'd bowled in a row, he also, seemingly, had problems remembering the number of his lodgings. As a visual aid, a bottle was hung from a tree in the garden to indicate which terraced house was his. All went well until the night he returned home, with no key, to find that all the gardens were bottle-less. Although he was irked, it was very late and being a thoughtful bloke, he didn't want to scare people to death by knocking on doors, none of which had doorbells. Fortunately, Charles then heard someone playing an old Frankie Vaughan song. This reminded him that his house was the only one with a green door. Despite losing his bottle, Charles was later awarded the 'no bell' prize for peace (and quiet).

Steve Jeffries took 112 wickets at 10.7 apiece in 1981 for Crompton. A South African ex-marine, he was only marginally shorter, yet slightly wider, than Charles. Jeffries was gifted enough to go on to take 10 for 59 for Western Province against Orange Free State, 8 Nottinghamshire wickets before lunch for Lancashire in 1983 and 5 for 13 for Derbyshire in the Benson and Hedges Cup Final versus Hampshire.

Hardly surprising then, that he was way out of my league. He was responsible for subjecting me to the most uncomfortable 30 minutes of my life, aside from taking my driving test and explaining to my wife that I would be playing cricket on her birthday and on our anniversary, again. Steve bowled left arm over, straight at your body, at speed. He was distinctly awkward, even on batsman friendly surfaces. Imagine, then, facing him on a hard track livened up by 10 minutes of rain. I was as frightened then as I was on my first ever flight upon hearing that the pilot was one Captain Skidmore.

Australia's Geoff Lawson had a career tally of 180 Test wickets. He got almost half that number of victims in his one season for Heywood in the early 80s. Geoff was so pacey that he almost got done for exceeding the speed limit against us. His body-line approach so upset 'Mr. Plod,' our sporting upholder of law and order that 'Plod' threatened to nick him for speeding if he got hit and Geoff then drove home after the game. Geoff did, actually, get nicked during our innings; by me, between fifth and sixth slip, which makes him sound much faster than the first and second slip it really was.

Ironically, a week later he almost fell foul of the law again. I'm told he left a toy shop with a Frisbee without paying for it. He was only allowed to go when he explained he didn't fork up because he thought it was called a 'Freebie.'

Entesham-ud-Din opened for Pakistan in five Tests. He was succinctly described by Graeme Fowler as 'a little fat bloke' who got him out at Headingley in 1982. In the same year, he played for Daisy Hill against Middleton in the Lancashire Cup. With club umpires, he was allowed to bowl from about 18 yards. That made him little, fat and rapid. In the event, we were fortunate not to end up pushing up the daisies.

There were also some nippy Englishmen around in the CLL as well. Heywood had Colin Lever, who received due praise in the previous chapter. He was partnered by the immaculate Kenny Stephens, who took all 10 wickets against Littleborough in the late 70s. Facing those two was like playing dodge the bullets in down-town Beirut. To this day, I still wince when I relive being hit in the Niagras (southern for nuts) by Kenny during the only game my mother ever watched me play in. That isn't because she still lives down south or because she doesn't like cricket. It's just that she doesn't think I'm worth watching.

My left gonad now had 'Readers' indelibly printed on it. Aware of the maternal gaze coming in my direction, I didn't know where to look or how to rub it. I do know that it was even more painful than the vasectomy I had years later under local, rather than general, anaesthetic. (We all make mistakes.)

Enough of that 'cock and ball' story, I stopped playing in the CLL when my daughter was born in 1983. I did so because my wife, Marg (she hates butter) had decreed that she also wanted a son. She didn't want 'Big Bird' or anyone else from Sesame Street to knock my rocks through my backside, causing me to become omnipotent, or something similar.

I went down the road, or downhill, from then on. Thornham played in the Lancashire and Cheshire League at that time. The standard of cricket amongst the amateurs is on a par with the Bradford and Central Lancashire Leagues. The only real difference is that the CLL generates more money to attract bigger named professionals and, thus, more spectators.

I naively assumed this meant I'd seen the last of really quick bowlers. I hadn't reckoned on Denton's money. By that, I'm not making a veiled reference to the vast wealth somehow accumulated by my headteacher, Denton Roper, who was once mistakenly called Swinton Stringer. This Denton is the club who almost hired Viv Richards but, to the chagrin of every batsman in the league, chose the one and only Malcolm Marshall, who mustered a mere 329 Test wickets in his time on good tracks.

I could have stayed at Middleton and crossed paths with Ezra Moseley and Curtly Ambrose. But no, I was advised, as I was now a father, that it was too dangerous. Lucky for me then that Malcolm was only about 10 mph quicker.

In fairness, Malcolm's philosophy was similar to Andy Roberts's before him. You were relatively safe if you dealt in singles. Short pitched deliveries were used sparingly unless you hit boundaries. As if. It then became personal and you soon wished you hadn't. That was Marshall Law for you.

When Malcolm moved to Leyland in the Northern League, he was replaced at Denton by another West Indian Test paceman, Kenny Benjamin. Lucky us. We got a double dose that season. As well as having to face Kenny, we drew Leyland in the Lancashire Cup. Marshall played, although it had been touch and go so they had Richard Hadlee on stand-by! Richard even turned up to watch and I accidentally trod on his foot in the bar. That was undoubtedly the only way I was going to be able to follow in his hallowed footsteps.

Kenny Benjamin was less placid. I was nearer 50 than 40 (years not runs) when I opened against him. From the outset, the omens were bad. The grape-vine had intimated that Kenny had drawn up a 'hit list.' I was on it. He also had a medium-to-strong hurricane blowing right behind him. He lovingly singled me out as soon as I began walking out to bat:

'That old man is not wearing a helmet,' he growled. (I look terrible in hats.)

Could this have been a mistake? For a split second, Asda seemed a preferable option. The situation deteriorated further when my partner, adorned in a glowing white helmet, as if to highlight my lack of headgear, upset our volatile adversary in the very first over. 'Yesah,' who is far more positive than 'Noah,' hit Kenny for a straight six. It wasn't that good. It was an edge which flew right over the wicker-keeper's head and got caught in the 'breeze.' I then foolishly pushed a single from the first ball bowled by the trundler from the other end. 'Yesah' predictably saw out the over, turning at least four ones into nones.

This left me to face the wrath of a man capable enough to take 6 for 66 against England in Kingston (Jamaica, not Surrey) the following year. No worries. Forget that he'd just been hit for six, I didn't think he was fast enough to put a helmet on for, my eyesight was little better than Stevie Wonder's and I was a marked man, or soon would be.

Unlike the bloke who always smells of onions, Thornham's 'Hot Dog,' I've never been a knife thrower's assistant. He and his wife visited us on holiday in Tenerife (pre-season, of course) and he was pulled out of the audience to be one. I do know just what it feels like, though. Kenny has prepared me for it should the occasion ever arise. Six life-threatening missiles whizzed perilously close to my body as I cowered in helpless submission.

The first ball was on course to de-core my Adam's apple. Somehow, I got my bat up in a reflex action in front of my throat just in time to avoid a nasty mess. The next one almost parted my hair straight down the middle, à la 1930's footballers. The third nearly did a Van Gogh on me and all but lopped off my left ear. The fourth ball confused Patrick Moore. He mistook it for a UFO. The penultimate delivery bounced even higher and almost needed a parachute to help it descend. Before Kenny let go of the final ball, I opted for a change of tactic:

'Bugger this for a game of soldiers' (a line which had come to me a few years earlier when facing Captain Nigel Knott who opened for the Combined Services), I thought. I hit the deck before he bowled. It was a maiden.

Ironically, 45 minutes later, another of Kenny's half-trackers didn't bounce as high as the rest had. I kept it down beautifully … with the point of my elbow. It wasn't humorous, although plenty of people chuckled. I couldn't grip the bat and retired hurt with a nice little red-inker and a not-so-nice enlarged red funny bone.

Then came the man who sounds like an Irish-built drain, Murphy Su'a. Murphy was born in Samoa but played Test and One-Day International cricket for New Zealand. He may go up in some people's estimation in that he effectively put an end to Dermot Reeve's Test career by dismissing him for nought in what was to be his last innings for England. Murphy played for Michael Atherton's former club, Woodhouses. He bowled slippery left arm over. Worse still, he swung the ball late in towards your toes. Unless you were a budding Fred Astaire, you were in severe danger of sore feet.

Blessed with footwork more akin to Red Adair, I had to convince young Murphy of the error of his ways. After five overs of tap dancing, not wanting to fall into the bath, I suggested that it was a waste of energy bowling quickly on such a slow wicket. Why risk burning himself out so early in the season? Take the pace off it and he'd be able to bowl for longer. He did and he did. 20 minutes later he stuffed me with a medium-paced jaffa which swung so far it made me go cross-eyed. Poetic justice.

From one Murphy to another. Tony Murphy was someone I should have heard of, but hadn't, back in the 80s. Throughout this time, the Lancashire and Cheshire League side had an annual fixture with the Cheshire County League. These tended to be reasonably amical affairs since both teams contained a fair sprinkling of Cheshire Minor County Players. The 1986 game was less run of the mill.

The opposition batted first on a typically benign Poynton wicket which played well throughout their 45 overs. During the tea interval, neither I nor my opening partner, 'Homer,' who wasn't a Simpsons fan but did have a dislike of playing away games, chose not to pass the 20 minutes nibbling cucumber and radish. We preferred to spend the time preparing for a, hopefully, long stay at the crease on such a beautiful batting surface.

My routine invariably involved quietly visualising the perfect execution of my full array of strokes (the forward defensive and the snick through the slips). Since, as Kenny Benjamin will testify, I did not wear a helmet, I was soon padded, gloved and boxed up, ready to visualise. 'Homer,' too, was not normally a helmet wearer. Why, then, was he sporting one and ducking and diving like a shadow boxer?

I am not a curious person but had to know what prompted this atypical behaviour:

'What's with the lid and the Henry Cooper impersonation?' I asked nervously.

'Get real. Didn't you know Murph's opening up for them?' replied 'Homer.'

I didn't but thought he said Smurf and was, therefore, curious as to why he felt the need of extra protection when facing a gnome. It transpired that Tony Murphy was a very large non-gnome who was Cheshire's top bowler. He was good enough and quick enough to go on to play for Lancashire and then for another first-class county where it doesn't rain so much, Surrey. He rose to fame by hitting the stumps twice in Surrey's inaugural 3-2 bowl out win over Oxfordshire in 1991.

Armed with this unwelcome news, my preparations now shifted to calculating how scarey he'd be on this excellent surface. As nothing before the break had got up to even box height, I concluded that no extra protection was necessary. 'Homer' and I walked out side by side. He was still jousting and then suddenly sprinted away from me to the bowler's end.

'Looks as though I'm facing then,' I said.

With Tony's first six balls being no more than gentle looseners, I wondered what all the fuss was about. Another maiden from his partner left me ready to face Cheshire's finest once more, but not yet. It chucked it down for about half an hour. Inexplicably, it took the home side nearly that long to drag the covers on. Murphy's first ball after the stoppage almost took my head off and we ran a bye. It would have been two had I not slipped! The next ball put a dent in 'Homer's' grill, prompting him to beg me to take a leg bye. This was really more of a chin bye, and without his helmet, could have been a goodbye.

These two deliveries prompted me to reason that flat and benign had become like one of the Spice Girls after a bath - wet and sporty. Half a chance then became none at all. With another rain cloud fast approaching, our skipper, 'Grumpy,' shouted:

'Go for it right away.'

Did he mean a helmet, the toilet, an appointment at casualty? No. He expected me to come out of my shell against a top-class quick bowler on a dangerous track before I'd even had the chance to get into my shell. To add to my woes, Tony isn't deaf. The lack of secrecy surrounding 'Grumpy's' plan had given him an inkling of what might occur next. Could I get us off to a flying start or would I get pinned to the sightscreen?

After careful thought, I made up my mind to enrol in the Peter Such school of batting. I would give myself ample room outside leg stump and swing in hope. Luck rather than skill saw me get away with three streaky fours on the bounce. With each delivery coming down more rapidly than the previous one, I had now peaked. I edged the next ball to the 'keeper and walked off almost as quickly as 'Homer' had run on.

I wasn't too disgruntled. I'd done as I was told and, with a touch of creativity, the snicks could easily become thunderous drives by the time I next saw my Thornham team-mates. My mood then changed somewhat. 'Grumpy' had just been reassured it wouldn't rain again and so instructed the new batsman thus:

'Forget what I told Jim. Play properly from now on. We've got loads of time and it will soon dry out.'

It did and under a clear blue sky we romped home by six wickets. Murphy's Law saw to it that he put his back out with the delivery which ended my fun and didn't bowl again in the innings. 'Homer' got 79 more runs than dents and was instantly called up into the Cheshire squad. I wasn't and 'Grumpy' was crossed off my Christmas card list.

I'm honoured to conclude my ramblings about fast bowlers with 'Gilly.' I had the pleasure and privilege to play with the late Roy Gilchrist for two seasons and against him several times. Thankfully, as an opponent he was well past his prime in terms of sheer speed. In his younger days, Roy was hailed as 'one of the fastest bowlers in the history of the game.' When he picked up 26 wickets in a series against India in 1959, he was deemed to be even quicker than the great Wes Hall. Michael Melford endorsed this view but gave a further insight into what you could expect:

'He was wild and had the reputation of being a greater danger to the batsman's head than to the stumps.'

That sums up Gilly.

His entire career was surrounded in controversy. Stories about Roy abound. If you picked your moment and bought him a beer or four, he was happy to confirm or modify a few.

'Gilly' had two spells at Thornham. He was the paid man in 1974 and he came back in 1983. After one game, he was in a reminiscing frame of mind and held court for a couple of hours. When asked if, given his time again, he'd prefer to come back as a batsman, he was most dismissive:

'No! I hate batsmen,' was his heartfelt response.

'Anyone in particular?' I mischievously enquired.

There was. It was an Indian Test player of bygone days who'd been Rochdale's professional in the CLL.

'Did you do him?' asked one of the more discerning audience.

Like any good storyteller, Roy milked the moment:

'It wasn't easy. He came out with cap on and towels everywhere. All I could see were his teeth. Skip looked at me as if to say, how about it Roy? I say to skip all I need is three balls. Third ball he's spittin' teeth.'

Well read Michael Melford.

Gilly was more succinct (southern for couldn't be arsed) when quizzed about the time at Crompton in a CLL 'game' against Radcliffe in 1965 when he let fly from 15 yards at a batsman who'd upset him. Don Bickley hadn't accused Roy of only being 'swift.' He had, however, foolishly appealed for 'obstructing the wicket' during Crompton's innings. It was now pay back time. Since Don twisted me out at Milnrow 15 years later, forgive me for not being as sympathetic as I should be.

Picture the scene. As an amateur cricketer, you've given up the chance of an afternoon at Tesco to spend a few leisurely hours playing your favourite sport. The only thud you're expecting to hear is that of leather on willow. Then, inexplicably, stupid arse that you are, you annoy the man known in world cricket as 'the Black Flash.' You have now made him extremely angry.

Even a night out with Russell Grant, conscription or shingles would be preferable. Well, options two and three would be anyway. You're desperately trying to remember whether, in your last will, you left all your worldly goods to your wife or your mistress. You are, in fact, so distressed that you can't even remember the difference between the two. (Answer – about four stone.) A tornado is heading your way and as my mother-in-law stated:

'Those torpedoes really do put the wind up you, don't they?'

Somehow, you regain your composure. You tell yourself:

'He is rapid but he will be 22 yards away. I can deal with that.'

If only. Gilly rushes in, arrives at the crease but keeps going. He eventually delivers the projectile, not from just over the line but from fully seven yards beyond it. Your two main concerns now are will you end up in an isolation ward and, if so, will you be there by yourself?

Our mild, genial superstar pooh-poohed our suggestion that this was tantamount to first-degree murder. (This is a charge not so alien to Roy: 'I was found not guilty.')

'A no-ball's a no ball!' he innocently remarked.

In the twilight of his career, 'Gilly' naturally lost most of his pace. Even so, his ability to analyse players' strengths and weaknesses ensured that he remained a force in league cricket. His reputation and achievements meant that he was highly regarded by most.

Two exceptions were Romiley's clean-living youngsters, 'Spic' and 'Span.' We went there for a cup game in 1983. We were riding high in the first division of the Lancashire and Cheshire League. They were riding low in the second division. With four overs remaining, Romiley were nine down and still required a further 150 to win. These two upstarts were in. Gilly was coming to the end of a good spell when it began to rain.

The rules stated that if a game couldn't be concluded on the Sunday everyone would have to come back on the Monday to finish it off. Romiley is bloody miles from Thornham and it's all over bar the drinking, so come on lads. We suggested a run out or a hit wicket:

'No way,' squeaked an adolescent voice. 'I didn't get a bat yesterday.'

Our powers of persuasion having failed and with the umpires beginning to wonder what it is that's making them moist, we looked to our celebrity to get us out of here. The tropical storm did not deter the batsmen. One of the little buggers proceeded to hit three successive fours off Roy. When the fourth ball received similar treatment, Gilly felt obliged to utter:

'Hey boy, don't you know who I am?'

He didn't.

'You're just an old bloke who can't bowl.'

If only it had been 20 years earlier. Dial 999. How would his adversary have been made to pay for this ill-advised comment? Would he be 'spittin' teeth?' Would he be treated to a 15 yarder? Would his 'head be in greater danger than the stumps? Gilly just smiled knowingly. The next ball was a beautiful leg cutter which defeated the misguided youth and bowled him neck and crop. (I've heard the expression used by commentators but haven't got a clue what it means. Does that make it research or plagiarism?)

'No, sonny,' retorted our wise old bowler. 'I'se the old bloke who has just got you out.'

Thanks for the memories, Roy. I know how much you liked to win but I also know you'd shake your head in disbelief at some of the antics described in chapter four.

Food for thought:

9.   Was England's 'Lumpy' Stevens ever allowed to make custard?

10. Why hasn't anyone written a poem about Northants and England fast bowler David Larter or Yorkshire's Bob Platt?

11. If Brian Brain of Worcester was dyslexic, how would his autograph turn out and would he keep a diary or a dairy?

12. If Wisden cricketers of the year CB Fry (1895) and CJ Burnup (1903) collided, would we end up with a Burnt Fry Up? Similarly, if the Palestinian factions, Fatah and Hamas, joined forces, would they become James Ormond, alias Fatas?

Chapter 4

WINNING AT ALL COSTS

It may now be far more cutthroat in the south, with league cricket having increased since my defection. Winning at all costs did entail batting on for 15 minutes past the half-way mark before declaring in a timed, 2.30–7.30 game. Nobody would have dreamed of stooping to such low-life tactics as one bald captain of Yorkshire. He secured a draw by ensuring that, in an era when three minutes for an over was considered sluggish, his side doubled this by bowling a ball a minute for the last quarter of an hour. I bet he was weened in the Bradford League.

One exception to the south's 'sporting' approach was more a case of not losing at all costs. A Public School Old Boys team was pitted against an XI made up of cricketers of African-Caribbean origin, possibly as a result of a phone call to the Central Bureau. The Old Boys' captain won the toss. Sensing some quick wickets for himself, he asked the opposition to bat. Four hours later, he plucked up enough courage to suggest that a declaration might be in order. Opting for clarity, his opposite number stated his position concisely:

'You put us in. You get us out.'

Another 'one off' took place in an Old Qs game which, of

course, had no appointed officials. An opponent was correctly given out caught behind. Instead of walking, as nearly everybody instinctively did, he refused to move. Like Bart's dad, OJ, he steadfastly protested his innocence, despite telling evidence to the contrary. It soon degenerated into pantomime:

'I didn't hit it,' protested 'Widow Twanky' (or something which sounded similar).

'Oh yes you did,' retorted 'Buttons,' the nearest thing we had to a stud.

As if to emphasise his intent, 'Twanky' sat down just short of a length, which in our case was anywhere on the strip. 'Twanky' looked a bit of a bruiser. Our attempts to make him see reason were, therefore, long-range, secretive efforts:

'Come on, old chap. Play the game,' had no impact and 'Porky' lost patience. He wasn't obese but it was rumoured he'd once gone the whole hog with a pig. He squealed:

'Put the dummy back in his mouth. He's crap so one more ball won't matter.'

Shortly afterwards, 'Twanky' got his lines muddled and was clean bowled. As he trudged off, the bowler 'Dunlop,' a Mick Jagger look-alike, informed him that his second innings was no better than his first.

Occasionally we came up against southerners who must have been to a Test Match at Old Trafford or Headingley. They had that northern mean streak in them, causing them to put winning before enjoyment. Old Fullerians' captain in the late 60s was a real tart. 'Bakewell' was so full of himself that he was probably a traffic warden. He was almost as smarmy as some find Michael Winner, ie off the smarmy scale.

Prior to the start, we agreed tea would be taken 15 minutes beyond the halfway point in proceedings. Was that cow dung I could smell? Ten minutes before the scheduled break, he declared, yet didn't, that his side hadn't got enough runs. I could choose. Pistols at dawn would be fine.

We could still have tea as arranged. The angel cake had been cut and, appropriately, he'd tossed the salad himself. If we did, they would carry on batting afterwards. This would then necessitate another break between innings. It was unheard of. It ranked alongside Fred Trueman completing a sentence on Test Match Special without nine 'ers' in it. It was as galling as when your wife or mother-in-law says:

'I don't know why you get so worked up. It's only a game.'

No it isn't!

Our second option was equally attractive. We could ignore our agreement and give them another 20 minutes batting before refreshments. Cheeky bastard. I put a third option to him. I'd read that the British Government of 1776 had put up a £5000 reward to anyone who could discover the North–West Passage. I was set to stake a claim but 'Bakewell' declined my offer. He confessed he wouldn't feel comfortable using his bat again knowing it had been thrust up the posterior opening of his alimentary canal.

Grudgingly, we opted for the latter. Despite the prospect of receiving 18 overs less than them, for once, we batted out of our skins, apart from 'Skeleton,' who didn't have one to start with. We got to within eight of our target with 10 minutes to go before 'Bakewell' struck again. He decreed that his own built-in light meter indicated it was too dark to carry on and took his team off. I gave him Queensbury's number and hoped they'd be very unhappy together.

Slightly more subtle, yet equally Trevor Chappell-esque (underhand) was Acton's captain versus Evershed whenever. They, too, weren't scoring as freely as desired. As the set time for tea approached, he ran on to the field to explain that the clock was running fast. There were actually 20 minutes remaining until tea, not two. In turn, I informed him I had Red Indian blood in me and the time by the sun was two minutes to tea time. We would be having our tea, peas and pies then. Otherwise, my pipe of peace might find a similar resting place to that suggested for 'Bakewell's' bat. My burly Irish vice-captain, Tom O'Hawk backed me up so despite their reservations we had our Wagon Wheels on time.

Any such scams in the northern leagues may well have resulted in 'fisticuffs,' despite being perceived as very lame. Up here, they don't merely bend the rules. They smash them to smithereens. Even if you are unable to bring yourself to condone some of the goings-on, you cannot but admire their ingenuity.

I've witnessed antics that would make Jeremy Snape's hair curl or Keith Fletcher's uncle Duncan smile. Cleaning the seam (northern for picking it with a bottle top) is commonplace. On wickets known to keep notoriously low, teams will use balls which are so soft that even the Old Quintinians would bin them. Pre-planned orchestrated appeals whenever the ball hits the pads are as regular as moans from the two Fergies, Sarah and Alex. It's not unheard of for fielders to appeal for catches when they know the ball has bounced. Wicket-keepers surreptitiously flicking off the bails when stood up and claiming a clean bowled is a scene witnessed as often as a scowl from Glenn McGrath. I've known batsmen to have been dobbed (northern for run out, backing up) as well as an appeal for a batter to be timed out when he'd been given permission to leave the field to take an aspirin.

As if that wasn't enough in one match (see chapter 11), bowlers often bowl at you before you are ready. It's not as if they need any extra help. The will to win at any price even extends to junior cricket. In a recent Lancashire County League u15 game, one side attempted to get its star batsman in for a second time by disguising him under a different coloured helmet. Playing over-age players is rife, with at least one instance of a supposedly u15 youngster arriving at a game in his own car. At least he left his wife at home.

Perhaps this philosophy of winning at all costs now prevails in the south, too. Such an approach can manifest itself in all kinds of abuse, both verbal and physical. These days in Lancashire, we have disciplinary panels expressly formed to deal with unacceptable behaviour. Anyone accused of being naughty is summoned before a jury to try to bluff their way out of their predicament.

Fortunately, some of these 'trials' do have a light-hearted side. Again, I use the LCL for my example. After a near riot, the two protagonists were cited by the umpires. The 'disagreement,' in their opinion, was worthy of inclusion in 'Gladiator.'

One culprit was a huge South African, not known for his diplomacy or his even temper. (No great surprise there, then.) The other was a small, volatile player of Asian origin. The latter had been dismissed by the former. Words were exchanged. The tiniest of the pair felt the need to arm himself with a stump. (His bat must only have been a size six.) Sparks flew.

According to 'David' and 'Goliath' it wasn't like that. One didn't know what all the fuss was about. It was just like that Shakespeare play.

The other suggested he did no more than say:

'Off you pop,' once the umpire had raised his finger.

Both received six match bans. Taking this into account, I assume Dennis Lillee is glad he didn't play in this league. After he kicked Javed Miandad in 1981, his punishment was a mere

£120 fine. (I believe there are those who felt he should have been paid that sum for beating them to the punch/kick.)

Occasionally clubs take matters into their own hands and mete out sentence prior to the 'trial.' A North Manchester league club banned one of its players 'sine die.' The League Committee must have been suitably impressed. They chose to take no further action. I suppose they could have asked for him to have been hung, drawn and quartered.

Physical abuse remains, thankfully, like how the French prefer their steak. Verbal stick, on the other hand, has become endemic. It is now an art form. When I started out in the capital, off the cuff quips were infrequent and almost apologetic. You might hear:

'They must be short today,' if you made a prat of yourself. (People didn't bother saying that when they played the Old Quintinians because they knew we always were.)

It's always been a trifle more vitriolic up north. Miss a ball and you'll hear something like:

'If it'll help, I'll put a bleedin' bell in it, you useless twat.'

Slightly more off-putting, I feel.

Things have come on. A master at a subtle form of sledging, ie. luging, was the fast bowlers' worst enemy, 'Pat.' Herein possibly lies why. 'Pat', a jovial man, who would make an ideal Father Christmas – big belly, red cheeks, unemployed – could put anyone off their game. Yet he made insults sound almost complimentary. He never swore or blasphemed. To add injury to insult, he always belittled opponents with a big smile on his chubby face. Many a rival was left undecided whether it was a smack or a snack 'Pat' was hankering for.

During a CLL game, I overheard him whisper to Walsden's Sri Lankan professional:

'Lionel…'

Lionel was a pleasant, meek gentleman who wasn't having a great season. (It ended with him averaging just 17 runs per innings and bowling only one over.)

'Lionel,' repeated 'Pat.'

'Yes, my friend,' replied this polite, placid fellow, who was struggling to get any part of the bat to within three feet of the ball.

'Lionel' (that was his name). 'You are, without doubt, the worst professional I've ever seen. Good luck, mate.'

Any slither of confidence thingameebob might have had, disappeared as quickly as a Roy Gilchrist 15 yarder. He did not trouble the scorers. (By that, do commentators mean he didn't call them names?) He was stumped off one of 'Pat's' floaters, trying to hit him off the strip. As he departed, head bowed, 'Pat' kicked the man when he was down with:

'Lionel. Stick to dancing with your sister, Joyce. You'll get more balls that way.'

Two decades later, 'Pat' was still at it. Like me, he had moved from Middleton to Thornham. Unlike me, he'd tried as many clubs as Andy Cole in the interim. His victim this time could play. It was the stout-hearted Murphy Su'a. Despite being over 50 years old, 'Pat' had scored a half-century in his own imitable style. This involved almost exclusive use of the long handle. (Southern for twatting it over cow corner.) The senior cricketer then took his pound of flesh by announcing:

'Isn't it funny? The quicker you bowl, the further I hit it!'

When a thoroughly drained Su'a came in to bat, he decided to give 'Pat' a taste of his own medicine. He failed. He, too, fell foul of the floater.

The master of understatement consoled him with these tender words:

'Son, you'll get nowhere in this game if you try to slog.'

The floater had become a sinker.

Our benign sledger didn't limit his silky tongued comments solely to players. He also played mind games with umpires. As a sub-postmaster for many years, he knew how to communicate with old-age pensioners – he shouted. 'Pat' spoke to every umpire who could hear him as if they were close relatives. He was so considerate that he would often help them out with decisions. When batting, if there was an appeal for lbw, he'd assist the man with the white coat/white stick:

'They can't trick you Venetian, can they? You know I got a little edge on that. Well spotted.' For a caught behind, he'd use: 'You know I walk, Beethoven. Great decision.'

As a bowler, he was equally helpful. Knowing a delivery which had struck a batsman on the pad was reasonably close but definitely not out, 'Pat' would act as judge and jury. There would be no appeal. Instead, he would insist it was close but not worthy of a shout. It was 'just missing leg' or 'a shade too high.' Having convinced the umpire of his integrity, he'd close the deed with a thoroughly credible:

'As you now know, I only appeal if it's 100% certain.'

The very next time he rapped a batter on the pad, he'd scream for blood at the top of his voice, even if it wasn't going to hit another set. I can't ever remember it not working for him. I think he learnt it from his cousin. He was equally devious but didn't smile as much. Accordingly, we christened him after one of the seven dwarves.

'Grumpy,' my favourite league team captain, plied his trade for Longsight. He was an outstanding club and Minor Counties cricketer. As such, we overlooked his resemblance to Charlie Drake. 'Grumpy' hated losing and some of his appeals were more outrageous than those made for 'Children in Need.'

As a most influential figure in the LCL, 'Grumpy' would

regularly get his own way. On the odd occasion he didn't, he could be either irrate or philosophical. I witnessed an example of the rarer of the two in another inter-league contest. Convinced he'd had a genuine caught behind and a plumb lbw turned down, he then clean bowled the same player. 'Grumpy' now put his own slant on Fred Trueman's:

'Nearly had him that time,' by announcing:

'I've never got the same man out three times in the same innings before. Does that count as a hat-trick?'

Now for 'Henry VIII,' as he is lovingly known. He's been married more times than Wayne Rooney's uncle Mickey. He's as intolerant of opponents as he is of women. He has to come out on top. Blessed, or so he believes, with the gift of the gab, one of his chat up lines is a cringing:

'You look like my fifth wife,' paving the way for a reply of:

'How many wives have you had?' to which 'Henry' would jump in with:

'Four.'

For him 'current affairs' means his latest conquest.

Like the man he was named after, 'Henry' is a music-lover. For the following incident to be fully appreciated, it is necessary to paint a brief picture of the fashion and music scenes of the time, the mid-80s. A bald head then, was to be avoided at all costs. Terry Wogan, Bruce Forsythe, Elton John, Shirley Bassey, Paul Daniels all tried hard. Indeed, the only two slap-headed celebrities I can bring to mind were Yul Brynner and the lead singer of the Flying Pickets. This group had recently topped the charts with 'Only You.'

Getting back to 'Henry,' he opened the innings for Prestwich, who were set to face Dukinfield in a LCL fixture. Dukinfield's opening bowler, 'Van,' was a driver for Morrisons and was too good for a, literally, shagged out opponent. 'Van' wore a wig to try to disguise the fact that he has either alopecia or amnesia. I forget which.

Anyway, 'Van' had been like well-used tyres since birth. He took it in good grace, as shown by his comment upon receiving a 21st birthday present:

'Not another bleeding syrup! You really shouldn't have.' (In hindsight, I should have called him 'Aaron.')

With his hairpiece firmly in place, the Dukinfield dasher got to the mid-point of his extremely long run up, only for the deathly hush to be broken by 'Henry' whistling the chorus of 'Only You' louder than even Roger Whittaker could. Everyone collapsed with laughter.

The bowler, however, did get the last two laughs. He struck 'Henry' squarely in the nads, so that he also now had his own Hampton Court. He then clean bowled the man who'd had enough mother-in-laws to make up a coven to make it more a case of flying wickets than Flying Pickets. 'Henry' retired soon after to become a gymnastics coach. This was solely because he discovered that the coach 'is allowed to mount the podium briefly during competition.'

I referred earlier to northern teams resorting to pre-determined, orchestrated appeals in their will to obtain unwarranted wickets. You can tell this comes from a bitter and twisted victim of the same. The master here, or more precisely, the choirmaster, was 'Cookie' in the CLL Too many of him certainly would have spoilt the broth. If he hadn't been so fond of biscuits, he'd have been dubbed 'Crookie.'

'Cookie' would post himself at first slip, having had a long gargle beforehand. He had the routine so well organised and practised, it was much the same as listening to a Welsh male voice choir. Both are unpleasant to the ear, unnecessary and designed to make you walk off.

I also mentioned a team wanting a batsman 'timed out.' This arose in a Thornham game at Stalybridge in 1984. Our number three, 'Rarebit,' was batting superbly, in spite of a headache. (A touch of irony here; a Welshman having, not causing, a headache.) We were on course for a deserved victory when 'Rarebit' asked the umpire if he could go off for a tablet. I sensed there would be trouble when a fielder cried out:

'Who do you think you are, Moses?'

As soon as 'Rarebit, had crossed the boundary, their captain, 'Pugwash,' appealed. I thought he was simply hungry and wanted a chocolate biscuit when he shouted:

'Time out.'

I can only imagine that 'Captain Pugwash' had sunk to such depths through ulterior motives. Maybe he was afraid that if our man got rid of his headache, he'd form a choir with one of the umpires, 'Dai' (who looked as though he could at any moment). The appeal was ignored. 'Rarebit' batted on in belligerent fashion. Boyo, did he Wrexham bowling figures thereafter.

In the same fixture the year before, or it possibly the year after (damn that alopecia), we witnessed another example of Stalybridge's friendly approach. Our fashion-conscious all-rounder, 'Trendy' had played a ball down at his feet. Being half-cut and about to topple over anyway, he indicated a willingness to pick the ball up for the fielder while he was down there. Such a charitable gesture in Chiswick would have met with a:

'You're most kind. I'll ask the bowler to reward you with a slow full toss.'

In the Bradford League, it may well have been greeted with a:

'Leave it there, you fat poof.'

This time 'Trendy's' offer was taken up with surprising gratitude. The nearest fielder, 'Dusty' (who wasn't a pre–

Madonna and didn't wear a blonde beehive wig and bucket loads of mascara; he was simply always covered in dust) cried:

'Cheers,' supplemented by a 'nobhead,' as he didn't want to appear too chummy.

'Trendy' duly stumbled a yard or so out of his crease to pick the ball up and tossed it helpfully to the bowler. Obviously very grateful, 'Mr Angry,' threw the stumps down and appealed for a run out. When this was turned down, he asked for an 'out, handled the ball.' It wasn't. 'Mr Angry' now ramped, champed and stamped so much that he became 'Mr. Incredibly Angry.'

It tended to be like that when teams played Stalybridge. I can't think why they never won the 'Sportsmanship Trophy.' Perhaps the answer lies in the club motto:

'Ad hoc, tempus fugit, winnus atas allus costus in loco parentis,' which loosely translated means:

'Screw you.'

Consider their opening bowler, 'Del Monte,' public enemy number one. Even before being banned for chinning 'Grumpy' – which upped his previously rock bottom popular appeal in some quarters – this man was already notorious. I labelled him 'Del Monte' due to his three favourite sayings:

'That's plum,' 'What a peach' and 'Good cherry.'

He saved his party piece for away grounds, so as not to upset his own groundsman. Whenever the umpires weren't looking – 'carte blanche' – 'Del' would deliberately seek to scuff up the wicket with his studs on a length outside off stump. When I witnessed this first hand, I asked him if he was a fisherman. He took the bait:

'What's your problem, you lanky streak of piss? What are you on about?'

I explained in words of one syllable that I thought he must be looking for worms. Digging deep for a witty rebuff, he composed an erudite:

'Eff off, wanker,' and advised me to: 'Watch your knackers.'

I thought I must have forgotten to tuck them into my jock strap. Then, after a couple of near misses, realised he intended to rearrange them for me. I went off tinned fruit after that.

Such underhand tactics are not solely the domain of the fielding side. Darcy Lever's overseas amateur in 1985, 'TinTin,' was hitting our bowling to all parts. For a lightly built man, he was punching far more than his weight. Intriguingly, the sound of the ball on his heavily taped bat didn't sound quite right. We had plenty of time to make our minds up as he batted right the way through for a hundred.

At the conclusion of the innings, we all saluted him (albeit with two fingers). 'Three point five' (Arthur Severn) called him an 'illegal alien' before 'Dibble' (you guessed it), who had suffered more than most, copped hold of 'TinTin's' offending weapon. He then grabbed his bat and began to rip off the tape. Detecting strips of metal chiselled into parts of it, 'Dibble's' subsequent cry of 'Ulrica' confused us. Had he found something or had he spotted one of Sven's old flames?

Put downs can also give you the upper hand. I have yet to come across one to equal this one provided by Liverpool's Cisse against Kaunas in August 2005. The Kaunas number five wanted to swap shirts with the striker. Cisse obligingly took his off and handed it to his marker. The delighted defender made as if to respond in kind, only for the Frenchman to shake his head and walk away empty-handed.

Almost on a par, a renowned bighead from Stand had been dismissed for 50 odd and was walking around the ground, intent on discussing his greatness with anyone who'd listen. He didn't reckon on KK (see chapter seven), who greeted him with:

'Hi. What number are you going to bat today?'

Similarly, when Denton West's pro, 'Retard,' another slow left armer, boasted to his counterpart in the Woodhouses team, 'Polly' (he's forever putting the kettle on), that he was the best slow left armer in England, 'Polly's' retort was:

'Come off it. You're not even the best slow left armer in this conversation!'

Occasionally, misguided (southern for drunk) spectators get the urge to contribute towards their team's cause. Middleton has always attracted sizeable crowds, many of whom are happy to let the game take its course and sleep through it. Then there's 'Brian the bus.'

During a home game against Littleborough in 1982, our verbose bus driver turned on Andy Roberts. Bad enough in itself, but Brian is endowed with the voice of a champion town crier. He felt Andy was being lethargic in his approach…and his delivery…and his follow-through. We all disagreed:

'Roberts, this is not Test class bowling.'

'Oh yes it is,' retorted 'Cinders,' whose real name is Bernie Cole.

Deluding himself that his admonishment of this world-class bowler was assisting us, Brian repeated his claim 'ad nauseam.' Well, it certainly made us feel sick.

After 20 minutes of this, even the laid-back Andy appeared to be taking stock of his credentials, salient as they are. Brian had to be quietened down. Another spectator, 'Xavier,' a lifeboat captain, came to our rescue:

'Brian, you're a nob. Shut up and go and collect some fares.'

He then threw him a packet of sausages and a fork. He told Brian to read the instructions out loud. Having heard his favourite word, he complied:

'Prick with a fork.'

'Exactly!' exclaimed our would-be saviour, 'Xavier.'

Just like my old Hillman Limp used to, it backfired:

'Prick?' boomed the busman. 'There's only one prick around here. It's that dick with the ball.'

Desperate measures were now called for. Before Andy started to hit us where it hurts, Brian had to be removed. Refusing to believe that he was wanted on the telephone by the Minister of Transport or the director of 'On the Buses,' an appeal to something dear to his heart was made:

'Brian, 'Party' (next in and panicking) has bought you a pint of lager. It's waiting for you in the far corner of the bar,' explained the celibate and none too choosey, 'Desperate Dan.' Once inside, and trapped in the corner by a carefully constructed maze of tables, Brian soon got the taste and eventually fell asleep. The 4.30 from Manchester to Rochdale had to be cancelled, but it was a small price to pay.

One's will to win or do well personally can cause even the most upright citizen to be less than honest. We struggle to cope with failure, either because we are worried about being dropped or due to our egos. Whatever the reason, most of us can find a means of blaming someone or something other than ourselves by unashamedly providing any excuse to justify our failures. With points at stake, the northerner's fiercely competitive nature renders him more likely to grasp at straws when things go awry.

We may not be as creative as the full-time professionals sometimes are, though. Take the Sri Lankans. When they lost to Pakistan in 2001, it wasn't their fault. Their clothes were too tight. They shouldn't have been so fat then, should they?

Nor are we likely to be as acerbic as one Zambian tennis player, Lighton Ndefwayl. (That's his name, not an anagram.)

He didn't get beaten due to his opponent playing better than him. He lost because his jock strap was too tight – not enough loose balls, I suppose. He also claimed that his rival constantly farted when he served. He obviously couldn't cope with the crosswind. This appears to be a case of the 'light's on' but no one's at home.

Can any of us come up with anything as classy? We often let ourselves down by falling back on old favourites. How often do bowlers blame the foot holes after a full toss or a long hop has been dispatched to the boundary? I've seen some call for sawdust in such instances on surfaces harder than the Kray brothers:

'That new ball is too slippery for me,' claimed Thornham's 'Eel,' after his first over went for 12.

Fielders are no better. Even those with 20-20 vision have been known to have suddenly been struck down like Saul of Tarsus upon spilling a dolly. Claims of:

'I didn't see it,' or 'bloody sun,' on days where there is total cloud cover are designed to convince all and sundry that the culprit isn't really another Frank Spencer.

Batsmen are, indubitably, in a league of their own when it comes to excuses. Brian Close takes some beating – as, in fact, he often did. Following a second ball duck, he contrived to blame the 12th man for his demise. It was he who'd given BC the wrong flavoured chewing gum.

The best one I recall from a team-mate occurred in the 60s during a school game. Dave ('Ali') Hupe was dismissed cheaply. (The bowler gave him 5p to spoon a catch.) His excuse was long-winded but worthy:

'You know when you write your initials in butter on a slice of bread and then toast it and the letters come out on the toast? Well, I did that for breakfast and now my right eye hurts.'

In his eye, no more needed to be said.

Only rarely do we admit to having been stuffed. I can readily convince myself, and hopefully my captain, that external forces worked against me. As for lbw, naturally, I've never had one which was genuinely out.

'It was too high.' 'I was too far forward.' 'I knocked the cover off it.' 'It pitched outside leg stump.' 'It was a no-ball.' 'He's bowling from too wide of the crease.' I use them all.

If, alternatively, I've been trapped right in front, ankle high, I have to think again:

'I wasn't ready.' 'Did you see that plonker walk in front of the sight screen (or white car) just as he bowled?' 'I knew he'd give it – third shout,' or 'I got cramp just as I was about to cream it through the covers,' will do.

It's not often that I'm reduced to confessing:

'That was wasted on me. It would have got God out.'

My bank of excuses, although overdrawn, is second-rate compared to 'Popeye's.' (He's not obsessed with Olive Oil; he used to be in the navy.) He was a team-mate at Middleton and detested losing. 'Popeye' was a good pace bowler, talented enough to play for the league side. His batting suffered by comparison. He was only number 11 because games aren't 12 aside. Yet, we all know that most bowlers love to bat and many kid themselves there's nothing to it. In reality, that's what they usually end up with.

Our ex-sailor was very much of this persuasion. Because he was so keen to do well but invariably didn't, he found solace in such a variety of excuses for being out that I re-named him 'Heinz.' Amongst his repertoire was:

'My bat slipped because my gloves are too sweaty.'

This prompted a doubting:

'But you only faced two balls,' from Thomas.

The old sea-dog had obviously planned ahead:

'I know, but it's bloody roasting out there.' (Roasting in Lancashire? The only thing roasting in Lancashire is a hot pot.)

'Heinz' did connect with the odd haymaker. One resulted in him being caught on the boundary:

'I couldn't possibly have hit it any better,' was his modest appraisal.

We all breathed a sigh of relief and were set to go to the tea room to see what type of lettuce was in store, when he added:

'This chuffin' plank of wood is like a polo mint. It's got no middle.'

He has even been known to blame a bowler's nationality for his downfall:

'I've never been able to get runs against Australians.'

This conjured up visions of him being clean bowled by a snorter from Rolf Harris or, more sublimely, being trapped leg before by Kylie Minogue's slower one. A week later, with most of us still drooling about Kylies' googlies, how we'd deal with Holly Valance's lack of control or Nicole Kidman's full toss, our walking encyclopaedia of self-absolution had brought another innings to a close. This time it was different. He'd made double figures. The consensus was that he'd be satisfied. He'd been stumped by a distance and would surely accept defeat graciously. Not quite.

'Heinz' had got his spaghetti hoops in a real twist. He was livid. Our traditional placatory:

'Unlucky matey' – we tried to make him feel all at sea when we could – was greeted by his bat being slung across the changing room. It wasn't boomerang-shaped but did find its way back to the thrower, via the back wall. To lighten the mood, I asked 'Popeye' if he always knocked his bat in like that. He looked perplexed for a moment, then threw his gloves at me and eventually refocused on his excuse:

'Just wait until I bowl at that short arse.'

By process of elimination, I took this to be a reference to the wicket-keeper, as the bowler was 6ft4 and neither Ricky Ponting, Harry Pilling, Pee Wee nor Jimmy Crankie were anywhere in sight.

Sensing a tale for a future book, I sought to exploit the situation, even though the rest of the team had abandoned ship and gone to tea:

'Why's that?' I enquired innocently.

'That naffin' dwarf took the ball a foot in front of the stumps. It was never out.'

If the dwarf had, he'd have needed one arm longer than the other, as, incidentally, the great Len Hutton had.

Creative as this was, it wasn't 'Heinz's' finest. He composed a piece of fiction worthy of the Pulitzer Prize in 1979. He'd patted a simple return catch to the bowler who pouched it with glee. 'Heinz' marched off with a face like thunder, if that's possible. Bets were placed. Would it be the bat, sweaty gloves or the fact the bowler looked like a kangaroo? Surely he couldn't blame the pitch. It was a shirt-front. (Perhaps the ball had deviated off a button.) We were way off.

Our customary passing reference to him being the unluckiest cricketer ever received his animated approval:

'You're telling me. And just when I had the measure of their pro, too.' (He's 6ft5.)

Playing devil's advocate, I suggested:

'The bowler's not an Aussie is he? He's wearing a turban.'

Not one to repeat himself, 'Heinz' ended the speculation:

'No. It was those bleeding kids.'

Thomas again expressed doubt:

'What kids?'

As far as we could ascertain, every youngster in the ground

seemed to be innocent. They had all been sitting down obliviously stuffing E additives into their unsuspecting mouths in preparation for some hyper-activity later on:

'Those kids up that tree,' continued our wounded mariner.

It now degenerated into 20 questions. Like the dog next to us, we began by barking up the wrong one:

'What tree?' asked Woody, in the knowledge that there wasn't even a lavatory on this particular ground.

'That one over there,' sighed 'Heinz,' pointing into the distance.

'Hawkeye' produced a pair of binoculars through which we could just about make out a line of trees in the neighbouring county:

'Oh, that tree,' echoed the chorused reply.

It was as harmonious as a 'Cookie'-led appeal:

'Did they put you off your stroke?' asked Woody.

'Yeah. They were jumping up and down.' (E additives?) 'I reckon they were chucking sticks up to knock down conkers.'

Thomas was unconvinced:

'Come off it. We're not falling for that old chestnut.'

'Heinz,' no longer full of beans, took a while to twig. Once he sensed we were 'pulling his pisser,' he smiled and shouted:

'Bastards,' and started to suck a Fisherman's Friend to acknowledge the termination of another potential match-winning innings and start considering his next tale of woe. Perhaps it would even be genuine. Imagine how much mileage he could have extracted if he'd suffered the same fate as Lionel Tennyson. His Lordship badly injured his hand while fielding for England against Australia in 1921 and, for a southern noble, showed undue grit. He batted one-handed and scored 63 in the first innings. In a reversal of fortune, he made 36 in the second dig, possibly because he used the wrong hand.

'Popeye's' petulance might have landed him in hot soup. It never did and nowadays he is a keen golfer. I wonder what he comes up with after a bad round:

'That tee was the wrong colour.' 'The hole's too small.' 'The bunker's got the wrong kind of sand in it' or 'What do you expect? I had to play one-handed.'

Whatever his excuse, it won't be as good as the one I heard prior to the 2005 General Election. When I asked Thornham's 'Monet' – he looks good from a distance but a mess from close up – if he was going to vote, he shook his head. Why not?

'Because I hate the smell of primary schools,' replied my impressionable friend.

Nevertheless, to his credit, 'Heinz' always went for variety. As far as I'm aware, he didn't use any of his 57 excuses twice.

Stalybridge's captain, 'Grim,' did. He was even more miserable than 'Grumpy' and was prone to telling fairy tales.

This sourpuss was the sort who would play Snap only with people who stutter. He would go to any lengths to win because he didn't have the talent to do so off his own bat or ball. 'Grim' really didn't have the bottle to face our quickie, 'Sharpy,' in 1985. He backed so far away from every delivery that we had to hail him a taxi after each one to bring him back into view. Not wanting to be accused of being a 'spineless dickhead,' 'Grim' felt obliged to justify his cowardly display:

'I'm not frightened. I've just had a vasectomy.'

We might have believed him had he not used the same excuse in the return fixture four months later. It was a case of one too many chips off the old block. Henceforth, 'Captain Courageous' became known as 'snip' rather than 'skip' and I'm told he retired from cricket to become an officer in the Egyptian army.

Most amateurs do place a heavy emphasis on coming out

on top but we haven't as much to lose as the paid men. Mentioning heavy, what about Shane Warne? His defence for testing positive for a banned substance in 2003 was to blame his mother. She'd given him a diet tablet to help him look slimmer. What was it, a miracle cure? Fat chance of that working, Shane. Appropriately, this is now followed by…

Food for thought:

13. When J.Decent made 45 not out for Bradford League club, East Bierley in the 1979 final of the Whitbread National Village competition, just how good an innings was it?

14. When D.Rought-Rought played for Cambridge way back when, was it a case of two roughts making a wrong?

15. Does India's Srinivasaraghavan Venkataraghavan ever have enough time or space to sign autographs?

16. Isn't it a bit harsh to say that Aussie Greg Blewett?

Chapter 5

THE PROFESSIONAL

While playing non-league cricket in the south, all the word 'professionals' signified to me was a second-rate programme on ITV to outgun BBC's 'Dixon of Dock Green.' Despite there being a conveyor belt of excellent players on the club scene around London, none, to my knowledge, was paid to play. The nearest thing to it was the Old Qs offer of free teas to the Melrose spectators who guested for us. Having tested one, they wisely decided not to jeopardise their amateur status.

I first became aware of such strange goings-on when I joined the Bradford League. The pro was supposedly the sole person to receive payment. Some clubs were confused by this ambiguous ruling. They paid several, or even all, first teamers.

Lidget Green, disappointingly, didn't. Only big Dave Ross was paid weekly ('very weakly,' he'd say). We did, nonetheless, have the opportunity to earn 'talent' money. Although Jim Davidson would struggle, I hoped that this might be a nice litte earner:

'How does that work?' I asked 'Shylock,' the treasurer.

I was praying for a pound per run, a fiver for every four, a tenner for a six, free beer all night for a fifty and a new car for a ton. His reply of:

'You'll see,' left me in limbo (a small village near Pudsey).

I wasn't sure whether I'd give them a run for their money or they'd give me their money for a run.

Imagine the air of anticipation when I somehow got 54 at Idle. They didn't make much of an effort to get me out, but I did receive torrents of abuse. Most vociferous in this was their off-spinner, 'Grand Canyon,' who was cursed with an enormous, gaping hole in the middle of his deformed face. He frequently commented on my questionable accent and the dubious quality of my shots. He even called into doubt the marital status of my parents, referring to my apparent similarity to a female's defunct private parts. Sometimes he even spoke in full sentences.

Still, it was worth it. If I could carry on like this all season, I'd be quids in. The odd bit of light banter and wit and repartee from a gently spoken, amicable northerner was a small price to pay for such riches.

After the game, there it was, that mythical brown envelope, stealthily hidden inside my bag. Unlike 'Grand Canyon,' it didn't seem very thick. I decided that it was an Emile Zatopek. I hoped that it would be like an Old Qs match ball and wouldn't bounce.

I waited until the envious eyes of my team-mates were fixed elsewhere - on the blonde waltzing past – before I opened it. It was an IOU. I composed myself – after all, it was an overture. I had earned the princely sum of £1.20. Was the decimal point supposed to be there? Was it a quid for the fifty and twenty pence bonus for putting up with the verbals? It turned out to be five whole pence for every run over 30. Wouldn't you be as sick as Indian Polly Umrigar if you were out for 29? 36, on the other hand, meant a Twix could be yours.

I subsequently discovered that the frugal nature of the

payout resulted from the treasurer's discovery that Austria had declared itself bankrupt in 1811. He didn't want the club to follow suit and advised me not to spend it all at once.

The mode of payment for talent money confused 'Acronym.' He has problems with initials. He had it in his tiny mind that the BBC's headquarters was at Lords and that Roger Daltry was the leader of the World Health Organisation. Consequently, I shouldn't have been surprised when he asked:

'Have you been given your OAP for getting over 30?' (Shouldn't it, therefore, have been over 65?)

This conjured up visions of 'Shylock' having a lock up near the M606 containing a shed load of past masters, such as George Hirst, Tom Graveney and Old Jack.

My next 'pay day' was at Spen Victoria. (When I first saw their name, I misread it and thought it was an order from David Beckham to his wife, telling her what to do with her money.) My innings of 34 was insufficient to help me overcome the chocolate withdrawal symptoms I was experiencing. All in all, I wasn't sufficiently talented to earn enough funds for a supply of gob-stoppers for 'Grand Canyon' and the 28,000 runs Don Bradman eased his way to in a mere 338 innings would have taken me 338 seasons.

I wonder how much talent money Messrs. Bastow and Mitchell received in 1942 from Lidget Green. Between them, they bagged 141 victims. No other bowler took a single wicket. I bet they really were pence in.

Dave Ross, being the first professional I ever played under, left a lasting impression on me. (He certainly would have if he'd fallen on me.) Dave was a nippy opening bowler – my choice of words, not 'Party's' – and, like almost everyone in the Bradford League then, apart from a few 'close relatives' from Derbyshire and just the one southerner, was a proud, dour

Tyke. Dave was good enough to have been invited for county trials (he was found guilty) in the form of nets at Headingley. Lamentably, he blew his chances by being proud and dour.

The man in charge, a Yorkshire legend who was very particular about his chewing gum and who could have been mistaken for the lead singer of the Flying Pickets, bowled. Dave smacked it. It ended up on the far side of the ground. 'Mr Juicy Fruit' told him to retrieve it:

'My name's not bloody Fido. Go and fetch it thy sen,' Dave replied.

Trial over.

Dave's trademark in the league was a gentle reminder to all batsmen that he didn't take too kindly to being hit for four. If you were foolish enough to do so you could expect the next ball to be a head-high beamer. Understandably, not many did.

Bowling Old Lane had a 'foreign' pro in 1974. He was from Derbyshire. Harold Rhodes had played county cricket for many years, taking over 1000 first class wickets at an incredibly low average of 19 apiece. (If he had played for Essex, he may have earned more than the two England caps he did get.) Intriguingly, he was paid per over. The more overs he bowled the more money he received. Perhaps this is what is meant by 'quid pro quo.'

Rhodes may have topped the first class averages in 1965 with 119 wickets at 11.04, but on both occasions against us he was taken off relatively early. It certainly wasn't a case of 'pro forma.' As you can imagine, he was not a happy Harry. I've never been able to fathom out how that worked. Clearly, the objective of the fielding side is to dismiss the opposition as quickly as possible. This didn't appear to be in Harold's interests. That said Bradford is in a league of its own.

There weren't many big name professionals in the Bradford

League in 1974. There was a leg-spinner who'd been inside for armed robbery, making him a pro and a con. We also had to contend with several ex-county players such as Derbyshire's Ashley Harvey-Walker, which is a big name, and John Harvey, as well as past and future England men, Doug Padgett and Bill Athey, who were, thankfully, all batsmen. Bill went on to play in 23 Tests and his first wicket stand of 193 with Graham Gooch against New Zealand is an England ODI best. Bearing in mind how slowly he batted in our two games, I bet Goochie got about 180 of those.

It was far more upmarket in the Central Lancashire League. (According to my father-in-law, they are 'not as tight' on this side of the Pennines.) During my time at Middleton, several paid men of varying quality were employed. The first, Gwynn Jones, wasn't a choirist. He was a stylish opening batsman from Rhodesia, an old man's name for those who can't pronounce or spell Zimbabwe.

Gwynn suffered from playing in a side containing players at least as good as him. Because of this, and due him being teetotal, he gradually slipped down the order. Gwynn finished the season at number nine but with his liver still in tip-top condition. He only stayed for one season.

JJ followed. He came highly recommended by a committee man who palpably wasn't teetotal. We were led to believe that this man was a mean pace bowler who'd performed well in Minor Counties cricket for Cambridgeshire. Our committee member did get one thing right. JJ was certainly mean. I can't remember him buying a round all season. His wicket tally was also very thrifty – an average of about one a match.

He did manage a five wicket haul against Heywood, although there were extenuating circumstances. It was a Sunday game. Heywood's captain had previously seen an article in 'the Good Wives Guide,' published in the 1950s. This enlightened tome suggests that:

'A good wife always knows her place. Don't complain if he stays out all night. You have no right to question him. Catering for his comfort will provide you with immense personal satisfaction.' (Verbatim.)

In the hope that his girlfriend had read the copy he glued to her forehead, he married her on the Saturday. The whole Heywood team had consequently turned up pissed as farts, a phrase which always brings to mind Bob Wilson's gaffe:

'He's pissed a fartness test.' (Was it a long-winded affair?)

JJ cashed in, just by being there, really.

After the game, the man who'd recommended JJ, 'Ray Charles,' tried to take some credit. He attempted to draw a comparison between this tormentor of a bunch of 'couldn't care less' drunkards and a Middleton professional of the late 1950s, Frank Tyson, perceived by many experts to have been the fastest bowler of his time:

'JJ puts me in mind of the great 'Typhoon' Tyson,' said 'Ray,' striving to sound convincing.

Unconvinced, 'Thomas' retorted:

'Yeah. They're both nearly bald.'

This isn't to say that JJ wasn't a trier. He was, but there did seem to be something of a language barrier. As a southerner, he struggled to decipher the broad Rochdalian brogue of our captain, 'Big' Ben, despite my attempts at translation. When told:

'Whatever you do, don't drop one short to Ralph,' JJ misunderstood the 'don't.'

Ralph effortlessly pulled the first ball of the match over the houses and into the main road, missing 'Brian the bus's' number 167 by inches. JJ only stayed one season.

Hasan Jamil replaced him. He was a top-class all-rounder

who was poached from us halfway through the season by the Pakistani touring party. Middleton's 'Party' was confused by this. He thought Hasan was Turkish. This was based him hearing a spectator call him a 'delight' to watch.

As well as being a fine cricketer, Hasan was also a generous man. We were batting together against Walsden. During a lengthy stand we found ourselves at the same end. (Doubtless, he hadn't been able to understand my weird accent.) Despite all my instincts to the contrary, I sobbed:

'I'll go.'

To paraphrase weatherman, Bill Giles, I was 'pissing against the wind.'

I was duly run out by what inflation now prompts me to consider was five country miles. After the game, Hasan, a man of few words ('You go' and 'I'll stay') came over to me. Like the Highway Code' when it tells you:

'Give way to trains at level crossings,' he stated the bleeding obvious:

'You gave your wicket away for me.'

He removed the socks he had on and presented them to me. No sweat. Smelling 'de feet' (we lost) I still chose not to turn my nose up at them. I didn't want to offend our pro. Anyway, I was short of socks.

They lasted two games before a hole as large as that big gob-shite's mouth at Idle appeared in one. I could say I kept them as a souvenir but, although Hasan was good, he wasn't that good. In hindsight, perhaps I should have done; a pair of Bryan Adams' soiled footwear recently fetched £550 at auction.

Be that as it may, my involvement in this means I can relate to Chris Cowdrey's slip of the brain regarding Pakistan's Moin (the lawn) Khan. Chris got his feet-related terms in a muddle with:

'Moin Khan has really earned his socks out there today.' As far as I'm aware, Chris didn't go on to point out that Saqlain was 'working his corn off,' but I am aware he does feel Mexican sheet music isn't worth the paper it's written on.

Returning to my personal hosier, imagine if he wasn't Hasan Jamil but 'Enjoy' Jamil, particularly just after tea. As mentioned, he abandoned us to play in a One-Day International at Lords. Our secretary sought compensation. He requested a replacement professional for our next game against Royton, rather than any footwear.

To our delight, the tourists agreed. We were all most excited. It didn't take much. Middleton has more in common with Lassa fever than it does with Lassa Vegas. Which of the six star players who hadn't been selected for Pakistan against England would they send? It was their baggage man.

At first, and second, sight our 'celebrity' appeared rather old and a touch portly. He put me in mind of that motorway sign which warns of an approaching 'abnormal load.' Moby' assured us he was a quality number six bat (just like mine had been) at first-class level. As such, he should really go in at three for us. (At least he didn't want to go in at two fifteen). Our porter also claimed to be a 'top flight off-spinner.' We believed him.

The batting order was rearranged. 'Moby' got a 35 minute duck, playing and missing more often than Nassar on a bad day. He apologised profusely and promised to take at least five wickets after tea. We believed him. Meanwhile, during the tea interval, we witnessed why he had the figure of Humpty Dumpty. He totally put 'Banger' to shame and cleaned up. We now eagerly anticipated him doing the same to Royton's batting.

He didn't. With figures as bloated as his figure – 0 for 36

from three overs which were looser than Bon Accord's back four when they lost by the same score to Arbroath – he was done, as we had been.

In something of a panic, our well-fed guest grasped at straws as avidly as he had at the sandwiches. He coyly asserted that he was a 'specialist' short leg. There was nothing to lose so we believed him. We were more than happy – which presumably made us ecstatic – to let him post himself at Boot Hill. This position, just a couple of feet from the batsman, is invariably reserved for the youngest or ugliest fielder, or the one least liked by the captain. 'Humpty' was no spring chicken but qualified with two out of three.

He held four stunning catches to help secure victory. 'Moby' was now as pleased as Neil Armstrong. He thanked us all, principally for the tea, and offered his services for the following week. 'Stanley,' who was forever exploring ways in which to upset people, quipped:

'Why? What do you think it is, tennis?'

It was only June, but our secretary, 'Porky the second' (he wasn't keen on pigs, he just told lies), fibbed that we had no games left.

Hasan stayed for one season. His replacement was Junior Williams. This was truly a misnomer. After a spell of eight overs, he looked even older than Bobby Robson. Junior was Jamaica's opening bowler along with the legendary Michael Holding. He was endowed with blistering pace, if only for about five overs. After that, he tended to go mysteriously off the boil. Nonetheless, he did bag 80 wickets at 14.5 apiece, earning him a contract for a second year.

Junior was so laid back that he appeared almost comatose for much of the time. Unsurprisingly, he'd never seen our kind of snow until a blizzard stopped play at Rochdale in May. The poor man was so cold that he looked even sadder than the Aussies did when Bob Willis finished them off with 8 for 43 in 1981. Henceforth, Junior played in long johns and a thermal vest under his whites in every game.

I invariably took him an apple on match days – 'an apple a day keeps the bouncer away.' Just like the half pint I splashed out, not literally, on Franklyn, this proved to be a sound investment. When Junior transferred to Royton, he always held something back when he bowled at me. Thank you, Granny Smith.

After Junior, we had DS de Silva. He played for Sri Lanka against England at Lords in 1984, taking 2 for 85 from 45 overs with his leg breaks and googlies. We found him to be a most intriguing man. No one could spot his googlies, possibly because he wore loose fitting trousers, and no one knew what DS stands for. The consensus is that his forenames are a mass of random consonants with more letters than that station in Wales.

This delightful man proved to be a superb acquisition. He took 105 wickets at 11.7 in 1981 and scored over 800 runs (albeit mostly off the spinners and medium pacers). It was rare for him not to get a collection for taking five wickets or scoring 50. The only occasion he failed with both bat and ball was in the final game of the 1982 season at Hyde. Annoyingly, he did just that. He couldn't be found anywhere. Not to worry, it was only the title decider. Whoever won this game would be crowned champions of the CLL. To add just a modicum of pressure, our captain was unavailable. I had to skipper the side for the first time.

It went down to the wire. One of their four pros, a park keeper/florist, the Hyde Ranger, concluded the match by restricting us to two singles. We lost by one sodding run. I felt as deflated as my six year old daughter would be five years later. She won her way through to the final of a disco dancing competition at a holiday camp only for her three year old brother to gate-crash the event and scoop first prize.

Opposing professionals inevitably included the seemingly endless stream of fast bowlers already mentioned. Mercifully, some clubs did engage batsmen. Milnrow foolishly signed an off-spinner, Derek Parry. Derek won Test caps for the West Indiesand in 1980 he had match analyses of 15 for 101 for the Combined Islands against Jamaica, the best figures ever in West Indies domestic cricket. He didn't do quite as well in the CLL. Everyone was so relieved to be facing a West Indian who wasn't genuinely quick that he took some fearful stick, so much so that he changed into a medium pacer half way through the season.

On the batting front, I was fortunate enough to have been in the league at the same time as such wonderful Test players as Rohan Kanhai (West Indies), Mohinder Amarnath (India), Bruce Edgar (New Zealand), Andrew Hilditch (Australia), Larry Gomes (West Indies), Trevor Hohns (Australia), John Dyson (Australia), as well as Harry Pilling.

As a proven run-getter over many years for Lancashire in the County Championship, Harry Pilling was hired (he had to be at only 5ft3) by Radcliffe for his artful batting. Hardly anybody, including Harry himself, was aware he could also, just about, bowl off spin. Murali he wasn't. Harry stole eight wickets in total in 1981 with his flighted filth. I was one of the eight. I cringe at the thought since this flighted filth was so polluted that it was verging on the obscene.

Good a batsman as Harry was, he wasn't in the same league as the incomparable Rohan Kanhai. Following a glorious Test career which produced over 6,000 runs at an average close to 50 for the West Indies, Rohan moved up a level in 1980. He signed for Crompton. He pulverised attacks to the tune of 1123 runs at an average of 75. This is all the more remarkable as he did so playing 50% of his innings on Crompton's wicket. Back then, their strip was as predictable as most wives at the wrong time of the month, exploding without warning.

This didn't hamper the master stroke-maker. With it being slightly more inclement in Greater Manchester than in Guyana, he erred on the side of caution. If he received a straight ball, he played it back. If it was so much as a centimetre off line, he hit it for four or six.

One shot he played against us remains as clear in my mind as if it was this morning. In an absent-minded moment, Junior chose to try and test this luminary with a bouncer. It was quick but it wasn't straight:

'Kanhai hit it for six?' Rohan asked himself.

He could. He hooked the delivery past a shell-shocked square leg. The shot was so powerful that it thudded against a wall 60 metres from the middle with such force that it rebounded back to within 10 metres of the perpetrator. The disbelieving fielder at square leg pinched himself, picked up what was left of the ball and tossed it back to Junior with the words:

'Bowl straight, son.'

'Brian the bus' was again on hand to say the wrong thing:

'Test batsmen don't hit it in the air, old man. It's time you thought about retiring.'

Rohan thought only about how quickly he was going to get another hundred. The wall was rebuilt soon afterwards and Brian was given directions to Heywood Cricket Club (by bus, naturally).

Right up there, too, is Bruce Edgar. In 1982, Bruce caressed a ton for Hyde at Middleton. It was an immaculate, chanceless innings. He'd obviously been listening to Brian's advice since every shot, bar one, was on the deck. It was elegance personified and, as a non-bowler, a pleasure to watch.

Classy as it was, it didn't meet with the approval of Brian's replacement. 'Abbey' Monkhouse constantly reminded Bruce that he was a 'pussy' and wasn't strong enough to hit sixes:

'There aren't any fielders in the sky, you pussy.'(Perhaps he thought Kiwis are called 'Black Cats' rather than 'Black Caps.')

For dessert, he also threw in:

'You couldn't knock the skin off a rice pudding. You're as exciting as Panorama.'

Bruce was undeterred. He continued to play every shot in the book on the floor until he reached 97. Only then did he alter course. He went to his hundred with an effortless lofted straight drive. The ball landed a gnat's chuff from our man with verbal diarrhoea, almost knocking the skin off more than his rice pudding and doubtless making him wish he'd stayed at home to watch Panorama.

Australian John Buchanan was Oldham's professional in the early 80s. He beat us almost single-handed in a Wood Cup semi-final. He batted at number three and, on a sticky wicket which was drying out in the sun, played what appeared to be a match-losing innings. John was there for virtually the full allocation of overs, made no attempt to accelerate and ended up on 38 not out in a meagre total of about 120 for 5. I was confident of a place in the Cup Final until I overheard what he said to his partner going up the pavilion steps at tea:

'80 is enough on that track.'

Wrong, John. 65 was. John is 6ft8 but didn't qualify for chapter three because he didn't bowl at 90 mph. What he did do was swing the ball in like a boomerang and get it to bounce awkwardly off a length. He took eight for not many. I tried to tell myself it's only a game. As with my batting, and the umpire's maths, I failed miserably. I was dismissed on the seventh ball of the over just 32 short of a collection.

As I've explained, the professionals I've encountered since 1983, with a few notable exceptions, haven't been of such a high profile. In the Lancashire County League, most paid men would meet with the approval of the League of Gentlemen. They're 'local.' My club, Thornham, is by no means affluent so we tend to pay pros similar rates to the talent money heaped out by Lidget Green.

During my long stint in the 1stXI we did uncover a few gems. Our policy of slave labour – get them young and pay them as little as you can – succeeded several times. In 1985 we won the league title (Lancashire and Cheshire 1st division) with Darren Rayton. Darren was quick enough to make me wish I'd never pretended to be a first slip and to make 'Snip' wish he'd stayed in the Egyptian army. We almost won it again the following year. Darren had moved on to Blackpool to play in the Northern League. We now had Garry Bolton.

I've always been wary of people who spell their first names incorrectly but it didn't affect Garry's cricket (or his appetite). As 'bulk buying' had proved successful, we adopted the same policy two years later by getting a crane to hire Manej Parek. He, too, did very well for us. Since then a line of, mostly young, hopefuls have come and gone without the same success. As if to emphasise this, in 2005 we engaged a Dutch Bangladeshi named Tufail. His woeful performances soon earned him a new Christian name – 'Bound.' Then there was 'Corkie.'

'Corkie' was the first professional I teamed up with at Thornham. You could not hope to meet a nicer man. He hardly ever stops smiling, just like the cat named after him. By his own testimony, although paid, 'Corkie' was no pro. He was a decent amateur in a good league. He was a dasher. For him, a dot ball was an admission of failure.

If 'Corkie' had ever made it to the dizzy heights of the county game and had been given the role of night watchman, I'm convinced he'd have approached it in the same vein as Robin Marlar did for Sussex. The Cambridge graduate – who probably didn't study maths – ignored the principle function of this specialist position. Instead of shutting up shop until close of play to keep wickets intact for the following day, Robin was, I believe, out stumped third ball for 12. I can hear 'Corkie' purring with approval.

In 1983, at Glossop, the biggest ground in the league, our dasher was middling the ball consistently and so was bound to get too excited before long. I'd already pleaded with him to settle down but that was as incomprehensible to him as don't bowl short to Ralph was to JJ.

Unperturbed by the inordinately long straight boundary and the gale force wind blowing into his face, our smiling slogger went for the big one. He struck his shot beautifully, getting underneath it sufficiently to get the desired height and distance.There was no long off. Why would there be? His smile was turned upside down as he was caught by mid-off who was only 25 yards away. The ball, having sailed well over the fielder's head, was blown straight back to him for an easy catch.

Even more embarrassing was his dismissal at Darcy Lever in 1984. The delivery with his name on it this time had slipped out of the bowler's hand. The ball rolled very slowly towards our over-eager batsman. Even Robin Marlar would have erred on the side of caution. Not 'Corkie.' His eyes lit up like

Blackpool illuminations. He came prancing down the track ready to meet the, then legal, daisy cutter, intent on slaughtering it. 'Corkie' had time to make three almighty swipes at it.

Needless to say, each flail failed. The ball eventually reached the stumps just ahead of the worm racing it. It kissed, rather than snogged them and one bail apologetically tottered to the ground. 'Corkie' was beside himself. He was concerned that his close friend Lynch might discover what had happened:

'Whatever you do, please don't tell Lynch,' he pleaded.

A quick phone call soon sorted that one out. After all, 'Corkie' did deserve to be 'Lynched' after playing a shot like that. Once again, he had thrown caution to the wind and paid the price.

As Worcester's Doug Bollinger does, rivalry between professionals can provide champagne moments. Take the time when Franklyn Stephenson and Junior Williams locked horns. A Jamaican face to face with a Barbadian isn't far removed from a Thames Valley Gentlemen v Rotherham Miners' Welfare Club clash. So long as you are only an onlooker, it's a contest to savour.

Each of these frighteningly fast bowlers believed himself to be quicker that the other. Fine, unless you were one of the amateur guinea pigs of Middleton or Royton. The RSPCC (with the 'C' for 'Cricketers') really should have been informed. Both men requested reassurance from the umpires. It was like the Wild West:

'Tell me I'ze quicker than he,' asserted Junior, only for Franklyn to plead:

'He's a tortoise compared to me.'

Well, I do know that Junior did compete in the Shell Shield. Matters came to a head, literally, when Franklyn came out to bat ominously early in Royton's innings. Their normally vociferous crowd was quite subdued, as you tend to be when danger threatens. Junior was still firing on all cylinders. He had already sent back numbers one to four. Franklyn's scalp would earn him a collection and that's the part of his body he concentrated on. Helmets were still a fantasy in Mike Brearley's mind so Franklyn opted for a cap. This was like placing an apple on your head with William Tell around. Target practice was about to commence.

With something tangible to aim at, Junior gave his opposite number a torrid time. Not surprisingly, it wasn't long before the cap and Franklyn parted company, thanks to a truly ferocious bouncer which almost caused 'Party' to pass out. (We hadn't batted yet.)

For what seemed like an eternity, a dazed Franklyn struggled to regain his bearings (and his cap). Daft Junior had appealed for a catch behind the wicket. He was a lone voice. We knew that we still had to face Franklyn after tea. The fact that Junior's eyes were bulging out of their sockets and the veins in his forehead were set to pop didn't work in our favour. His hostile appeal woke the umpire from a deep slumber and he raised his finger in a reflex response.

We were doomed. The 3 million plus heartbeats reserved for each of us over an entire month were used up in the next 30 seconds. When it finally dawned on Franklyn that he'd been triggered (as, rumour has it, Roy Rogers was on a regular basis), it was too much for him to take. He stood there shaking his head in disbelief. Like 'Widow Twanky,' he wasn't for leaving.

Although apparently still breathing, neither umpire intervened. We left it to 'Den,' a Millwall fan, to send the man on his way. An inoffensive:

'Off you pop, my friend,' would have been my first choice but 'Den's' words were more direct, even if the mode of delivery was somewhat furtive.

Using the cupped hands as camouflage in front on the mouth approach, 'Den' passed sentence. (This time the sentence had come after the appeal.)

'Eff off, Franklyn, you're out. If you hang about much longer the bar will be closed.'

Franklyn spun round like Torville or Dean in a vain attempt to identify the villain of the piece. I smiled and shook my head:

'Call me Noel, darling!'

In fact, we all put on our 'it wasn't me' expressions. Even 'Ethelred,' who never seemed ready for anything, was the picture of innocence. None the wiser, but a touch miffed, Franklyn picked up his cap, scowled at Junior, the umpire, our 'keeper, 'Teflon' and anyone else foolish enough not to be looking down at their boots. Hitler had just invaded Poland.

Our innings was more of a whirlwind than a breeze. Any speed cameras would have over-heated. The ball suffered severe grass burns but Junior avoided batting. Somehow or other (the other being scores of extras), we won. Mercifully, Franklyn was snapped up by Sussex and then by Nottinghamshire, becoming the last 1st class cricketer to do the double in 1988. He was also the leading wicket taker with 125 wickets at 18 in the County Championship.

Equally competitive, but far less dangerous, was the rivalry between three Middleton star amateurs in the late 70s. The trio, 'Owen,' who bought everything on credit, 'Bob' and 'Viv', both of whom were as backward as one another, setting up a charity for 'blind dogs for the guides,' each took a season out of the CLL to pro in slightly less high profile leagues in the north-west. To add a bit of spice, they had a weekly wager as to which of them would make the most runs in each match. They always met up in our bar afterwards to compare scores. On one memorable Saturday evening, 'Viv' came in cock-a-hoop (which had already won him a goldfish):

'Tough titty, boys. two more than the trombones today. 78 beauties.'

'Not enough to lead the big parade,' chuckled 'Owen.' '101 dalmations for me. 'Bob,' you're quiet. Didn't you contribute, you waster?'

'Bob' grinned knowingly:

'I did. 223 times. My round, I think.'

Influential as they undeniably are, even the professionals are likely to be upstaged by another body, well, two bodies but possibly no pulses – the umpires.

Food for thought:

17. Was Daniel Bottom of Derbyshire related to Hampshire's A.Bowell?

18. Was Somerset's Bill Alley a batting or a bowling Alley?

19. Did the great Australian Victor Trumper ever confess?

20. Was Warwickshire's Jack Bannister easy to get hold of?

Chapter 6

OFFICIALS

Be it in Scarborough or Southend, umpires are like curries. They vary. A good one fills you with a warm, satisfied sensation. A bad one churns you up. Whereas the men in the middle up here are qualified, certified, neutral and appointed by the leagues, those in the south weren't. Any ice-cream salesman, doctor or lab.technician could find himself donning the white coat. I swear a young David Blunkett gave me out lbw at Putney in 1967.

Back in the 60s, it most often fell to members of the batting side to do a stint in Old Quintinian games. My first taste of unbridled power was imposed on me as an inadequate 14 year old. I was making up the numbers in Watford against the inappropriately named Sun Sports. (I'd filled in once before a year earlier but didn't bat, bowl or field the ball – faultless, but not quite as impressive a debut as that of Kiwi, A.Moss. He took 10 Wellington wickets for 28 in 1889-90.) We batted first and I was soon summoned. My training for the role was intense:

'Get six stones and don't give front foot lbws or caught behinds. We all walk.'

Who needs courses? I was spared making an arse of myself

since it chucked it down almost immediately, as it was bound to do in a fixture where the opposition tempted fate by naming itself Sun Sports.

A year later, I witnessed an example of the brain-power required for the role at the Polytechnic Ground in Chiswick. This huge expanse is sufficiently spacious for four games of cricket to be played simultaneously. It also has an ample car park. This did not deter 'Stirling,' the William Ellis umpire, from going directly to his intended destination. He did not pass go. He did not collect £200. He should have gone straight to jail. Believing himself to be taking part in the GB Rally, he drove his mini straight across two of the previously pristine squares. He then circled the outfield and came to a halt at deep square leg, presumably because his tank, like his head, was empty. He got out of the car and excused himself with:

'Sorry I'm late. How many balls are left in the over?'

My gesture indicated that there were two.

In the same season, on the same ground, Imperiads were batting against the Old Qs. One of their players was as happy as Pinky, Perky or Porky in muck. Where else could you ruin someone's weekend merely by raising one finger? (Answers to Claire Raynor…) He had no intention of being accused of procrastination. Why put off until ten to three what you can do at half past two?

An Imperiads player, appropriately called Heron, fished at one. It appeared to have clipped his front pad on the way through to our keeper, 'Cymbals' Dave. Since Dave actually held on to the ball, he appealed, as did our slip, 'HonkyTonk,' a piano tuner. The white-coated megalomaniac seized his moment. He goose marched down the track to cross-examine Dave:

'What are you appealing for?'

'I'm convinced it was out, pal.'

Stopping short of asking him to swear on the Holy Bible, 'Rumpole' continued:

'I'm not your pal. Not why. What for?'

'Leg before,' pleaded Dave, resisting any temptation to call on character witnesses, which was just as well.

Giving nothing away, 'Rumpole' now turned on 'Honky Tonk':

'Why are you appealing?'

This presented 'HT' with the opportunity to respond with:

'I've got big blue eyes and a large tuning fork.'

He resisted and opted for:

'Caught behind, you honour.'

'You're wrong,' put Dave in his place.

This was no surprise since Dave even made mistakes when painting by numbers (four and seven look so alike) and believed aerobics were chocolate pens.

The umpire's itching gangrenous digit now sought out 'HT':

'You're right.'

Finally, the batsman got the verdict:

'You're out. You hit it.'

He hadn't but he made no protest. It had all taken so long he had lost the will to bat. He retreated over the boundary, just like the Italians, offering no perceivable resistance.

Admittedly, our power-crazed pointer was an exception. Generally, players acting as umpires did a good job back then. This was also true of the clubmen who accompanied most teams at Evershed. We had Little Willie and Ray Shaw. Despite his apparent inadequacy, Willie was an excellent umpire. It helped that this was an era when nearly everyone walked for caught behind. Indeed, appeals only tended to be made when the fielding side genuinely believed the batter was out. As you can tell, hardly any Aussies played in the south then. Ray was less decisive and so gained an extra initial. R.Shaw became RU Shaw.

Parents acting as umpires can be dodgier. This word brings to mind a conversation I overheard after a junior net practice in 2005. A youngster boasted to his mother thus:

'We played dodge ball today and Sir said that I'm the dodgiest boy in the class.'

But not as dodgy as some dads, who can be inclined to show undue favouritism. (Southern for be as bent as a nine bob note.)

'Howzat, Dad?'

'Well bowled, Son.'

The worst case of nepotism I've come across arose in a London Schools u19s game against Essex in 1968. Son was facing in Essex's innings. Dad was umpiring at square leg. Son tracked our leg spinner, 'Irish' (Scott Welsh). He missed the ball and was left stranded six yards out of his ground. He was stumped fairly and squarely. Anyone with a 'scru' (half a scruple) would have given in graciously. Not son. 'Scru you,' he concluded. He strolled back into his crease, replaced the bails, muttered something about the wind and gazed innocently at Dad.

How could Dad possibly come to his rescue? It took a stroke of genius, which was more than Son had managed:

'Sorry. I must admit I wasn't watching so I can't give it out.'

Son, blessed with more front than Blackpool, resumed his innings, totally unmoved and seemingly immovable. Dad had a long and fruitful career as a Conservative MP.

Perhaps less sinister but certainly more liberal was the performance of a Canadian umpire a fortnight later. He had accompanied the Canadian Colts u19s on their tour of England. London Schools played them at the Bank of England ground, Roehampton. He accumulated a Ray Julianesque nine victims in our innings, but curiously failed to increase his tally in theirs. He gave seven of us out lb and two more run out. He raised his finger so often that on several occasions he put up two fingers at once to save time. Oh no, sorry, that was us.

In his defence, there were extenuating circumstances. As Peter Smith explains:

'Cricket is still played in Canada but the climatic conditions coupled with the influence of the French, have resulted in the game not becoming a leading national sport.'

If in doubt, blame the French.

Secondly, our finger-happy destroyer was of the Brendan Behan school of thought. He'd seen the advertisement encouraging you to 'drink Canada Dry' and had taken it as a personal challenge. Consequently, he probably saw six men at third man but was somewhat disappointed at the drinks break. The tea lady commented that it was bitter, an innocent reference to the temperature, offering him merely soup.

Whilst 'studying' at the City of Leeds and Carnegie Teacher Training College, I felt the full force of one over-exuberant umpire from Bingley College during a British Colleges Cup game in 1972. 'Bent of Bingley' normally played for them but was injured and had volunteered to officiate. No one could have doubted his enthusiasm. It is possible, however, to get carried away and he should have been. He began by celebrating dismissals in the belief that 'impartial' meant he was so open-minded that he didn't mind how we were out so long as we were.

Going one step further, he then appealed for a caught behind from square leg. To complete the set, all that now remained was to do so with the bowling at his end. He did and upheld his own appeal. He alone shouted when I was hit on the pad (front foot).

Unimpressed by this show of hyper-zealous officiating, the next man in passed me a tissue and muttered:

'He's really incontinent, isn't he?'

I was confused by this comment from 'Belly.' (His surname isn't Bell. He's simply fat.) Was he implying that 'Bent' was a shitty umpire or intimating that he was no good?

Not far from Bingley is Bradford, hence the building society. This contrivance leads me on to league umpires. My recollection of those in the Bradford League is, like their eyesight, somewhat hazy. There must have been a few good ones but I also sometimes convince myself I don't eat enough salad. Pirates wore ear rings in the belief it improved their vision. Unfortunately for the league's batsmen, the only accoutrements anywhere near the umpires' lobes in West Yorkshire had batteries in them.

My first contretemps occurred, coincidentally, against Bingley. It involved the captain of the league side, ie God, and a stone cold run out. Eleven of us appealed in unison, as opposed to Welsh. 'The Chosen One' was so far out that the only consideration was if he'd been run out or abandoned. The umpire wasn't his dad, so he was looking. That said, to dismiss the captain of the Bradford League side was, I discovered, as likely as the away team getting a penalty at Old Trafford. The umpire shook his head. I took this, initially, to signify that he was distraught at having to give out the single most important person in the county. I was mistaken. Rather than:

'Why me?' it was: 'Not me. I've got a wife and a squadron of racing pigeons. I don't want any of their heads pulled off. Not out, Sire.'

The other batsman then lovingly singled me out for special consideration. Could it possibly have been my accent? He advised me to retract my appeal. If I didn't, he'd relocate his bat down my throat. I'm paraphrasing. My old mate at Old Fullerians came to mind, even if that was concerned with the southern end as opposed to the northern one.

I declined his kind offer with:

'I've already eaten thanks, although for what little use you're making of your bat, it might as well be somewhere else my good fellow.'

Unsure as to whether I was referring to pizzas or gangsters, my northern neighbour sought to close the deal with a witty:

'I'll do you later.'

I was already in hot water so decided I might as well get scalded:

'I hope your impressions are better than your batting.'

'Impressions? I'm not a bleedin' painter. Piss off back to Sydney.'

This hit a nerve. Did he think I was Australian or queer? Either way, the connotations were disturbing. Should I change the way I talked or the way I walked?

There was one umpire with his own built-in stereo system – a hearing aid in each ear. He seemed to rely on lip reading to give guards and on integrity for caught behinds. We called him 'Misguided' because neither worked and, despite many visits to our ground, he regularly got lost, even without us telling him to.

But even he looked positively youthful compared to 'Ton up.' He came to games on a motor bike and had both gout and Alzheimer's. Strangely, it didn't bother him:

'At least I haven't got gout,' he was overheard saying to his uncle standing at the other end.

The CLL had some first-rate umpires in the 70s and early 80s. (Decades and ages.) Inevitably, they were cancelled out by a few loose cannons, including George Gunn's son, 'Tommy' and Paul Reiffel's uncle, 'Air.'

They didn't come any looser than Phil 'the Leak.' Phil isn't Welsh. He merely likes his beer. He easily persuaded himself that a couple of pre-game pints calmed his nerves. This had no adverse effect for the first hour. Thereafter, it became an endless procession. Even the most outrageous appeals got the nod, followed by Phil rushing past the dumbfounded batsman on his way to empty his bladder. Once the seal is broken... Collections for five wickets were up for grabs amidst this chain reaction:

'Bugger, I need a piss,' was invariably followed by an 'howzat' and a raised digit.

Thankfully, Phil had the decency to leave the field before relieving himself. 'Slasher' didn't. He went for instant relief. He watered the spot at square leg where he was standing. Calls for sawdust and his removal from the list immediately followed.

Sam 'the Claw,' aka 'Frostbite,' always gave you a cool reception. He was convinced he was like one of Diana Ross's backing group and reminded me of a deserted hospital – he had no patience. Word has it that, despite being even older than the Queen Mother, he only stopped skydiving because his guide dog was scared of heights.

In a game at Castleton Moor, everyone (except Sam) was enjoying themselves. Then, out of the blue – it was a nice day – he struck. Without a word, he walked off. Was he making his way back to the nursing home? The other umpire, 'Gerry,' had a pacemaker, giving him two reasons not to rush to get in front of Sam. As bemused as the rest of us, he enquired:

'What's up, Sam?'

'It's raining,' replied Sam.

Ironically, the man who was incapable of spotting anything during the game was now seeing things. In desperation, our pro, DS de Silva, climbed onto the roof of the score box. He thrust his hands towards the heavens à la Moses on Mount Sinai and disagreed:

'It is not raining.'

Sam was not taken in. We were. DS felt moved to complain of sunstroke as Sam sipped his third cup of tea and made several futile attempts to dunk a custard cream before the eventual restart.

Rupert didn't wear flashy checked trousers. The poor sod, like Aussie bowler, Stuart R Clark, was actually christened Rupert. He was known for taking no nonsense from bowlers. He responded to appeals in kind. If a bowler shouted 'howzat,' Rupert shrieked back 'not out.' If, at the end of an over, the disgruntled bowler grabbed his sweater, Rupert would do likewise at the beginning of the next one. Nor did he take kindly to excessive appeals. He took the wind out of the sails of a whinging Walsden bowler, 'Ellen McArthur,' who thought any ball not middled (plus some which were) was worth a shout, by coming back at him with:

'Bloody hell! You make more soddin' appeals than Oxfam.'

If you asked Rupert how he was, he'd lull you into a false sense of security with a reassuring:

'Mustn't grumble,' yet would then do so.

This made him as popular as Douglas Jardine is in the Dominions.

Cliff scaled great heights as an umpire, just as he had done as a fine opening batsman for many, many years. He must have hated shopping with a passion. Predictably nicknamed

'Chalky,' he was something of a purist. If you were struck on the pad playing across the line you were doomed. He would do a regal 'tut' – despite having no Tongan ancestry – shake his head and off you went. He would invariably justify his decision thus:

'He must learn to play straight. Cow shots are for cowboys.'

With more and more unorthodox batting creeping into the CLL, it all became too much for Cliff. He began looking very pale and so retired to Kent for the sea air. Herein, he became one of the White Cliffs of Dover.

The 'Sergeant Major' was a clone of that pillock from Imperiads. They both strutted around as if they owned the place à la Giscard d'Estaing. Their goal was to spoil your day. In a popularity contest both would probably push Graeme Le Saux, Gyles Brandreth, Shakoor Rana, Margaret Thatcher, Edwina Curry and Matthew Hayden for last place.

This objectionable man was so far up his own bum that whatever kind of 'ectomy' that would need wouldn't have saved him. After overnight rain at Werneth, the sun was shining and the ground had dried out. A decent, rather than indecent, crowd had gathered. Everybody was changed and warming up. No one had the slightest concern about not starting on time. We didn't. 'He who must be obeyed,' proclaimed:

'There is a wet expanse in front of the sightscreen. You're not starting until that's dry. Wright's the name and I always am.'

I wanted to tinker with this to make it:

'Twat's the name…'

We went to investigate and found a small, dampish spot of little significance (Skegness?). The captains objected but the tyrannical tit would not back down. A suggestion for common sense was made, only for the know-all to reject it:

'No way. We're having none of that here. If you agree to start, I'll bring you off after one ball. I'm in charge.'

We had to wait for fully two hours until the ground became moistureless. Our wicket-keeper, 'Claude' (he was forever being scratched by his cat), called him a 'doddery dictatorial dickhead' and got a three match ban. It should have been six but the disciplinary committee doubtless agreed with 'Claude's' assessment.

Rumour has it that 'the Sergeant Major' and 'Frostbite Sam' were both so into ruining people's leisure time that they'd started out as Butlin's Red Coats and followed this up by becoming Mike and Bernie Winters. In their quest to upset as many people as possible they finally swapped red for white and made an art form out of being as miserable as Greg Chappell every weekend.

Almost without exception, the men in the middle in the Lancashire and Cheshire/ Lancashire County League are, or were, lovely old men. This is especially true of those who umpire in the second division (for 2ndXIs) which is where I have largely been confined to since the late 1990s due to lack of talent and limb seizure. The 'lads' who (just about) stand in these fixtures are like horses in that they can fall asleep whilst vertical.

Norman 'Raspberry' Hartley, an octogenarian, or some other kind of surgeon, arrived at Thornham on a beautiful Saturday afternoon. He duly complimented us on the condition of the playing area. Unusually observant we thought. He soon blotted his copybook, however, by pointing to the nets lodged on the edge of the sloping farmer's field on the far side of the ground:

'It's a pity the practice wicket is looking decidedly rough.'

'Raspberry' had blown his cover.

'Creepy' Crawley is the only umpire, other than Dai, I've seen who looked distinctly unlikely to finish the game still in this world. Plenty are well past retirement age but 'Creepy' looks ready to meet his maker at any moment. He soldiered on for longer than Thora Hird before calling it a day. When he did finally pack up it was a relief to us all and to 'Donald' – he never scores any runs - in particular. He had lost the toss and was one assigned to give 'Creepy' the kiss of life should the need arise.

'Senseless' was the second umpire I met who sports two deaf-aids. He was a permanent fixture for many years until, in 2001, he came to watch rather than officiate. Just like Radio 5 commentator John Murray did in December 2004 with:

'The referee is a Spaniard, Manual Alonzo, from Spain,' I said it as I saw it:

'Not umpiring today, old boy?' I bawled.

Fully aware, ie deaf aids full on, 'Senseless' answered:

'No. I've got cataracts so I'm only on the reserve list this year.'

Reassuring in itself, but it does go to show that adversity doesn't make a blind or deaf bit off difference to these men. It also explains Geoff Boycott's mixed message in 2008 as to how one should deal with sledging:

'Turn a blind ear,' does make sense, so long as you are as deaf as a bat.

'Carol Vordeman' isn't cute or smart but does have a thing about numbers. To his credit, he looks the same now as he did 30 years ago. He looked bloody ancient then, too. He's old enough to have attended Geronimo's funeral and is a genuinely lovely man, but he's innumerate. You can never be sure whether an over will last for seven, five, four or even six balls. I suppose I can understand why. When 'Carol' first started way back in 1774, all overs were of four balls. He then witnessed a move to the five ball over throughout the 19th century and the change to six in 1900. Mercifully, he didn't emigrate to Australia after World War1. They opted for eight ball overs. 'Carol' would have been so confused he wouldn't have been able to tell a boolabong from a Goolagong.

Fair enough. We all make mistakes and we can all learn from them. Not necessarily. In 2003, our answer to Pythagoras got it wrong for three successive overs with a good poker hand, three sevens. The bowler, now four inches shorter and struggling for breath, wasn't amused:

'I was unaware the ECB had sanctioned an extra delivery in each over starting 20 minutes ago and only from the Rochdale Road end,' he panted.

'Carol' looked as perplexed as if he'd been asked for nine consonants and a vowel:

'Was that a seven ball over? I can't recall having done that before. I must be getting old.'

One out of two, 'Carol.'

I wonder if 'Carol' was responsible for D.Hill of British Guyana bowling a 14 ball over (all legal deliveries) in 1964ish. It should have been eight and Conrad Hunte had cause to be miffed at the miscount. He was out lbw to the 14th delivery.

'Carol's' problems with numbers even extend to the time. In 2004, when asked how long there was before the end of the tea interval, our ever-helpful friend again had his finger on the pulse:

'Oh ages,' he concisely informed us upon looking at his watch, prior to stuffing more angel cake between his dentures.

Furthermore, when asked who was standing with him in a game against Prestwich – bearing in mind he was 82 at the time – 'Carol' replied:

'I can't remember his name, but it's that old bloke who always brings his dog' (as a guide perhaps?).

When 'Botox' officiated you could be sure he wouldn't smile. He was also bound to do something controversial and, at some stage during the match, would walk off without warning, not for a piddle but to visit the score box. This would be under the pretence of querying the score. The real reason was to have a drink of milk for his ulcer.

I knew I shouldn't have told him only babies drink milk. He got his own back with a vengeance. I wonder if he thinks I'm Australian. In his defence, he was always most approachable. (I'd have liked to approach him with a cattle prod and a book of rules.) Just like Brian Clough, he'd pretend to listen to your side of the story. He would then explain why you were wrong and he was right. He really is as friendly as a funnelweb spider.

Ironically, it's 'Botox' himself who looks as if he'd been bitten by the scary, aptly Antipodean arachnid. He constantly seems depressed and continually froths at the mouth. The philosopher Chrysippus died laughing. That is never going to happen to 'Botox.' He is far more likely to peg it of unnatural causes while watching 'Les Misérables.'

Dear 'Botox' managed to give me the finger of doom twice in one weekend in 2002. After his first aberration on the Saturday, he rubbed salt in the wound by making me relive the torment. Perceptive, if nothing else, he stated:

'You didn't look happy with that lbw, Jim.'

To my knowledge, I've never guffawed when I'm out. I resisted making any reference to the visually impaired but an uncontrollable urge to make him see the error of his ways remained:

'No,' I blubbered. 'If my front foot had been any further forward I'd have run a single.'

'Botox' remained oblivious. (I'm heartened that synonyms for this word include blind, unconscious, deaf and ignorant.) He countered by fibbing that he, (only he?) had received a letter from Lords instructing him to give 'those out' to stop batsmen padding up. I did sob, even though it's no use crying over…

The next day, there he was again, at Glossop. I tried to avoid any repeat by batting outside leg stump and two metres out of my crease. I could almost shake hands with him. It was to no avail. A stifled appeal, accompanied by an immediate 'sorry' from the wicket-keeper, was sufficient. Once more, he insisted on his pound of flesh:

'Got you again!' he smirked.

Unable to come up with any insults using 'sterilised' or 'semi-skimmed,' I intimated that the ball had pitched well outside leg stump:

'Yes, I know,' replied the imposter, 'but it would have hit the wicket.'

This was almost as galling as when I was given out stumped by a one-armed umpire in a London versus Yorkshire u19 game. Illogical, I know, but I felt I only had a 50% chance of him doing so and was surprised to hear him tell me to 'sling yer hook.'

It's not as if 'Botox' has any redeeming features. He could hardly be described as sympathetic. An opponent, 'Jack,' a stocky lad strong enough to lift up a car single-handed, was felled by a sharp delivery which caught him on the inside of the knee behind the pad. He went to ground quicker than Arjen Robben. As he was being helped off, 'Botox' consoled him thus:

'Don't worry about hurrying back….you're out leg before.'

Scoreless and limping, 'Jack' was the epitome of a 'lame duck,' but if Lords tells you personally…

Sometimes these men hunt in pairs. Eric and Eddie did. We

called Eric, 'Noddy', not because of his red and yellow car, but because Eddie has big ears. Eddie packed up, literally, when his plastic hips melted on a very hot day at Roe Green. Good old Eric didn't. (One of those two adjectives is accurate.) He persevered long enough to have been involved in our league for 60 years as player and umpire. What an achievement, made even more remarkable by the fact that he didn't start playing until he was 55. (One of those two statements is true, too.)

At their peak, 'Noddy' and 'Big Ears' regularly had a game done and dusted by tea-time. This prompted a change of nicknames to 'Simon' and 'Garfunkel.' No sooner had they arrived at a ground than they were 'homeward bound.' These two thoroughly pleasant old-stagers were simply too kind and trusting. They worked on the principle that if the 'honest-looking, nice bowler' appealed in the belief that it's out, then it must be. They would have even trusted Harold Shipman, finishing their careers with more victims that Courtney Walsh, Murali and Shane Warne combined.

As mentioned, 'Garfunkel' did go solo after 'Simon's' retirement. He lived locally and as a consequence of being electronically tagged and unfit to drive his brightly coloured car, he was all too often appointed to Thornham's 2ndXI home games. Before a match in 1999, he confessed he was bewildered as to why he kept getting low marks for his performance. I advised him that he would benefit from distrusting all bowlers and wicket-keepers totally. I failed to add that a new battery for his hearing aid and eye transplants would not go a Dennis (a miss).

One word from me... He gave a typically gung ho performance to earn a collection by doing a 'Canadian' and adjudging seven of the opposition out leg before. We talked again after the game. Using sign language as back up, I decided to be more 'factual.' Working on the assumption, as Cher has, that you can do almost anything with figures, I invented some statistics.

I lied that for every 10 appeals for lbw made in Test Matches, only one is upheld. I added that Test class bowlers bowl far straighter than our opening bowler, 'Jammy' Jamie, who had just benefited to the tune of four wickets by hitting the pads four times and shouting.

'Garfunkel' seemed visibly moved by our tête à tête. This could have had something to do with his internal problems. Irregular ball movement is common on uncovered pitches. A not-so-common 'Garfunkel' was plagued by irregular bowel movement. To summarise a previous observation, he was incontinent as well as incompetent. This was why enquiries about his health were unwise. As a matter of courtesy, one tends to ask the men who give up their time for us how they are. Those who hear the question normally come back with a 'Rupertesque':

'Can't complain.'

Some utter a more sinister:

'Not bad, considering.'

The 'considering' is a warning to move swiftly on to another topic of conversation.

'Garf' is one of those who respond to a 'how are you?' by telling you. There's no such thing as too much information.

'I had an enema up my rector last week,' he once admitted.

I curbed my desire to correct him by saying 'rectum' as he'd have probably said:

'No. It did them some good.'

It wasn't that simple with 'Simon,' either. He genuinely does have two plastic hips. He can't hear or see very well but can he do the twist. If it wasn't that he makes Kate Moss look like a heavyweight boxer, I'd rename him 'Chubby.' His affinity for dismissing batsmen, even before any appeal, earned him an unheard of third sobriquet, 'Quickdraw McGraw.'

Returning to his partner in crime, 'Garf' has undergone numerous operations on his inners and I was convinced he shouted 'no bowel' when a bowler overstepped the mark. By that I don't mean the offending party called him a 'senile old sod.' I just mean his front foot was over the line.

Ever since I've known him, 'Garf' has had 'failed' rather than 'failing' eyesight. On a rare occasion when I actually middled a long hop, pulling it for four just behind square leg, he signalled leg byes. He couldn't have been expecting it and I was lucky no one appealed. As Gary Linekar is accused of saying:

'He exhumes confidence.'

Far be it from me to dig up commentators' slips of the brain and Gary has obviously made a packet out of his crisp adverts etc. so he must know what he's on about. The same can't be said of 'Garf.' In 2001 I saw him walking his dog around Woodbank's ground during the LCL's 2ndXI Hulme Trophy final. He was making his way to the barbecue. (Maybe he needed a haircut.) Steering clear of asking about his defecating problems, I chirped up with:

'Going for a hot dog, Eric?'

His reply bewildered me briefly:

'Yes. We've only had it three months. I had to have the Labrador put down.'

It must have been too heavy.

As I've said, 'Garf' does own a deaf aid but doesn't always put batteries in it. To me, that's no different to having Mark Butcher at slip. You know it won't work, but you have to put it somewhere.

'Garf' once asked for a lift home after a game at Cheetham Hill which had finished early, even for him. It, too, was washed out. Thinking ahead, I obliged. I discovered that he lives close to the M60 motorway. I asked if the constant noise of the traffic got on his nerves. It didn't:

'The wife can hear it, but I can't.'

Moving back to his love affair with lbws, this old codger's response to my fictional Test match statistic was dramatic. He applied it totally in his own way and, henceforth, contrived to uphold only one appeal per innings. The upshot of this was that his wife became suspicious as to what he was getting up to until 8.30 on Saturdays when everyone knows cricket matches always finish at 4 o'clock.

'Garf' eventually gave up the ghost in 2003, before becoming one, having confessed that his memory was going. Everything else now appeared fine but like the man caught in revolving doors, he didn't know whether he was coming or going.

In a bid to negate the duo's trigger fingers, prior to an Irlam versus Denton St Lawrence 2nd XI fixture in the mid-90s, the captains, 'Riff' and 'Raff,' made a pact. Nobody would appeal for anything which hit the pads, thereby prolonging the event beyond mid-afternoon. As such, they followed the example of TN Pearce's XI and the Australians in their 1961 fixture.

I wonder how this pair would have gone on if they'd officiated in Australia in the 1880s where one of the prominent teams was 'Deaf Mutes.' No appeal necessary with 'Simon,' so no problem.

I should, however, state that none of the umpires mentioned is as short-sighted as a Welsh colleague who thought he saw a kangaroo in Cardiff in October 2004. It turned out to be a fox with a limp. Taffy couldn't have been wearing ear rings.

It's easy to poke fun at umpires, yet we can't play without them. Moreover, it's not an easy job. Calling no-balls can be especially problematic.

In 1972, I was reduced to umpiring for Evershed at Old Latymerians. I should have been playing but I'd lost my right contact lens whilst batting at Surbiton the previous Sunday. As a leech on society (northern for student), I couldn't afford to keep a spare pair. I had to order one, which took about a fortnight. As an interim/inter lens measure, I opted to play in my glasses. One ball in the nets, ie groin, proved I couldn't. The prescription was more out of date than the packet of chewing gum I'd just found in the bottom of my bag. It was like batting in a sauna.

I had a brainwave. I knocked the left sided glass lens out of my specs, kept the right one in and wore the specs plus my remaining contact lens in my left eye to get the best of both worlds. You know that feeling when you haven't slept for 72 hours? My eyesight was on a par with 'Garf's.' This made playing out of the question. I saw no reason why I shouldn't umpire, however.

The opening bowler, Allcock, was soon guilty of overstepping:

'I'll warn him next time,' I thought, calling upon the vast experience gained umpiring at Sun Sports 10 years before.

I did. It wasn't long before he transgressed again. (Allcock and no balls came as no surprise):

'I'll call him next time.'

I didn't. I was struck down with a dose of the George W's. My brain and mouth were incapable of working in tandem. It was akin to being embroiled in a monologue with your wife. You are contemplating when to butt in to announce you have six double week-ends in a row. You know the situation calls for you to speak but you can't spit it out. You settle for the easy option of putting it off, hoping there will be no repercussions later on.

Like umpiring, it's a special type of person who takes up scoring. Exactly what that speciality, or peculiarity, is tends to be confined to the under 15s and over 60s. Youngsters often score because it's preferable to getting up at the crack of dawn to do a paper round. Either that or they are press-ganged into it by their cricketing dad who is only allowed to continue to play by his wife on condition that he takes at least one of the kids with him. The more mature scorers give up their weekends for the free tea or because they don't play Bingo or go to Beetle Drives.

Naturally, the Old Quintinians didn't have a scorer. If we had, he or she would have ended up making up the numbers to 10 each time. The opposition, likewise, rarely brought a 'number cruncher.' It was, therefore, left to the players on the batting side to cobble together something which vaguely conveyed events – hence the expression 'do the book.'

Other than when I swear I broke Hanif Mohammed's, then, world record score of 499 at EMI in 1967, only to be accredited with a 'measly' 54, I can't recall a single disagreement taking place. We did get a few bowlers' names wrong, though.

Having asked: 'Bowler's name?' we were convinced we heard, and consequently wrote down, 'A.Duffer.' It was, in fact, 'A.Duffy.' He was, however, more like the former.

We also got the wrong vibrations when we thought a bowler was called 'Barbara Ann.' We didn't want to offend him so we wrote 'Beach Boy' for Bob Moran. It would have been more embarrassing if we'd have made a mistake over 'Asif Balok' and written down what we believed was said. Fortunately, we didn't make a balls of that one.

Similarly, if Prince Hassan had ever turned out against us, I'm convinced we'd have got his name, his title and even his sex wrong. Just say his name quickly and you'll hear what I mean. If England's scribe was hard of hearing, he might have written down Monty Panacea, in the hope that the spinner would turn out to be the answer to all our problems. Not paying attention could even make an intended compliment sound like an insult. For instance, during Euro 2008, David Pleat described Cesc Fabregas as 'a cunning little…. passer.'

At Evershed, every team had its own scorer. Ours answered to 'Paddington,' partly because he looked like a bear and partly because he was a rail clerk. He was more hirsute than Rasputin and made Pavarotti look positively emaciated – more like a fiver than a tenor. Not built for playing, he got involved by intermittently waddling out of the score box, not in search of honey, but to say his piece. His proclamations were invariably directed at the umpires or our captain. This soon became restricted to the former. 'Paddington' became more reserved after our captain's response to the advice aimed at him. 'Poker,' who was good at two things other than cricket, shouted back:

'The scorer now arriving at platforms six, seven and eight is coming in sideways.'

It did the trick, or more appropriately, it was just the ticket.

When 'Paddington' found out I was moving north to play in the Bradford League, he threatened to join me. I pointed out that it would be very expensive to travel up each week. It wouldn't. He had a railcard. I finally dissuaded him by mentioning that I'd heard the teas were rubbish.

At both Lidget Green and Middleton the scorers were reliable and of train-spotter, rather than train employee, stock. Both score boxes were situated high up out of harm's way. Neither had the inclination nor the speed to be anything other than unassuming so you can assume that there is nothing to report there. Nothing, that is, other than that Middleton's scribe was named Fielding. When we first met, he introduced himself thus:

'I'm Fielding.'

This provided me with the perfect opening to reply with:

'Where?'

There is more mileage to be had at Thornham. 'Tony' Woodcock made little of his obvious affliction to become a most proficient scorer. An added bonus for the club was that he always spent his match fee in our bar after games.

'Charlie' didn't, although she still made her presence felt there. As the world's most well-endowed scorer, apart from being able to see her coming around corners, she always gave you somewhere to rest your pint (or your head if you were lucky) if the tables were full. Even though she shared an apartment with a friend, in no way could she be deemed to be a flat mate.

'Ivor' Hickey, alias 'Love Bite,' was equally efficient, although his handwriting is so scruffy that he could have been a doctor. He was far more amicable than the notorious 'Ginger' Dave. Despite not being talented enough to get a game himself, he was never backward in criticising the players:

'That crappy shot you played cost us the game,' certainly shut me up. 'Why can't you bowl straight?' similarly boosted the confidence of the man who hates hard biscuits, 'Dunker.'

Less opinionated was the boy with long legs and a subsequent lack of oxygen to the brain. 'Daddy' was never going to pass even Key Stage 1 maths but he could draw dots and count to six with the aid of a calculator. After we'd beaten Longsight by nine wickets in 1995, he devised a novel way of making the batting and bowling figures tally.

'Walter' – he was saddled with this nickname because he came to home games on a Raleigh pushbike – had batted right through. His score had been shown correctly on the board all the way to the end. When the winning run had been hit, he stood on an impressive 84 not out. Unfortunately, 'Daddy's' Latin was as good as his maths. He wasn't cognisant with 'adsum,' so he took some off. Within 20 minutes, 84 had been pruned to 57. An understandably vexed 'Walter' enquired about this 'minor' discrepancy. 'Daddy' explained:

'I was 27 out on the batting and bowling so I took them off your total as you had the most.'

Imagine if 'Daddy' had been on duty when Arthur Collins amassed his 628 in a junior house match. The scorer of the game added his own rider:

'Plus or minus 20, shall we say.'

'Daddy's' supplement may have offered more scope:

'Somewhere between 500 and 1000.'

My son, James also did a stint until he became old enough to get a game, bearing out my earlier point about Dad's 'baby sitting' to obtain permission to play. Incidentally, he and I can probably claim a unique father-son (mis) feat. We both dropped the same batsman off the same ball in 2007. James was keeping and was standing up to 'Housewife,' who invariably bowls a nagging length. I was asleep at first slip. The batsman got a thick edge. James moved quickly to his right and did well to parry the ball up softly towards me. I moved slowly to my left and did less well to fumble the ball even more softly towards the turf.

Of the more mature scribes, the cake loving 'Madeira' excelled in the way he avoided confusing batsmen. Next to each name, he made notes of distinction. It was always totally politically correct. You would never find comments like 'beer belly,' 'midget,' 'lanky,' 'greasy bugger' or 'salad dodger.' This was most evident when Denton West opened with a 'Little and Large' combination. One was small enough to have appeared in 'Lord of the Rings.' His partner looked like Mike Tyson. Rather than state the obvious, 'Madeira' came up with 'green bat grip,' 'black bat grip.' A true gentleman.

'Mogadon,' has been called many things in his time at Thornham but never a true gentleman. Listening to him can be like trying to read a book on the history of anaesthetics:

'We should have scored 400 off that bowling today.' 'I've seen better bowlers in the primary school down the road.' 'Those umpires want shooting.' (I doubt if they do.) 'Who's eaten all the angel cake?' 'Raquel Welch's left boob is bigger than her right one.' (It's not.) 'These ice-cubes are too bloody cold.' 'He's that clever Dick who did the organ recital' (Now that is a clever dick!)

Nothing pleases him and he has an opinion on everything. 'Mogadon' really could start an argument just by looking in the mirror:

'You're fat.'

'I'm not. I'm big-boned.'

Despite his negativity, our soporific scorer is a club man at heart. When we are desperate, he can always be relied upon to do the book for us. In this role, he is a mixture of 'Daddy's' maths, 'Lovebite's' writing, 'Ginger's' criticisms and 'Paddington's' predilection for going AWOL. He is not averse to leaving his post half way through an over.

'Mogadon' took this to extremes at Wythenshawe in 1986. Not only did he desert the score box, he also left the ground mid-way through our innings in search of an ice cream. He returned 10 minutes later clutching a half eaten, quarter melted 99. This was certainly as close as he ever got to a ton. His action might not have been so significant had not his opposite number also abandoned the box some two minutes earlier to pay a visit. It became another case of post-match creative accountancy à la 'Daddy.'

The book also tends be inaccurate when youngsters are on duty and the opposition has an attractive female doing the honours. Sitting side by side in a confined space definitely affects our boys' concentration (northern for hormones). They seem to need more stretches and toilet breaks than normal. You can easily become stiff when cooked up in a tiny box.

Under the banner of officials, I must also pay tribute to those behind the scenes. This includes that special (needs) group who make up the selection committee. In my experience, they have much in common with school governors. You'd expect both bodies to be well-informed and on the ball. In reality, what you frequently get is a bunch of egotistic wind bags who can't distinguish posteriors from humeruses.

Picking teams can be a sensitive process. Alternatively, you could adopt the slightly more 'laissez-faire' attitude that one chairman of selectors of a northern first-class county reputedly did. The story goes that he debated the eleven for the next game with the captain over the phone along the lines of:

'We'll go with you, Bob and Pete. No, not Pete, Phil. Pete retired last year didn't he? Give Tom a game if he's fit. Then there's that big ginger lad who can bat a bit and the quick bowler. You know the one who likes fish and chips. How many's that? Only six? Bugger. Who else is there? Oh aye, that spotty lad who drives the Escort and his mate with big feet. Have I forgotten anyone? Who, Don and Mike? How could I forget them? Who's Mike? Is that 11? Only10. OK. You choose the other one. Cheers!'

Even such distinguished pundits as those who select the

Wisden Young Cricketer of the Year can leave themselves open to criticism. Whoever did so in the 70s really knew their stuff: 1971 – J. Whitehouse; 1972 – D. Owen-Thomas; 1975 – A. Kennedy. They all made the big time! Up to now, no one from Worcester has ever been chosen. Aren't they glad?

At club level, too, some selections beggar belief. With the Old Quintinians, of course, there were never any disagreements;

'Who's available next week? All nine of us? Great!'

Elsewhere, cricketing ability isn't always the deciding factor. I remember enquiring why one player seemed to be an automatic choice for Walsden's 1st XI in the CLL when the consensus was that there were several better players in the 2nds. It all fell into place when I was told:

'There are, but they didn't build the wall round the ground, did they?'

That's a new slant on the expression:

'He's cemented his place in the side.'

In a league with such kudos, one would assume that selectors would have a sound knowledge of the game. It's not far removed from making a Scotsman Chancellor of the Exchequer – horses for courses, as the two Geoffs, Lawson and Arnold, would say. At Middleton, we were privileged to have had one selector, 'Phil,' a dentist, who was bordering on the psychic.

Prior to the start of a match at Heywood in 1979ish, I overheard 'Phil' telling the mere mortal by his side, ie the psychic's side-kick:

'We must bat first today. That wicket won't last.'

His associate, thirsty for more knowledge, asked:

'Why? Have you had a good look at it?'

'No,' replied 'Phil.' 'I don't need to. I can tell just by walking on the outfield.'

One of 'Phil's' colleagues was equally clued-up. Following a delayed start at Oldham after a deluge, amidst mopping up and sawdust aplenty, 'Dizzy' – he just is – phoned a friend. He explained that our spinners would win the game for us:

'It'll take spin right away. You should see it. It's like a dust bowl out there.'

My most disheartening experience regarding selection came in 1988 when I was involved in the selection of the Lancashire and Cheshire League side for a prestigious inter-league fixture against the Bolton League. I'd been given two weeks prior notice of the meeting and, knowing it to be an extremely important event, took my duties most seriously. I studied the previous season's averages in the league handbook, looked at current form – only three players were in prison – and listed every player I felt worthy of consideration, even those I didn't like. After hours of deliberation, I finalised my choice. There won't be any arguments there, I concluded.

There weren't. The day of the meeting duly arrived. It was almost an hour's drive but I didn't mind. I saw myself as David Graveney, although not quite as bald, overweight or boring. I was genuinely excited at the prospect of announcing my eleven. I had loads of evidence to back up my reasoning. There was no need to consider wall builders or car owners. (In an era when minibuses weren't an option, the London Schools selectors invariably left one spot open for a player with a car.) This would be a team capable of beating the Bolton League. I was confident that, after due deliberation, my fellow selectors would back my judgment, even though I hadn't gone for the bloke who liked fish and chips.

I arrived to find 'Rod,' who loves fishing, and 'Frank,' who nearly always speaks his mind, pulling into the car park. We went into the function room (southern for cellar) and sat at a table. My heart was racing. Should I speak first or accept that it was no different from being at home and wait until I was given the nod from 'Rod?' He got us started... and finished:

'There's your team,' he proclaimed, reeling off 11 names from a cigarette packet.

Before I could ask who Benson and Hedges played for, 'Frank,' concurred:

'Right,' said Fred, I mean 'Frank,' without even looking at the names.

Rod' then confirmed my being surplus to requirements:

'Don't worry about the batting order, Jim. I'll cast an eye over that before Sunday.'

It occurred to me to ask if I should bring my own coin. Instead, I plumped for:

'Do you want to see my list?'

They didn't. I might as well have spent all that time picking my nose instead:

'Must go,' said 'Frank.' (Did he need to get changed into euros?) , leaving me in need of a stiff drink. A glass of starch would have done nicely.

I can't let tales on officials pass without reference to 'Tolstoy,' the LCL secretary. This top bloke produces, single-handed, the best toilet read imaginable, the league handbook. It has enough fascinating information to see you through a lengthy stay yet is small enough to hide about your person when your wife shrieks:

'Why are you taking so long? You're reading in there, aren't you?'

You can deny this without having to throw any incriminating evidence out of the window. It details every statistic imaginable, including how many runs each of the 26

Leech brothers of Denton scored and how many southerners are on hit lists.

'Tolstoy' also doubles as master of ceremonies at the League Dinner, held at Old Trafford every October. He can always be relied upon to come up with put downs. One which sticks in my mind came in 1996. Denton had won the league title again. This wasn't surprising as their professional was Lancashire's Steve O'Shaughnessy, the joint record holder of the fastest ever first-class hundred (35 minutes). He'd plundered a mere 1552 runs, although 'Daddy' had him down for 625.

Our MC called upon Denton's captain, Glen Bullock, to receive the trophy. 'Tolstoy' informed his captive audience – we were all tied down with rope – that Glen's lifelong ambition was to have a pub named after him. Those of us sober enough to care tried to think ahead. Would it be 'Glen's Boozer,' the 'Duck and Bullock,' or 'Load of Bullocks? Not even close. 'Tolstoy' announced that he was sorry, they just don't name pub's 'big, fat, ugly bastard.' 'Tolstoy's' a real character. Fortunately, he's not alone.

Food for thought:
21. Why did John Hampshire play for Yorkshire?
22. One William Shakespeare played for England pre-Derek Underwood but was he barred because he did not play right? Did he ever appear with Surrey's Julius Caesar?
23. Did Mike Buss of Sussex become a coach?
24. Whenever Somerset's Wally Luckes failed to make his ground, was it a case of 'Luckes run out?'

Chapter 7

CHARACTERS

Geographical location imposes no limit on the distribution of cricketing characters. In this case a 'character' is anyone who has made me laugh or cringe on or off the field. Herein, they fall into one of two camps – character or wazzock. As with genious and idiot, there is often a fine line. To judge, ask yourself would this person brighten up the place by their presence or by going home?

I go back to 1967 for my first oddball. A 13 year old, named Delanie, was set to bowl in a school game in Willesden. The umpire posed the obligatory:

'What are you bowling?' expecting right arm over, round or optimistic.

He received only a blank look. He repeated his question, not thinking to rephrase it. Again, Delanie looked bemused, as if he'd been asked to name every state in the USA in alphabetical order. The umpire tried once more, adding:

'I need to tell the batsman what you're going to bowl.'

'Ah,' muttered a relieved 'Delboy.' 'You can tell the batsman I'm gonna bowl real fast.'

He did.

My good friend, Kevin – we dislike the same people - told

me about the next candidate for the Dream Team. 'Hoss' Cartwright was playing for Liverpool University in the late 70s against a well-to-do club side who would doubtless have rated themselves as 'very strong.' It didn't take long for the opposition's opening batsman to have the same effect on 'Hoss' as Keira Knightley has on most straight men. He became all hot and bothered. The toff was dicked in a cravat and a Douglas Jardinesque hooped cap.

The bombastic batsman opted not to call in English and indulged in his own version of French cricket. 'Hoss' had to endure cries of 'oui,' 'non,' 'attendez.' The 'Entente Cordiale' went out of the window. 'Hoss' was incensed but it wasn't long before his bonanza arrived. He trapped his man lbw and made full use of his 'A' level French skills to send him back:

'Allez au fuckin' hutch, twat! (Northern French for off you pop to the changing room, Monsieur.) Vous êtes prune.' (In this case, a prune's a plum.)

Another one-off was provided soon afterwards by a hard-nosed village cricketer from Wiltshire. I'll call him 'Holly' because he is a prickly character and his wife's name is Ivy. 'Holly' has forearms like a post-spinach Popeye and was good enough to play Minor Counties and County Seconds. He scored a couple of centuries against Evershed and is not a man to mess with. When acting as twelfth man in a County Second XI game in the south-west, he was summoned to run the captain's bath. The captain was a no-nonsense, tough ex-England player who didn't like trialists smacking him from one side of Headingley to the other.

'Holly' did his duty, yet, having been told rather than asked, ran the bath cold. That scuppered any chance of a county contract but he believed it to have been well worthwhile, experiencing both the air and the captain's arse turn blue.

Maurice Edgar Wickens was the first club cricketer I revered. Mo (his favourite shot) had the ability, if not the fitness, to play at a much higher level (11 a-side) than he did. (9 versus 11.) He was the Old Qs' answer to Garfield Sobers, although if I'm being fastidious, Mo is shorter, fatter, less agile, white and right-handed.

On the plus side, Mo would bowl relatively sharply for a while and then change to bowling useful off-spin. He once did so to devastating effect against Heston Nomads. They were 101 for 3, chasing 110. Mo had reached the stage where he could no longer run up to bowl. He reverted to walking two paces and giving us all a good look at his tweakers. The Nomads kept wandering out of their crease and we won by seven runs.

Maurice combined his skill with a good cricketing brain. He gave me plenty of sound advice in my formative years – stuff like don't eat too much swiss roll before you bat, never trust a South African wicket-keeper and drink the mild not the bitter.

He was renowned for having a fuse as short as a Chinese firework. Frightening as this could be, his volleys were often rendered less explosive by his turn of phrase. Mo had a command of vocabulary which Nancy Reagan lacked when she uttered that immortal line:

'I believe people would be alive today if there were a death penalty.'

Compare that to Mo's offering when being pestered by a dog during a drinks break. Minus a couple of vowels, his instruction to man's best friend was a masterful, unambiguous:

'F-ck off you canine c-nt.'

Now acutely aware that this cat-lover was not to be crossed, Rover moved on and started sniffing around Max ('Olga'), who, true to form, dropped the hound when it jumped up into his arms.

Not one to worry about his fibre intake, Mo's fragile mood could be adversely affected by attacks of piles. On such occasions, he made Placido Domingo appear as docile as Ghengis Khan. We witnessed this first hand in May 1965 at Chiswick. Mo was obviously suffering. He was mincing around like Dale Whatshisface and decided to take his discomfort out on the batsmen.

Going off on a tangent once more, on the piles front (or rear), I did play a couple of seasons with a wicket-keeper at Middleton named Roydes whose daughter is named Emma. Back to Mo, now Maurice is no dancer but he could make the batsman look like they also had two left feet with his nippy outswingers. On this particular day, he was bowling too well for our opponents, our wicket-keeper and our slips. Despite his swollen veins, our mercurial all-rounder surprisingly accepted a couple of dropped catches behind the wicket with a mere shrug of the shoulders. Soon after, two more edges were grounded off successive balls. Mo could contain himself no longer. All of the toys left the pram. It was tantamount to a tantrum. Until now, I'd been happily redundant at first slip, hiding behind our mint-sucking, petrified keeper, 'Marco.'

My plump physics teacher, 'Ohm sweet ohm,' was next to me at second and third slip. He had already erred twice. Consequently, when the next chance flew in our direction, he chose sod's law over Boyle's law, bawling:

'Yours, boy.'

I dived, well, flopped, to my left. I took what appeared to be a half-decent tumbling catch. I say 'half' decent. I spilled it. The ball, having fortuitously found its way into my hand, immediately found its way out again. Nobody knew it had since it lodged under my prostrate body. Before I could say a word, shed a tear or run for cover, a jubilant Mo shrieked:

'At last! Well held, Jim. I knew I could rely on you, son.'

In my defence, the batsman was already three parts of the way back to the pavilion, convinced he was out. What a dilemma. I was only 15. I really wanted to live to be 16 so that I could legitimately go to the cinema to watch 'X' rated films. Mo was so happy. I wrestled with my conscience and, in true wrestling tradition, went for the shady option. I gave the smiling bowler a slap on the back rather than risk him giving me a slap in the mouth. No one would know. I'd soon overcome my embarrassment.

But I hadn't reckoned on my eagle-eyed physics teacher. Suspecting malpractice, he whispered:

'Did you drop that, Carnegie?'

I was crap at physics and in no position to be cute. I came clean:

'Yes sir, I did.'

'Oh well,' he said knowingly. 'Welcome to the club.'

'Matt' and 'Luke' are brothers. Both were outstanding league cricketers in the 70s and 80s. Both are also extremely amusing men and neither suffers fools gladly. Nor was either one shy of controversy. In all my years of playing, I've only come across two cases of players being 'dobbed.' (Northern for run out backing up too far.) In London, this was a no-no. For 'Bros,' it was a yes-yes.

'Matt's' was the more straightforward. It involved an Aussie so he wasn't chastised in any way. Playing at Milnrow for Crompton in the CLL in the mid 70s, 'Errol' Flynn middled one to second slip. Would you believe it, he didn't walk. No less surprising, the umpire was caught unawares and didn't send him packing.

'Errol's' disinclination to depart was not met with universal approval. Phrases containing words like 'dishonest,' 'convict,' 'beguiler' and 'hoodwinker' (or thereabouts) were uttered. 'Matt's' good nature permitted the crooked antipodean to get to 50. His more competitive side then took over. 'Matt' spotted the cheeky cheat about to steal a single by backing up too early and too far. Ignoring protocol, without the customary warning, he pulled up in his delivery stride and whipped off the bails. A startled umpire, 'Jack,' a crown green bowler, was instructed:

'He'll have to go this time.'

'Jack' acquiesced and 'Errol' had the nerve to call 'Matt' something akin to a 'treacherous knave.'

Not to be upstaged, 'Luke's' effort arose in the Milnrow versus Stand fixture a year later. 'Luke' was a flamboyant cricketer, talented enough to play for Lancashire. In the first meeting between the sides, he had pushed gently forward to a ball but, instead of opting to leave it where it was, he then whacked it to the fielder at square leg, presumably to save time. His thoughtfulness was not appreciated. A WG Grace-like appeal (1878 South v North) for 'hit the ball twice' was made and upheld. (His WG should have been replaced by DIS thereafter.)

Mildly irritated, 'Luke' waited for the away encounter before striking back. Without warning, he dobbed Stand's main man for nought. His response to boos from the home crowd and disapproval from the opposition was to shout:

'One all!'

The boys' efforts, whilst noteworthy, aren't in the same league as 'master-dobber,' MA Wahind of Ceylon, as was. He did warn the opposition's number eight before dobbing him but failed to extend the courtesy to numbers nine or ten. They both went the same way in quick succession. A unique hat trick, I suspect, but it begs the question if the number nine was slow to catch on, how dense must the number ten have been?

Possibly dense enough to believe that Vlad the Impaler relieves asthma or that fjords are Norwegian cars?

Despite knowing 'Luke' quite well, whenever I faced him he'd bowl me a bouncer first ball, followed by a wink and a smile. I'd always duck and remind him only to hit each delivery he faced just the once when it was his turn. He'd then get me out.

I've known 'Matt' for longer. He has always been a real kidder. Having played a ball past him at Middleton for an easy single, he ambled after it as if to coax me into a dodgy second run. I was undecided until he fell over in a heap, turning it into a comfortable three. Typically, 'Matt' glossed over it with a:

'Back to the drawing board. Don't back up too far, Jim.' (My accent again, I suspect.)

His next brainwave seemed to involve a most vigorous 'cleaning of the seam,' which could be why his following delivery deviated more than David Bowie and did me.

For the fond memories 'Matt' and 'Luke' have provided, I dob them the true 'Chuckle Brothers.'

'Chopper' is also guaranteed to make you giggle. Before any female readers try to find out his address, disappointingly for him, his nickname is derived from his attachment to a push-bike rather than due to the size of his willy. 'Chopper' isn't the sharpest axe in the woodman's armour. This is borne out by his quiz clangers that Fred Trueman was President of the USA in 1945 and that Gloucester's Sam Cook was a soul singer in his spare time.

As a consequence of being done for drink driving, 'Chopper' invested in a two-wheeler to get to and from Middleton's ground. He assumed his gave him free rein, or free handlebar, to hit the 'pop.' After one session, he rode his bike, and his luck, up to the rear of a parked car and stayed there for ten minutes, believing himself to be in a queue of traffic. I watched him from my front window. Once I'd stopped laughing, I went out to assist him. I'm glad I did. He needed to piddle before he could pedal, so I'd helped to avoid a paddle in a puddle.

A month later, he was moved to tears when he was pulled by the fuzz for being 'intoxicated whilst on a bicycle.' (Southern for pedalling booze.) He didn't get any points on his licence but was banned from competing in the Tour de France for five years.

This setback coincided with a slump in 'Chopper's' form. In truth, he'd been short of runs for a lifetime and was now so disappointed with his drought that he opted for a measure likely to put him on a par with many umpires. He, too, would enter the world of deep sleep. He visited a hypnotist. The idea was that the hypnotist would implant the suggestion that 'Chopper' couldn't get out until he'd scored a certain number of runs. Unfortunately, nobody thought to hypnotise the bowlers so the only score of note from 'Chopper' was the 20 quid he paid for each session.

Most cricket clubs have a member or two who love the sound of their own voice. Does this make them a character or an arsehole? For instance, in which camp does Dominic Cork fall? Should that 'r' be a 'c'? I bet he felt a bit of one when he went for 96 off only eight overs against Notts in 1993.

Once again, the Old Qs were an exception, having no one who was up themselves. Nobody took themselves seriously enough to brag and none of us ever did anything good enough to brag about. Whereas a 'good season' for Don Bradman constituted six double hundreds (1930), to us it meant avoiding food poisoning from the teas and no cardiac arrests or nappy rash.

Evershed, too, tended to be blessed with bashful rather than boastful players. We had several talented individuals who could have sounded off about themselves. Instead, they preferred to take the mickey out of each other and the opposition - my kind of people. None could be accused of being as self-possessed as Roy Keane or as cock-sure as David Platt. In 2007, Roy began a sentence with:

'I, myself, personally,' just in case we thought he might not be self-opiniated.

David followed up with:

'That was certainly definite,' regarding a foul committed in the Carling Cup in 2008.

My favourite character at Evershed was 'Speedy Gonzales,' the south's forerunner, or forewalker, to the soon to be vaunted, 'Treacle.' If these two should ever meet for a 100 metres race, it would be more of a stroll than a dash. Uranus takes 84 years to orbit the Sun. 'Speedy's' would take twice as long.

'Speedy' became thus after he'd taken so long to 'chase' a ball that the batsmen ran a five. The bowler, 'Gurkha,' who loves small pickled cucumbers, exclaimed:

'He's as slow as a disabled donkey.'

Granted he is more like a three-toed sloth than a peregrine falcon and wouldn't be quick enough to avoid a nip in the nuts from a squirrel. However, rumour has it that things have improved. 'Speedy' now uses 'Lively Blond' shampoo.

Just about the only time I saw 'Speedy' get his arse in gear was at Lords in 1963ish. This was following a visit to the Oval where he'd been impressed by the actions of an OAP. This old gent had spotted Surrey's Mickey Stewart fielding on the boundary, near to where he was sitting. He fumbled in his pocket and shouted:

'Refresher, Mickey?'

Not hailing from Yorkshire, he didn't seek any payment from the England opening batsman as he threw the packet of sweets to the star. Mickey graciously accepted one before returning the rest. Low and behold, when Surrey came to Lords to a few days later, the same sweet-toothed sportsman was positioned within chucking distance of us. 'Speedy' saw his chance. He rushed to the confectionary stand and spent his bus fare home on Mickey's favourite candy:

'Refresher, Mickey?'

'Speedy' was disappointed to hear an emphatic rejection before he even got his purchase airborne, leaving him as the sucker.

Lidget Green had one strong candidate for the 'Mr.Big Head' title. The wicket-keeper, 'Narcissus,' staunchly believed he was God's gift to everything. As you can probably tell, he ran me out once or twice. I had a soft spot for him – a boggy marsh in the middle of Exmoor. He had played a few games for Yorkshire Second XI and decided this qualified him as a super star. Like being named Beverly Mills, Judy Punch, Sid Carr, Catherine Wheeler, Shaun Warne or Shane Wayne, it was a case of so near yet so far.

Middleton is a big club with plenty of larger than life 'characters.' One who would not be ignored was a 15 year old. He stood out for two reasons. He was full of himself and he was ginger. A cocky, teenage carrot-head was as welcome as mumps. To be fair, and I bet he wishes he was, we all knew that 'Shrinking Violet' would become a very good bowler.

After performing well in a number of other leagues in the north-west, he came to pro at Thornham in1990 odd. Officially an 'amateur' up to this point, he took a pay cut and brought his less than useful brother along. He saw it as 'two for the price of one.' As neither could claim to be a thing of outstanding natural beauty, we saw it as a famous Clint Eastwood western.

On a par in the self-confident stakes was KC, minus his Sunshine Band. Whatever anybody else did, he could do it better:

'If I'd been in as long as you, I'd have scored twice as many, Viv.'

Maybe, but he was never in that long for us to find out. In the five years we played together, his highest score as a top six batsman was 33. This still did not prevent him from constantly trying to convince us he was Superman. What a pity there was so much kryptonite around. Like 'Alexander' before him, KC considered himself to be a 'great' cricketer. Great, as in Great Yarmouth? OK, I confess, he also ran me out three or four times. I'm guilty of having something in common with a sick prince…ill will.

Staying in the north, Thornham can boast, and this duo most certainly can, two past masters of the Max Bygraves academy:

'I wanna tell you a story…about myself.'

'Ribena Man' and 'Treacle' are legends in their own minds. The former isn't keen on blackcurrant drinks but does go the colour of one after minimal exercise. The latter is lightning slow. 'Treacle' couldn't have beaten Douglas Bader in a sprint. Incidentally, it's a recorded fact that Bader was captured by the Germans in 1941. How difficult could that have been?

'Run, Douglas. Oh shit, I forgot. Tell them nothing.'

'Ribena Man' endeared himself to all at Thornham through his humility and wisdom. I always think of him when Test Match Special is interrupted to bring us the highlight of the day – the shipping forecast. He is that 'slow moving, deepening depression spreading over the north-west.'

'Ribena' is as dear to us as Peter Roebuck is to Ian Botham.

He sees himself as the fountain of cricket knowledge yet is unable to come to grips with much of the terminology. For him, a night watchman is a kerb crawler, a reverse sweep is a peews and economy rates are how often you buy a round.

When you are barely good enough to play for the 3rds, such modest comments as: 'I'm the best wicket-keeper in the area,' 'I'm the best leg spinner in the league' and 'I'm the best opening bat Thornham have got,' are best kept to oneself.

The purple-faced windbag didn't enhance his popularity when, upon returning to the club from an away 3rdXI fixture, he heralded his entrance into the bar full of 1stXI players and supporters with a typically humble:

'Somebody buy me a lager. I've just scored 50.'

Even a curt:

'Piss off, big head,' didn't deter him.

'In that case, I'll have bitter,' was met with a:

'Go and play with the traffic, shy boy.'

'Treacle,' although equally self-obsessed, is far less obnoxious and can at least laugh at himself. Sometimes he has no option. He can empty a room in seconds when he starts pontificating about how he only scored seven but it proved to be a match-winning innings. That said, 'Treacle' is not a bad player and because he is a nice bloke, we put up with him pontificating from time to time to time to time to time.

After the opening game of the 2004 season, 'Treacle' scored an excellent 60 for the 3rd team. We overheard him consoling a less successful team-mate with:

'It's lucky I'm in such a rich vein of form. I was able to bat for the both of us.'

(This prompted me to consider what constitutes a good trot. My answer is AE Trott. In 1899 and 1900 combined, he took 450 wickets and scored 2512 runs at a canter.)

'Treacle' has never been able to run at a moderate speed and so continued to show his paces through what I'll charitably term 'one-upmanship.' A few games after having batted for two, his parting shot to an opponent was a cheery:

'See you next season. I'll try to hit you for three fours in an over again then.'

In 2002, I was at the other end when the man who is too ponderous to eat 'fast' food, pulled a full toss sweetly for six in a 2ndXI game at Denton. Knowing I'd regret it, I praised the shot. 'Treacle' was as dismissive of the compliment as he was of the delivery:

'My dad says you should always hit full tosses for six,' giving the bowler a 'don't bowl that crap at me,' look.

Perhaps his eyesight began to fade – he is single – but a day later he only managed a four off another full bunger. Was it deflation? The bowler was certainly depressed. His comment this time was:

'My dad says you should always hit full tosses for four.'

Our standards must drop as we get older. Hence, a year after this, he justified his failure to score off a similar gift by stating:

'My dad says you should never get out to a full toss.'

Horror of horrors, several games later, he was caught off one. I resisted the temptation to ask what his dad would have said. I reckon it could have been:

'You should never be bowled by a full toss.'

Blessed with a dodgy memory, 'Treacle' maintains he never drops catches. In reality, his hands are as safe as Brixton or Moss Side. Born with the reflexes of a corpse, he can turn a dolly into a difficult half-chance in one laboured movement. He will also attempt to convince anyone who'll listen that he was a capable bowler in his youth. Foolishly, I brought this up during a pre-game knock up. Dexterously, 'Treacle' turned my passing comment into a detailed account of a 50 he made for Thornham u15s during the Depression. He gave this self-indulgence credence, having heard my snoring, by confessing:

'And my bowling went down hill after that innings so I decided to concentrate on my batting from then on.'

Our urbane friend's exploits extend way beyond the cricket field. The mention of a dolly leads me on to a tale told by one of his ex-girlfriends. She must have discovered that he'd described her as 'less than gorgeous.'

'She's no looker, but she'll do for now,' constituted a possible proposal of marriage.

Her put-down was to tell us that 'Brad Pitt' is no dab hand at housework. When asked by her to hoover the front room, he performed the chore with such uncharacteristic speed for someone who is too slow to run a bath, that she was moved to enquire:

'Have you done it already?'

Her expectant partner responded in the affirmative, sensing that this dolly might be thinking of rewarding him with more than a mere hello. His baffled lady friend went on – as 'Treacle' himself often did – to say:

'I didn't hear any noise from the hoover.'

'Treacle's' reply dashed any chance of another great knock:

'Oh, I didn't know you had to plug it in to make it work.'

'Treacle' is equally adept at driving. Northerners are renowned for their nowse but he accepts he is an exception. His excuse is that he works in an office full of southerners. In 2003, 'Treacle' thought he was playing skittles in his car. He contrived to knock over half a dozen wheelie-bins on the way to a game. Pardonnable, perhaps, if you're drunk or if it happened on a blind bend. This was on a main road.

Days later, he left Longsight without staying for a post-match drink. 'Fool' Hardy had drawn the short straw and was riding shotgun with him. (It's a bit 'tasty' around Longsight.) It's only a 15 to 20 minute drive back to Thornham, depending upon how many times you get car-jacked. 45 minutes after they'd set off, Hardy popped his head around the bar door and whispered:

'Can someone tell us how to get back to our ground? We've just been all the way to Stockport.'

In global terms, that's the equivalent of setting off from London for Manchester and ending up in the Isle of Wight.

'Treacle' then excelled himself by contriving to crash into a stationary panda car. Luckily, neither Chi-Chi nor An-An were inside but 'Treacle' knew he'd made a pig's ear of it. His only way out was to plead insanity. When a policeman spotted his Neil Diamond tapes he almost pulled it off, only to blow it by asking the officer if he liked bacon butties.

This indiscretion resulted in him being summoned to attend a Driver Improvement Scheme. It proved ineffective. As the penultimate driver of a convoy on the way to a game at Woodbank, he went through a red light at a busy junction with three lanes of oncoming traffic. Rather than get out of the way, our screwy driver cut his losses and pulled up. Mayhem. The advancing vehicles had to treat the intruder as a roundabout, as the oblivious 'Treacle' whistled 'Sweet Caroline.' Once bitten…

At the next set of lights, 'Schumacher' became confused by the filter, which was on red, and his lane's lights, on green. He opted for caution and stopped. When informed by the convoy's back marker that it was in order to go through, 'Treacle' was adamant:

'Oh no! You're not catching me out again.'

Whilst the lovable 'Treacle' and the squeezable 'Ribena Man' were together at Thornham, everyone's nightmare was to be collared by both simultaneously. That was a fate worse than facing a wind-assisted Kenny Benjamin without a helmet when you're past it.

It nearly happened once. Several of us had gone back to Thornham after a 1st XI game in the early 90s. We were having a leisurely stroll around the ground, watching the 2nds. We spotted 'Treacle' approaching from the left. Only belatedly did we notice the pincer movement from the right by the 'world's number one all-rounder.' We were trapped.

'Brace yourself, boys. Hot air from both sides in sea areas Dogger, Ford Sierra, Vauxhall Astra and Thornham imminent,' came the warning via a mock Radio 4 announcer.

A wicket fell. 'Botox,' had given another lbw. We all looked anxiously at one another and, without a word, sprinted across the ground to safety past astonished fielders and batsmen. Far from engaging in that renowned activity on the River Severn called 'Chasing the Bore,' we had done exactly the opposite.

The two immovable forces collided perilously soon afterwards. None of us dares to ask who got the upper hand. It certainly wasn't short-winded. I'd guess 'Ribena Man' ran out of juice first, mainly because he'd been fitted with a defibrillator which presumably prevented him from telling any more lies. Even so, I expect he will have tried to take credit for inspiring near namesake Rubina Humphries in her astonishing feat of taking 10 for 0 whenever.

Compared to these two, 'Spaceman,' or 'Yuri' to his friends, is a mere apprentice, despite being as mad as a triathlete. As a surfer who rolls his own (smokes not waves), he is in a world of his own most of the time. 'Yuri' takes his cricket seriously, although he could not be considered to be the fountain of all sporting knowledge, believing Alice Springs to be an Aussie triple jumper and drag racing to be exclusively for transvestites. He once overheard some of us fawning over the 3Ws. When he heard the name of Everton Weekes, he thought our discussion concerned summer holidays in Merseyside.

Nor is geography his forte. At Thornham, in the off-season we hold a quiz night on the first Saturday of each month. 'Yuri' turned up only once. He tried to convince us Chile is so called because it snows a lot there and that its capital is Con Carni, whereas Khartoum is definitely the capital of Disneyland.

Predictably, he saved the best 'til last, which is where his team finished. By muddling an 'n' with a 'v,' he contrived to say 'Viagra Falls.' When corrected, he inadvertently provided more ammunition with:

'Blimey. That was a stiff one.'

In a rare appearance for Thornham 1stXI in about 1995 at Denton St. Lawrence, 'Yuri' dismissed Lancashire's Gary Yates, albeit with a rank long hop. Gary hit it like an exocet to the man on the mid-wicket boundary who somehow held on to it. 'Yuri' regularly heralds his moment of triumph, explaining to the infirm:

'I did him with my slower ball.'

Reality does kick in occasionally. Irlam's teenage wicket-keeper, 'Rantipole' (old southern for pillock), was really getting under our skin in 2002 with his whinging and time-wasting during a 2ndXI game. I thought 'Yuri' was going to do something we'd regret when he shouted:

'That's it, you little snot!'

I went over to him, thinking I should inform Houston that we'd lost control. (If I had, he'd have assumed I was referring to that station near King's Cross.) I told him not to do anything daft. (This would have been like telling Gloucester's Gilbert

Jessop to take it easy – Gilbert smashed 11 tons in under an hour.) His response bordered on the responsible:

'I'm a man so I can't hit a 15 year old kid but my brother can. I'm going to get him up here and twat the little shit.'

I managed to hide his mobile but he did inform our tormentor how his body parts would have been rearranged had he made the call.

We could have done with 'Tippex' – his pet phrase is:

'Correct me if I'm wrong,' to counter our obstreperous opponent on that day.

A Prestwich v Thornham game was delayed by rain in 1993. This afforded the home side's professional with an ideal opportunity to proclaim his greatness in the bar. He was about 10% of the way through describing his latest masterful innings when 'Tippex' struck. He 'innocently' ushered the other home team players outside. They all returned five minutes later, sporting earphones. 'Tippex' then said all that was needed:

'Carry on, pro.'

During the same match, catching sight of the team-mate who'd just run him out, arm in arm with his well-stacked girlfriend, he muttered:

'Here come the three biggest tits in the club.'

'Tippex,' like his ex-mate's girlfriend, has been around. So had the aforementioned old Ernie, with whom he bore an uncanny resemblance.

A brief comparison of these two characters throws some light on the north-south divide. 'Tippex,' a Lancastrian through and through, is more down to earth and had his own vocabulary for the 'wasters' in his team. A 'nomad' is someone who is always wandering in the field. A 'kipper' is likely to fall asleep when fielding. A 'wide-boy' can't bowl straight. A 'drop out' can't catch. A 'goblet' is any loud-mouthed juvenile. A 'huskie' is an accomplished sledger and a 'larder' is overweight.

Ernie was a cockney and seemingly less confrontational. Ernie wasn't a milkman, although he did like a pint. He wasn't given to histrionics. Having been around for longer than barbed wire, he'd seen it all and knew how to humiliate without insults or sobriquets.

Despite his lack of 'Tippex's' directness, Ernie could still get his point across. As useful as a stapler with no staples himself, he demanded high standards from everyone else, even though it was the Old Quintinians. Herein, 'Wonderloaf,' (Keith Baker) failed to escape Ernie's wrath at Eton – the club side, not the school, although we did have Penguins at tea.

Keith was our best fielder, being able-bodied and under 70. He'd made a valiant attempt to hold on to a real stinger. The ball had been hit with such force that, despite Keith's intervention, it still had enough on it to go all the way to the boundary. Instead of receiving a 'great try' for his magnificent effort, Keith got a reprimand:

'Get up and fetch the ball, then bring it back here,' pronounced a stone-faced Ernie.

Keith did as instructed.

'Now toss it to me,' continued the stalwart.

The old boy proceeded to pouch the gentle lob and concluded the lesson with:

'There. That's how to catch a ball. Don't miss the next one or you'll be walking home.'

In a game at Richmond, for reasons known only to him, Ernie gave me a bowl. After three overs of mediocre tripe, he asked me:

What are you trying to bowl, son?'

I'd heard Richie Benaud mention 'off-cutters' on the radio. In an attempt to impress, I borrowed the term. My captain may not have been convinced:

'Just as long as you know. Carry on, Brian Statham.'

A mammoth four over spell ended when the inappropriately named Tony Toogood dropped a skier. Guess what ritual he had to go through.

You certainly couldn't criticise Ernie or 'Tippex' for being indecisive. Neither ever fannied around like the International Astronomical Union. Is Pluto a planet, a big rock or a cartoon character? Just decide!

Nor did they blame themselves for poor team performances. I couldn't imagine either doing an Arthur Shrewsbury. Arthur was England's skipper when they were dismissed for 40 odd in a Test Match. He must have felt a modicum of guilt because he later shot himself.

My next character/penis bonce, 'Basil' has already surfaced in chapter three. I also refer to him as 'Vidal' for his obsession with his hair. His dapper appearance apart, he had a reputation in the CLL in the 1970s and early 80s for club hopping. By this, I don't mean he divided his Saturday nights between the Hacienda, the Ritz and Smokies.

Not wishing to have his looks or locks spoiled, he tended to follow the most fearsome bowlers around. This saw him have spells with Royton, Werneth, Middleton and, when Joel Garner was signed by them, Littleborough. Some would say this made 'Vidal' smart, in both senses of the word. Others might be tempted to add 'arse.'

Moving around didn't prevent 'Vidal' from one brush with a West Indian quick at Middleton. Neil Phillips of Stockport got him above the eye with a real brute. In spite of losing enough blood for anaemia to set in, 'Vidal' made the taxi driver taking him to hospital hang on. One last, lingering look in the mirror convinced him it was the need for cosmetic surgery that was the most pressing. Hence, he called out to his sweet wife:

'Honey, comb my hair for me before I go. I mustn't look a mess in public.'

We were all in sutures well before he was.

Predictably, prior to team photos, our own Beau Brummel spent ages ensuring not a single strand was out of place. Imagine, then, the extra time and trouble he'd taken to appear gorgeous for the official colour photograph commissioned to commemorate our 1977 Wood Cup Final success. Eventually, he was satisfied and gave 'Lord Lichfield' the nod.

Our cheesy grins soon graduated to howls of laughter. With his finger poised on the button, 'Lichfield' was moved to abort due to a scream of anguish. Robin Barnard (who'd got so close to being a Robin Bastard) had taken this as his cue to put his ideas on alternative hair styling into practice. Robin had ruffled 'Vidal's' feathers, and his pristine locks, into a Ken Dodd formation, exclaiming:

'Who's a prissy pussy?'

In between grooming sessions, 'Vidal' did score plenty of runs. He was on course to notch up the magic four figures - 1000 runs for the season, not 99 pounds 99 pence for a haircut – going into the final game in 1976 at Werneth. He required a very gettable 41 but it wasn't looking promising. Werneth had batted first and had slumped to something like 50 for 7, partly thanks to 'Frostbite's' unique interpretation of the lbw law.

Drastic measures were called for. Even though he didn't condescend to bowl in the nets, presumably because it would have played havoc with his parting, he brought himself on for some 'buffet' (help yourself) bowling. He loosened up by way of a squirt of Harmony and sent down a succession of pies, gentle enough for even 'Popeye' to dispatch.

Werneth got to 180 before it was time to sit down for the real savouries. 'Vidal's contentment was short-lived. He was brilliantly caught by their keeper a mere 41 runs short. It was a case of 'well kept' rather than 'well kempt.'

Robin took time out from re-styling 'Vidal's' hair on a Saturday in July 1979 to act as a master chef. Robin, my wife, Margaret and I were chatting over a beer – we couldn't afford one each – in the tea room after Middleton's home fixture with Oldham. Their Aussie professional, who I now tag 'Shearings,' because he is a famous coach, had just beaten us almost single-handed. His exertions had obviously made him hungry. We noticed him purloin a raw egg from a table and place it in his trouser pocket. Why none of us said anything was solely because we were all still guffawing at 'Septic' Tank's latest gaff which involved him telling us that he'd just got back from practising on a rifle range and he now had shooting pains in his arm.

About an hour later, the light-fingered pro who now qualified for that criminal record our Old Etonian international believed you need to get back home, returned to the tea room. Once he'd he picked up his bag, which he had packed himself, Robin called him over and made as if to shake his hand. Instead, Robin patted him hard on the pocket with the egg in it, saying:

'Good luck for the rest of the season. You'll have to have it scrambled now.'

The lanky Aussie left with egg on both his trousers and his face, probably vowing never to poach one again.

The incomparable 'Pat,' the man with the uncanny knack of winding up giant West Indian pacemen, did manage to turn this to his own advantage just once. He'd reached the final of a single wicket competition in 1981. For the uninitiated, this didn't involve playing with only one stump. It's a one versus one contest in which you bowl a couple of overs at your opponent who then reciprocates, with 10 mugs volunteering to merely field all afternoon. This was more popular in the mid-1800s when getting 22 players to the same place on two mules and a goat was as easy as getting on the front foot to Joel Garner.

The prize was a most acceptable £50 for the winner, which our innumerate umpire, 'Carol Vordeman,' reckons is worth at least £35 in today's money. That was the good news. The bad news was that 'Pat's' opponent was the biggest, nastiest, fastest West Indian around at the time. They had crossed swords before and were as close as Kevin Pietersen and Graeme Smith.

'Pat' knew he would be head hunted. This was confirmed by a spot of friendly banter before the final:

'Fat boy, I'm gonna knock you out.'

There were, of course, two equally unattractive ways to interpret this. 'Pat' responded true to type – sledging with a smile:

'Let's face it. I'm merely an amateur. You're a highly rated international cricketer. If you don't beat me, you'll be letting yourself, your profession and your country down. How's that for pressure? Good luck, paid man.'

Having won the psychological battle, 'Pat' also managed to stave off the moment of execution by winning the toss and opting to bowl first. A last minute:

'Your country expects,' ensured a frenzied approach from a now seething opponent.

'Pat's' 'buddy' was sufficiently intimidated to seek to smash the first ball, a gentle off-break, all the way back home. It bowled him. Only one to win. More pleasanteries were exchanged. Guess which protagonist announced:

'I've already booked you a bed in casualty to save time later, Slim.'

Unphased, 'Pat' upped the ante with a brave, possibly foolhardy:

'That's the first time I've been threatened by someone with halitosis.'

This was bound to cause a stink. Either the hit-man would know what it meant and be infuriated or wouldn't know, considering it an even bigger insult than it was. Bad breath or bad blood?

Known for his good fortune - he backed the winner in the 1922 Grand National when only three of the 32 horses finished – 'Pat' wished himself luck and took guard as the very quick, incredibly angry giant raced in off an extra-long run up. As he released what was a stone-cold certain bouncer, 'Pat' immediately started running – not towards square leg but to the other end. He gleefully watched the ball sail harmlessly over his head en route to the wicket-keeper who was positioned three parts back to the boundary. Not content with the cash, 'Pat' signed off by deliberately getting his word wrong:

'You really do falter to deceive, big boy.'

'Tiddles' is a one-off. We were at Leeds Carnegie together. He is the funniest person I've ever met, excluding Cannon or Ball, naturally. As well as having the capacity to make you laugh, 'Tiddles' was a genuinely brilliant goalkeeper who went on to play in the top flight for Leicester City. Even so, his nickname owes more to him drinking milk out of a saucer than to his prowess between the sticks. This true character was the first person I heard actually use the chat-up line:

'You don't sweat much for a fat bird, do you?'

He also confessed that his ideal wife would be a bloke with tits. Hardly surprising, therefore, that the only thing he pulled at college was the chain.

'Tiddles' was a tidy swing bowler. He began by coming on as first change but soon got asked to open when it became apparent that Bill Peak would never live up to his name. Tidy he was, but he did manage figures of 1 for 10 against Doncaster in a British College Cup tie in 1972. Nothing wrong with that, you might think. Normally, there wouldn't be except Doncaster were all out for 12, with 'Bacon' Ryan taking 9 for 2. All the former could do was protest he'd been put on at the wrong end.

He was more successful at Manchester University in 1973. He and 'Bacon' took three early scalps apiece. This brought their number eight to the crease. He asked for a guard, presumably because he was either frightened or rich, in an unmistakably broad Scottish accent. 'Tiddles' waited until the new batsman had faced a couple of balls before calling over to him:

'You're looking good, Taffy. You should be playing for Glamorgan.'

A short while afterwards, he cemented the relationship further with:

'Tell me your name so I can say I knew you before you were famous. You're the best player I've ever seen from a third-world country.'

The unsuspecting batsman obligingly played along:

'Simeon,' he confessed, hoping to get off scot-free henceforth.

Unfulfilled, 'Tiddles' went for the jugular:

'Simeon! What kind of name is that? Couldn't your parents spell Simon?'

Simeon's concentration was now shot. He was summarily dismissed for zero. Ever one to hit a man when he's down, his tormentor ushered him on his way with a thought provoking:

'As a foreigner, if this was a two innings game and you did equally well in the second innings, would you qualify as an au pair? Give my regards to your mum and dad down there in the valley.'

Simeon saw the funny side of it and foolishly accepted 'Tiddles' invitation to sit with him at tea. Once he'd had his fill of curled up potted meat sandwiches, Simeon was shown the dessert options, gâteau and meringue. Both were adorned with strawberries and so looked alike. Our Scottish friend needed assistance. He pointed to one and asked:

'Is that a gâteau or a meringue?'

'Tiddles' put him right:

'No, you're not wrong. It is a gâteau.'

Simeon tucked in, unaware that he'd just played the straight man, which was more than could be said for his batting.

After the game we were all hungry – Simeon had scoffed most of the dessert - so we frequented a chippy near the ground. (By that, I don't mean it was built on stilts.) When 'Tiddles' was handed his food, he politely asked the server, 'Fritz,' if the vinegar was free. When told that it was, he nearly got battered by continuing with:

'In that case, I'll have nine bottles, please.'

Talking of brown liquid, 'Tiddles' was no stranger to the amber nectar. After playing St John's York, an opponent bet him a bottle of Newcastle Brown that he couldn't drink six pints of it in an hour. Despite this beverage being as thick as 'Treacle' and as potent as absinthe, he made it with two minutes to spare. He put that time to good use. He rejected his prize, professing that he never wanted to set his cat's eyes on the stuff again. No sooner said than undone. He decorated himself and his immediate company with the fruits (and diced carrots) of his labours, before ordering a pint of Guinness to wash it down.

In his drunken stupor, 'Tiddly' blew any chance he might have had of a dalliance with the well-proportioned beauty, Sue Fosbrey. Half-cut, like his hair, he publicly pronounced her 'Miss Menstruation,' as her periods came fortnightly instead of monthly.

Sue was unimpressed. She made it clear that the discharge of blood and cellular debris from the womb of a non-pregnant woman was her concern and no one else's, especially not a 'balding, immature country bumpkin who couldn't hold his drink.' 15 all, I'd say. Fortunately, she didn't live up to her first name.

Apparently, this fall out may have been a blessing in disguise. Rumour has it that middle age has taken its toll on the once magnificently formed Sue, providing another case of the 'Fosbrey flop.'

Such setbacks did not deter 'Tiddles' on either the drinking or lady fronts. We went into a pub in the centre of Leeds following a game at Leeds University. An old man in the corner asked if we fancied getting drunk quickly. The local was completely off his face. He advised us to try a mixture of Barley wine and Tetley's bitter. He called the concoction 'a pint of pain.' When asked why, he explained:

'It gives you a pain in your forehead when you drink it.'

The old fella ended on a note of caution:

'Be careful, I've had three but I'm used to them.'

We all tried one and concluded that the mixture was appropriately named. 'Tiddles' confessed:

'It's a similar feeling to when I got nutted by that Jock at Butlins.'

Before seeking clarification, I noticed the beer was cheaper by the jug. Three of us bought one each. Then, once they were empty, 'Tiddles' poured forth. He admitted that, as a youth, he did get into the odd scrape or two. This one occurred in Blackpool during 'Glasgow Week.' Having chatted up what emerged as the wrong girl with one of his 'smooth' lines:

'Where's the scaffold? I want to build my whole world around you, darling,' 'Tiddles' and his alcoholic pal, ironically named Drinkwater, were minding their own business when they were surrounded by a dozen irate Glaswegians.

They were not best pleased with our feline Romeo. They knew he was better than any Scottish goalkeeper and their leader also fancied doing some construction on the young lady his rival was leching over.

Despite the odds, 'T.' and 'D.' decided to stand up and be counted. Well, one did. 'D.' ended up lying down and being counted out. The unfavourable odds of 6-1 against soon doubled. Our goalie threw an expansive right hook towards the ringleader, Mark. It missed its mark and hit its own tag-team partner. The punch floored 'D.' and knocked him senseless – not a difficult task for someone who believes Calais is French soap and Al Qaida is one bloke.

'Tiddles' was rescued from this Scotch mist by the timely appearance of four hefty security men. They had heard the ensuing laughter and came to rescue the 'one hit wonder' before he punched his own lights out.

My next star, 'Mogadon,' the aforementioned ever-willing scorer, will go down in the annals of Thornham Cricket Club for two unforgettable incidents.

In the late 60s, Thornham 3rds visited a ground which, unthinkably, had no bar. Their contingency plan was to ship (by car) a crate of bottled beer to the venue, situated near a stream. As it was an extremely hot day, the skipper instructed the gopher, 'Mogadon,' to transport the drinks down the slope and leave them in the cooling waters of the stream until after the game. Knowing he had no chance of a bowl unless he obliged, the surly, sturdy serf duly complied.

He returned soon afterwards, looking more than usually bewildered. The term 'smooth flow' had yet to be applied to beer and he'd discovered why. The crate wouldn't stay put in the water due to the strong current. The prospect of warm beer was as appealing as dysentery, so the skipper asked if there were any rocks lying around. 'Mogadon's' baffled expression multiplied. Perhaps he was toying with asking:

'What flavour?'

'Large stones. Are there any large stones?' enquired his anxious captain, showing early signs of withdrawal symptoms.

There were. 'Mogadon' duly placed the heaviest ones on top of the beer to good effect. As soon as the game was over, our man trotted off to fetch the refreshments. Rather than return within the expected couple of minutes, 'Mogadon' was absent for nearer 20. Worried that he'd disappeared in search of another '99' or was guzzling the beer himself, the skipper sent out a search party. 'Ferret,' a pest controller, was assigned to sniff out the beer first and the pest second.

'Ferret' eventually spotted 'Mogadon' emerging over the top of the slope. He was dripping with sweat, panting profusely and his eyes were bulging like Marty Feldman's. Sadly for him, this wasn't because he'd done six rounds with Miss World. He'd acted like a soft-nosed expanding bullet – a dumdum – and had carried the crate, complete with beer and rocks, all the way up the hill. I've heard of whisky on the rocks, but not beer. I suppose it was lucky he was carrying 'light ale,' since, unlike ants, who have no trouble in lifting stones 50 times their own weight, our porter had.

The same man's luck was also out three years later. He was on strike (facing the bowling, not refusing to cool down the ale). He had received one of those rare deliveries which slips out of the bowler's hand and nestles harmlessly three or four strips away. Most of us chuckle, call the bowler a waster and wait for the umpire to signal 'dead ball.' Only Aussies, Tykes and Andy Moles insist on a free hit for four unearned runs. 'Mogadon' must have had a pint of 'Fosters' and a yorkshire pudding (the list is endless) for lunch because, like the one-legged, ethnic homosexual on family benefits, he demanded his rights:

'Leave it,' he barked, sensing a career-best personal score.

He swaggered up to the immobile pill with the confidence of Lee Westwood set to tee off. It became be more like Vivian Westwood and eff off. We'd been telling 'Mogadon' for years that he'd chosen the wrong club. He definitely had this time. Instead of the orb speeding off to the boundary, it was the batsman who did. He topped his shot (and should have subsequently done the same to himself). The ball rolled a couple of feet to a grateful fielder. The recipient chuckled, picked it up and ran out a flabbergasted, stranded batter.

Wisely, he retired from playing soon after. The turncoat then used his Saturdays to go shopping but was equally unsuccessful. I'm told he was reprimanded by his partner, Ruth, who left him soon after, making him ruth-less, with:

'Why have you bought eight tins of cat food when we've only got a dog?'

'Mogadon's' ineptitude put me in mind of his hero, Ronald Regan. Ron's classic:

'Trees cause more pollution than cars,' prompting one wag to counter with a sign which read:

'Cut me down before I kill again,' was on a par with 'Mogadon's:

'Does the Hoover Dam collect much dust?'

No less entertaining was 'André Previn.' This conductor (bus not music or lightning) opened the bowling for Middleton throughout the 1970s. As laid-back as a limbo dancer, he struggled to concentrate unless he was bowling. One typical lapse resulted in him not having the faintest idea about a simple catch on the edge (as most people are) at Ashton. He was totally unaware that the ball had plopped beside him because he was watching a model aeroplane circling overhead. Oblivious, he exclaimed:

'Did you see that?' pointing to the offending object in the sky. 'Awesome!'

The bowler responded by pointing his own offending object to show his appreciation of the miss.

'Andre's' laid back approach does give credence to the Archbishop of Canterbury's view. In 1925, the would-be pontiff/plaintiff described cricket as 'organised loafing.' (As a primate, he was accustomed to getting up to monkey business.)

'Andre's' wife, 'Stella,' who loves Belgian lager, is as easy-going as her husband but is less street-wise. During a post-match drink, she spotted a tramp sitting across the road from our bar:

'Fancy going out on a Saturday night dressed like that,' she naively exclaimed.

'André' is by no means verbose. You would never catch him, nor would he catch you, pontificating with such long-winded phrases as 'at this particular moment in time,' when 'currently' will suffice. He applauded Marie McDonald McLoughlin Lawrie for becoming Lulu and would doubtless refer to the Reverend Sir John Robert Laurie Emilius Bayley Laurie, who hit 152 for Eton v Harrow in 1841, as Vic, thus saving 46 letters. 'André' has always favoured the direct approach. When asked his opinion of one Middleton captain, he was typically succinct:

'He's a shit.'

We all knew exactly what he meant.

During a lengthy career, 'André' got more wickets than runs. He only batted higher than number 11 once. 'Sick note' was taken ill again so 'Andre' went in at 10 and it gave him a nosebleed. Noughts are easy to add up so he only really troubled the scorers when he pestered them for loose change. Fare's fair, after all.

Following another score of less than one, I sympathised, only for 'André' to put me right:

'You won't see that happen very often.'

Isn't virtually every Saturday 'very often' I wondered? When he did manage to get eight or nine at Crompton, I was quick to congratulate him:

'Well done, pal. You were in full flow today,' expecting a characteristically terse:

'Tanks' – he thought I was called Sherman. I got more than I bargained for:

'No. If you see me in full flow, you cry!'

'Flicker' loves a flutter and has equine features without the accompanying fleet footedness. Again, it's for you to decide how to label him. He came to Thornham in the late 80s with the reputation as a hot head. I witnessed his debut for the 3rdXI. He opened the bowling and had a catch dropped by a youngster fielding at point. There was no discernible reaction, not even à la old Ernie. We therefore decided that reports, like Richard Branson's hot air balloon, were misguided.

They weren't. At the end of the over, the culprit was singled out by the panting bowler. A point to the point was to the point:

'Twat,' resounded around the ground, leaving the club

treasurer searching for the swear box and one elderly spectator to ask:

'Why is he appealing now?'

If 'Flicker' isn't already in Greenpeace, he should be. He hates wasting energy. If he saw a sign at a swimming pool which read 'no running,' he'd say:

'Suits me.'

Like 'Inzi,' he chose his moments when to move. He steamed in quickly enough to bowl or when he hit the ball. He has even been known to almost exert himself if his brother was bowling. Otherwise, he preferred the sedentary approach:

'Why run if you can walk, and why walk if you can sit down?'

Why, indeed?

He did get his legs pumping at Longsight when a delivery from 'bruv' crept past him. By the time he'd caught up with the ball, the batsmen had run two. They only opted to take a third because they knew 'Flicker' threw like a three year old girl with rickets. They hadn't reckoned on plan B.

The now breathless fielder set himself for the underarm return. Many of us with no arm feign to throw the ball in mightily and then toss it back with a gentle underarm lob which reaches its goal in the time it takes to hard boil an egg. 'Flicker' mistimed his return, as Ken Dodd and Lester Piggott must have. The ball sailed back over his right shoulder. It landed straight into the appropriately named 'Whizzer's' hand. He could have rivalled Robert Percival who reputedly threw a ball 140 yards in 1881. 'Whizzer' whizzed it in like a tracer bullet right over the stumps for an unlikely run out. 'Flicker' tried to insist that his gross act of incompetence was intended. As he hasn't got eyes in the back of his head, we know otherwise.

His brother, 'Dopey,' turned out for the thirds on occasions. By that, I don't mean when it was someone's birthday or on Bank Holidays, I just mean sometimes. Although he is a pleasant chap, 'Dopey' is greater than a right angle. For years, he assumed people from Italy were 'italics' and those from Crete were 'cretins.' Before one game, we were discussing a fatal crash on a nearby stretch of the M62. 'Dopey' chipped in with a less than erudite:

'Was anybody killed?'

'Dopey' really is easily confused. To this day, he steadfastly maintains that an inmate is your batting partner. A Dane, Rasmus Rask spoke 235 languages (qualifing him as a Great Dane). 'Dopey' has difficulty mastering one. During a chat about a future cup game for the 1sts, the consensus was that we were the underdogs. A straightforward enough assessment until 'Mensa Man,' who'd found out that Coca Cola was called 'Brain Tonic' in 1886 and subsequently overdosed on it, asked:

'What kind of animal is that?'

By accepting that it was similar to a scapegoat, he confirmed that he would cause confusion if asked to take a 'dope test.'

The deadly duo had combined forces a year earlier to provide a rib-tickler on the boundary edge at Thornham. 'Flicker' was doing his bit for energy conservation at third man. 'Dopey' was strolling gently around the ground – it must be in the genes – listening to the football scores through his radio earphones. He took the earphones out as he approached his brother and announced:

'Bury are drawing one all.'

'Flicker' replied:

'Bury are drawing one all?'

'Dopey' came back with:

'Are they?'

My next cricketer who refuses to be ignored is 'Blue Peter.' He's as profane as Gordon Ramsay and has an endless supply of girlie magazines for when the team needs uplifting. Peter was described by one umpire in the LCL as a 'balanced' cricketer. He took this as a compliment, believing it to be a reference to his textbook stance, until the official explained:

'You've got a chip on both shoulders.'

Peter is a whole-hearted cricketer (southern for can't bat or bowl but dives about a lot in the field) and you wouldn't fight to have him in your quiz team:

'Good thinking, Peter,' aren't words you'll hear in the same sentence.

Verification of this came at Longsight in 2003. Not known for his boyish good looks, Peter had been assigned to field at short leg. The ball was hit past him and he set off after it. Once this man opens his legs there is always a problem, only this time it was a leakage of runs rather than gas. Peter knocked off his helmet to pursue the ball. Presumably, he thought that minus this excess weight, he'd be able to make up the 12 seconds it took to remove it. He eventually retrieved the ball but chose to roll it back to the bowler rather than throw it. It rolled straight against the helmet. A comfortable two had become a charitable seven.

During a, mercifully, rare bowling stint for the seconds, Peter was getting severe tap and was as keen as we were for the over to end. Consequently, he asked the umpire how many balls were left. Three was the answer.

'Sorry, is that three gone or three left?' asked the bewildered bowler.

Don Topley of Essex is attributed with a similar slip of the brain but Peter assured us he hadn't known this:

'I just wasn't thinking,' he admitted and I'm convinced.

We kidded Peter that England's bowling coach, Kevin Shine, is Polish and that Vic Marks is Karl's grandson. (He can't spell.) However, when I tried to persuade him that the 'A.' in A.Kumble stood for Apple, he called me a pudding. This convinced me that he is not as gullible as 'Dopey.' He was unable to ascertain who the only non-1st class cricketer is out of Ron Hooker, Ryan Driver, Geoff Pullar and Road Sweeper.

There is one area where Peter is in a class of his own (which is the best place for him). I made passing reference to it a short while ago - excess wind. Here, it's flatulence rather than verbosity. He can clear a dressing room quicker than Ken Bates. Thornham has its own wind farm. Consequently, when anyone tells you Peter has dropped one, it has nothing to do with catches.

Graham Gorman was a wit and raconteur. Graham was associated with Glossop for many years before passing away at the turn of the century. Known as 'Bags' for being well off, we regularly swapped stories. He used some of mine for after-dinner speaking. I'm not sufficiently eloquent to perform such duties so I'll merely steal a couple of his to use now.

The first involves another Glossop veteran (southern for old fart), 'Tofty.' In the late 90s, 'Tofty' was unlucky, or drunk, enough, to have fallen from a ladder. He broke his leg. 'Bags' visited him in hospital for some free grapes. (Most rich people are tight.) He discovered 'Tofty' was in a ward in which every other inmate had broken bones while playing sport. Before reaching 'Tofty's' bed, 'Bags' noticed a man in traction. Being of a sociable disposition (southern for nosy bastard), he enquired:

'Is it a sporting injury?'

'Pardon?' replied the patient, concerned about jeopardising a possible:

'Are you the victim of an accident which wasn't your fault?' claim.

'Your leg,' continued his inquisitor.

'Did you break it playing sport?'

'Oh. Yes,' said the patient (and it's just as well he was).

'Which sport?' coaxed 'Bags,' realising that extracting information here was harder than eating soup with a fork.

Expecting football or rugby, 'Bags' was surprised to hear:

'Crazy golf. I got a hole in one. I jumped up to celebrate, landed on the windmill and broke my ankle.'

'Bags' nodded in appreciation, made a mental note for a future sportsman's dinner and wished him well:

'It could happen to anyone. I hope you recover in time for the Open, Seve.'

He then caught sight of a young lady in plaster. She was a cheerleader who had successfully negotiated the human pyramid, only to fall foul of the basket toss. 'Bags,' for once, was lost for words.

Rumour has it that Graham made the daily press in his own right in the 1970s. On the point of parking his Rolls Royce in the last available space in a car park, he was beaten to it by a hippy in a Mini. The 'flower power' boy had nipped into the spot uninvited and boasted:

'You have to be cool to do that, man.'

Peeved, but ahead of the game, the stranded 'Bags' equalised by parking his Rolls on top of the Mini. He reversed it in, flattened the hippymobile and cemented his victory with:

'You have to be rich to do that, boy.'

Like me, 'Bags' wasn't afraid of borrowing material in an attempt to get a laugh. Was it Wilson Mizner who stated:

'Taking from one source is plagiarism. Taking from more than one is research.'

Or was it Wilson Pickett?

When he'd been clean bowled by someone with an extremely dubious action, 'Bags' felt obliged to pass comment as he walked off:

'Umpire, can you clear that up for me? Was I bowled out or run out?'

'Bags' confessed this was not an original. He'd 'borrowed' it from Doug Insole of Essex who'd expressed similar sentiments when bowled by Surrey's Tony Lock. Suffice to say that Tony's action was as kinky as George Michael and he was frequently asked by team-mates to 'chuck' them a few in the nets.

Disgressing yet again, Doug Insole is a past England chairman of selectors and was an excellent amateur footballer in the 1950s. He played for a highly regarded side called Corinthian Casuals in the twilight of his career. I justify including this tale in a book ostensibly about cricket because of the club's Surrey connection. Their manager in 1970 was Mickey Stewart of Refreshers fame, while ex-England captain Johnny Douglas also played there, as did Mike Willett, Bob Willis, Alec Stewart and Mark Ramprakesh.

I had several games in goal for their reserves that year, before moving north to Leeds Carnegie. I might not have done had I known they play in chocolate and pink quarters. Anyway, before my first game, the hefty Mr. Insole, introduced himself thus:

'My name's Insole. I own this club. When you get the ball, throw it to my feet. I'll be standing on the right wing.'

An order's an order. When I eventually managed to catch the ball, I looked to my right and there he was, in oceans of space. I bowled the ball out. It rolled gently to where I'd intended – about a foot in front of him. I was, appropriately, tickled pink that I'd obeyed instructions. My self-satisfaction was short-lived. Doug stood motionless and watched the ball roll out of play for a throw in to the opposition. He glared at me and shouted:

'To my feet, boy, I said throw it to my feet.' (More like arse'ole than Insole.)

'Bags' had a son. I forget his name, so I'll call him 'Baguette.' He captained Glossop's 2nds for a couple of eventful years in the late 90s. I appreciate Glossop isn't far from Iceland and the one tropical thing about it is the sun bed shop in the High Street. Even so, 'Baguette' is the only cricketer I've seen field in a woollen hat. (At the other extreme, in a Middleton v Rochdale game in 1976, Geoff Gowland fielded in white shorts. Middleton is of course very tropical.)

This certainly wasn't done to keep 'Baguette's' brains warm. His thermal underpants were doing that. His dad told me how, in a match at Denton West, he got his son out of hot water. 'Bags' was at gully and was very impressed with son's field placing. Three overs had elapsed, no runs had been scored and the batsmen couldn't find any gaps in the field:

'Well worked out, Son. You've used your loaf for once. You've got three men there, two there, a couple here, three more over there, a keeper and the bowler. Hang on. Oh shit, that's 12.'

For each ball of the fourth over, 'Bags' edged a few metres back, until he was right on the boundary. At the end of the over he sneaked off, got changed and then came out to watch the game in his civvies. Nobody said a word.

On the theme of unusual headgear, I should pay homage to Crompton's Les Whittle. Les beat even Mike Brearley to the punch regarding protective headwear. Always his own man, Les – brother of Mel of chapter one fame – made his own fashion statement by facing the fearsome Joel Garner wearing a yellow navvy's, sorry that makes him sound like a coward, a navvy's yellow hard hat. As if Joel needed any encouragement. Les had played it by ear and nearly ended up deaf.

Going back even further for my next 'card,' Paul 'Joker' Watson was a team-mate at Quintin Grammar School, in St John's Wood. The school is only five minutes from Lords and on the morning of a Test Match against New Zealand some of us were revising for our forthcoming 'A' Level poker exams in the sixth form common room when we spotted the great John Snow walking across the car park. I can only think that he was the celebrity designated to present the award for being the laziest person ever born to our PE teacher, 'Killer.' Whatever the reason, there he was.

It soon became a case of there he wasn't. He fell over. Before we could rush to his aid, he was up and off but it didn't prevent Watson from shouting out:

'Snow falls in July in north-west London!'

Talking of snow, it's a little known fact that the highest score by an England lady in a Test is E.Snowball's 189 against New Zealand in 1934-5. She then got so hot she melted, causing tongues to wag regarding a possible liason with Middleton's 'Scoop.'

In 1966, Paul made a conscious decision to wear the same cricket socks for every game of the season. Seemingly nothing strange there, Steve Waugh had his red hankie and plenty of players have favourite items of kit. Moreover, Watson didn't know Hasan Jamil so he had no access to freebies. Very strange, on the other hand, if you decided you were not going to wash them from game to game. Paul played for the school 1stXI on Saturdays and for the Old Qs on Sundays in the same pair. They were left in his bag to fester from one weekend to the next. This could be where the Cockney rhyming slang for socks, 'Brighton rocks,' originated. By the end of that season, they certainly had a hard enough crust on them to be considered 'sedimentary, my dear Watson.'

Paul retired from cricket halfway through the following season after complications involving a similar plan with his jock strap. A course of antibiotics eventually sorted him out, enabling him to take up a place at Exeter University studying hygiene. Incidentally, he chose Exeter because they gave out the nicest pens of all the institutions he visited at Open Days. Mentioning institutions, he now works in a mental hospital. There's a fine line...

Like Paul, most characters are confident people. This confidence can sometimes be misplaced. Loads of policemen play cricket and some (I'm being charitable) have a swagger bordering on arrogance. 'Dibble,' who even looks like Surrey's Bernard Constable, is such a man. He performed well enough during his time at Thornham in the early 80s to be selected a couple of times for the Lancashire and Cheshire League side. This gave a far from needed boost to his ego. It prompted him to announce:

'The name of 'Dibble' must be worth at least three wickets to Thornham before we even start a game.'

Our wicket-keeper, Mike (he's got a booming voice) disagreed, or so it seemed:

'Bollocks!'

Undeterred, 'Dibble' plodded on, explaining how his mere presence was enough to unsettle even the best opposing batsmen. 'Dibble's' drivel prompted Mike to bring the debate to a close with a conclusive:

'You'd be unsettled, too, if you were facing a bowler with a flashing blue light on top of his head.'

Perhaps Fred Trueman should have joined the force. Not only was he brimming with self- belief, he was also really clued up on the laws and fully alert. As such, he was able to make these two statements:

'That was a tremendous six. The ball was still in the air as it went over the boundary,' and 'I'm the finest bloody fast bowler that ever drew breath.'

My favourite character, the lovable KK, had as little in common with Trueman as the Old Qs had with any decent cricket club. As a youngster, he contracted polio. This caused him to walk with a limp but did not deter him from giving his all for Thornham 3rds. In fact, KK was so enthusiastic that at the age of 62, he paid to go to nets at Old Trafford for individual tuition.

His wry sense of humour even led him to joke about his affliction. He maintained that if he'd been like Chandrasekhar and had contracted polio in his arm rather than in his leg, he, too, could have been a great Indian leg spinner. Leg puller, more like.

Not the strongest of men, KK's only realistic chance of a boundary was an outside edge, or 'thin middle,' as he called it. He was so lacking in power that his doctor prescribed some tablets to build up his strength. They didn't help. KK couldn't get the lid off the bottle. Despite all this, he remained ever cheerful and as keen as Durham's wicket-keeper.

His major claim to fame arose in 1978 when he somehow managed to bat for fully 26 overs. This was by far his longest ever innings. The trouble was he didn't score a single run. He was typically philosophical about this and always laughed at his mode of dismissal. (He joked that he'd been trying to emulate Kiwi, Jock Sutherland. Jock carried his bat for 0 not out in 1976, playing for the inappropriately named, Wakatu. Wakatu, Jock obviously couldn't even push a one.)

'I was out 'ookin'' (northern for playing the hook), proclaimed our stonewaller.

KK, like a contemporary of his, Lancastrian RG Barlow, wasn't made for 20/20 cricket. He claimed that Barlow was his mentor. The strokeless opening batsman carried his bat for a mere five not out in 1882 out of a total of 69 all out against Nottinghamshire. To prove that this was no fluke, he'd previously amassed 10 not out from a team score of 47 all out versus Yorkshire. On the other hand, he did show that he could slap it around as well with 34 not out against Kent out of 187 all out in 1876.

KK was a real kidder. He was watching Denton St. Lawrence's professional Steve Dublin carve our bowling to every corner of our ground in 2004. Dublin went on to break the league six hit record for a season of 35, by just 30. Steve recorded nine of these during this match, and later hit eight sixes in one eight ball over (two no balls) to enter the record books, causing KK to comment that if he'd been a foot taller and five stone heavier, he'd have given Dublin a run for his money. He further amused bystanders as one big hit bounced off a bovine beast in the farmer's field bordering the ground:

'What a cow shot. Bull's eye!' said it all.

Unable to command a regular place in Thornham's 3rds, KK unilaterally appointed himself 'team manager' to the 2ndXI. He saw role as 'just being there in case.'

He deliberately caused a stir at Sale Moor by announcing he would be playing. To make it fair, he'd put all the names of those who 'assumed they were playing' on pieces of paper into a cap and would pull one out. Bad luck, Peter Foy.

Peter looked as happy as Nicky Boje bowling to Adam Gilchrist in full flow, until he unravelled a second piece of paper:

'Peter Foy.'

KK had written Peter's name on all 11 bits of paper.

Intent on causing more mischief a month later at Woodbank, KK had arrived at the ground early to execute his plan. He'd relied upon our fiery professional, 'Byron' – he'd seen himself bowl on video and described his own action as 'poetry in motion' – also being one of the first to arrive. He was. 'Byron' hated losing and had as much of a sense of humour as the equally ginger Shaun Pollock.

These two factors were central to KK's plan. He greeted 'Byron' enthusiastically and made sure the pro noticed him getting changed;

'What are you doing?' enquired a frantic pro.

'There's been a last minute cry off. I've been asked to fill in,' retorted the prankster.

Mischievous as ever, he threw in:

'I always score runs here.' (Even the singular would have been an exaggeration.)

'Byron' was horrified. He frantically contacted the pre-warned skipper on his mobile. 'Skip' played along. The pro was apopleptic. His blood pressure hit the roof when KK asked him to bowl him a few. It was only when the whole team arrived that the pro could relax. Even then, KK did not crack. He threw a pseudo-tantrum:

'That's the last time I give up a Saturday to help you lot out. I'm going somewhere I'll be appreciated.' (Peter Foy's house, perhaps?)

My final memory of the late KK came at the last league dinner he attended in 2004. Ronnie Irani was the guest speaker and, presumably because he'd run out of things to say, he asked if anyone had any questions. KK had. He asked the Essex captain:

'In light of recent events, are you glad you're not called Ronnie Iraqi?'

'Hercules' of Prestwich may be physically stronger than KK but so is my neighbour's six month-old baby. 'Hercules' is by no stretch of the imagination bashful (a word one could never use to describe KK's batting). Despite being a heavy smoker, he describes himself as:

'16 stone and super fit.'

Or did he say 'super fat?'

More tellingly, although playing again now, he did announce his retirement, either in the Times or the local free paper in 2002, declaring à la Nasser that he wanted to go out while still at the top. This confused me. At the time, he was batting at number six for their 2nds. All in all, though, 'Hercules' is an affable bloke and positively retiring, for the second time, compared to Thornham's 'Marilyn Monroe,' our very own blond bombshell.

'Marilyn' has more self-belief than Imran Khan and carries a full-length mirror in his kit bag. Whenever he fails with the bat or ball, which is most days beginning with 's,' he remains up-beat. When most of us were thinking he's a waste of one, 'Marilyn' professed:

'I bowled out of my skin today. I really hit the straps.'

'Really?' said 'Dubious' Dave. 'Don't you mean you really hit the middle of the bat? What did you end up with, a Michelle?' (Five for.)

'No. 0 for 69,' lamented 'Marilyn':

'I didn't think we played double headers in this league,' stated Dave.

Whoosh.

'We don't. I was too quick for our slips. They couldn't hold on to a banister.'

Our kidder in chief, 'Billy,' told him not to be so blond. He suggested that, since his quick stuff was too hot to handle, maybe he should slow down:

'We all know some like it hot, Marilyn, but you're generating as much warmth as Idi Amin. Try bowling some slow stuff.'

'Marilyn' seemed interested, especially when I said a similar move worked wonders for England Women's off-break bowler, 'Spinning Jenny.' He went off the idea after hearing that most spinners, including 'Swanny,' harden the skin on the spinning finger by dipping it in urine.

'You're taking the piss,' exclaimed 'Marilyn.'

'I'm not, but you'd have to,' I replied, adding that it was a preferable option to what Spaniards used to do with their wee. They cleaned their teeth in it.

Despite his lack of success, 'Marilyn' persisted with the quicker stuff and asked me to compare him to other bowlers. I told him his action reminded me of Zimbabwe's S.Peall. This meant nothing to him because Peall's name didn't ring a bell. I also informed him that even he had a long way to go before sinking to the depths of R.Grubb. During a Queensland country match in 1969 he excelled himself by going for 62 from a single eight ball over – plus four no balls. The man who smacked him for nine sixes and two fours was R.Morely. Perhaps he should be renamed R.Greedy. There's food for thought, Mr. Grubb.

In 2004, 'Marilyn' convinced himself that he was invincible. While attempting to bat, a delivery struck him on the chest. The ball rolled down what he perceives to be his perfectly formed body towards the stumps. He tried to knock it away with his bat. He emulated 'Corkie' and missed. He then sought to kick the ball away, missing it again. As a final, futile gesture, he flicked it with his hand and walked off, out 'handled the ball.' That's rather like playing Russian roulette with six bullets in the gun. He must have thought if it was good enough for Graham Gooch (Old Trafford, 1993), it was just about good enough for him.

'Marilyn' regularly informed us what a great fielder he is. To be fair, he has a good arm – as did Len Hutton. (One good, one shortened.) If only blondie could have given as much to our team as Len did to his. Going back 50 years, John Snagg, who was more famous for commentating on the Boat Race, found himself reading out the county cricket scores in the days when Yorkshire ruled. Astonished, he reported that the champions were all out for a lowly 232. He soon realised why when he announced:

'Hutton ill,' only to correct himself with: 'Sorry. Hutton 111.'

Plain Len was so good that he became Sir Leonard. Sir Marilyn won't happen but imagine if Liz got it wrong and canonised people. The actress, Helen Mirren would be spoilt for choice. Depending on whether she is a rugby or a football fan, she could be either St. Helen(s) or St. Mirren while Burl Ives, the fat American singer, would double as a holiday resort in Cornwall.

Returning to 'Marilyn,' he makes no allowance for distance. Five or 55 metres from the wicket, he fizzes it in with all his might. As with circumcisions, this has its drawbacks.

In his second, and last, season with us, he let loose from about 10 metres, vaguely in the direction of the stumps at the bowler's end. The skipper, 'Tom' (he's moody) was directly in the flight path and was almost taken out. Four overthrows.

'Marilyn' bowled the next over. A ball was played to 'Tom' in the covers. The batsman opted not to run. This did not deter the still smarting skipper. He put all of his considerable weight behind his throw, which was destined straight for 'Marilyn's' knackers. A back flip helped them escape demolition but resulted in four more overthrows. (We were infamous for not bothering to back up.)

The blond bomber then showed why he is to overthrows what Inzamam is to run outs. (Inzi was totally unaffected when the speed limit was raised from 4mph to 14 mph in 1856.) Mishearing 'twonker' for 'encore,' he put on a repeat performance in the next over.

'Third man both ends, airhead,' commanded 'Tom,' convinced 'Marilyn' was unlikely to cancel out the eight runs he'd given away when he batted.

Ignoring his lack of success at Thornham, 'Marilyn' nevertheless decided to ensure that he will always be remembered. Before emigrating, he donated a trophy for the best fielder in the club and nominated himself as the first recipient.

Far more modest is the ever–smiling Abdul. He is a taxi driver so I've lengthened his name by placing a 'c' in front. Our benign slow bowler is as mysterious as the Bermuda Triangle and has a few idiocyncracies which warrant his inclusion. 'Cabdul's' bowling action is as straight as a horseshoe and he invariably travels light. He arrives at grounds ready-changed. This includes cap and boots. After games, he politely excuses himself and leaves likewise. None of us knows what colour his hair is or even if he has got any. For him a changing room is no more than a stand and watch when it's cold room.

'Cabdul' turns up in like fashion even when he is named as reserve. He will quietly make his point by asking the captain if he is due to play, despite knowing he isn't. He then hangs around for an hour before driving off in his cab to pick up some startled fares in Rochdale who must think they've hailed either a ghost or John

Travolta, as in Saturday Night Fever. This is in stark contrast to the Nottinghamshire county side of 1930. They all walked on in civvies at the start of the third day's play against Hampshire. Admittedly, Hampshire did only need one run to win. Perhaps an extra ball the night before might have been helpful.

Even though his bowling action is as suspect as a nine month old chicken sandwich and his batting stinks like 'Blue Peter's' aftershave ('Skunk'), this lovely bloke is a team man. He is a real trier and has turn of phrase Old Quintinian, Mo Wickens would appreciate. Arriving at the crease as the number 10 on debut for the 3rds, with Thornham on 90 for 8, chasing double that, 'Cabdul' reassured Titus thus:

'I am looking forward to a long and fruitful partnership with you, Tit. Don't worry. I can bat. We will win.'

They lost by 90. This setback didn't dampen his spirit one iota. The following week, when told he'd be at 11, he remained philosophical:

'That's a tad low. Never mind, I'll just enjoy watching the lads knock them off.'

No wonder he's a hit with the ladies.

Food for thought:

25. If JJWarr and JWH Makepeace were up for the same spot, would the decision go: 'Makepeace, not Warr.'

26. If South African master batsman Barry Richards had been Irish and a good mixer, would he have been christened Morphy?

27. Did Leicestershire's Graham Cross get so many noughts that it made him angry?

28. Was South African Lennox Giddy more playful than Indian Amar Singh(about)?

Chapter 8

AROUND THE TEA ROOM
AND THE BAR WITH THE LADIES

Predictably, the refreshments, like the beer, vary in both halves of the country and from club to club. Rock bottom for teas, as well as for nearly everything else, is the Old Quintinians. This won't go down well with those who regard Chiswick as the centre of 'haute cuisine' in the Western World but it was the teas which were hard to swallow.

The steward throughout the 1960s, or to give him his full title, the bar steward, at the Polytechnic ground thought 'cordon bleu' was a shade of Duluxe paint. He charged an arm and a leg for bread and butter plus a brew strong enough to stand a spoon up in it.

If you wanted 'jam on it,' ie a third course, you paid extra and put it on yourself. This man put a new slant on the adage 'all proper tea is theft.' In case you didn't feel stuffed after such a feast (particularly by the price) you did get one slice of the omni-present, galloping towards stale, swiss roll to finish off in style.

One solitary piece of swiss roll certainly wouldn't have done for Middleton's 'Banger.' 'Banger' is so named, not due to his predilection for using his sausage, but, as with Marcus

Trescothick some 30 years later, because he is largely responsible for the British consuming 20 tonnes of them every hour. It wasn't just sausages that 'Banger' ate plenty of. His idol was King Farooq of Egypt, who ate himself to death. I witnessed 'Banger' demolish an entire plateful of chocolate swiss roll single-handed at Norden soon after rationing had ended:

'That's mine!' left us in no doubt regarding any neutrality about this swiss roll and the only protests came via a woman with a crop from Greenham Common sitting in the car park and Bob Dylan wailing away on the radio.

Getting back to Chiswick, I rarely availed myself of the option of spending my paper-round money on a couple of dry pieces of aerated white bread but I was pleased I did in June 1967. The occasion was the annual School 1stXI versus Old Boys fixture. This was the one sporting event in the year to which our head teacher, 'April' (he was a fool) was allowed out unaccompanied. Medically speaking, morons are more intelligent than imbeciles, who, in turn, have more nowse than idiots. 'April' easily qualified as an idiot.

We were confident he'd be instrumental in something memorable happening. This was based on a string of previous gaffes. The first involved the Tannoy system at school. Each classroom was equipped with a loud speaker (we had a second - form captain, 'Mucker'), which was directly linked to the Head's office. Keen to verify its efficiency, and with little else to occupy his time, 'April' carried out a weekly check. He employed this howler every time:

'Any classroom which can't hear this announcement must send a messenger down to inform me.'

Amazingly, he never received one messenger, not even Melinda.

He dropped another brick during a school assembly in 1964. In front of 700 lads aged 12 to 19, ranging from the incredibly puerile to the unbelievably immature, 'April' recounted how Mr. England, our geriatric metal work teacher, had been placed third in an international inventors' convention in Belgium. It transpired, thankfully before he expired, that Mr. England had entered two inventions, a bath with a door and a pickaxe with an additional handle on the side to reduce the work load. The bath flopped, or more precisely, leaked. The pickaxe did considerably better.

Unfortunately for 'April,' he chose the wrong words to express his admiration, bearing in mind the make-up of his audience. This is verbatim:

'I'm sure you'd like to join me in congratulating Mr. England who won a bronze medal for exhibiting his tool in Brussels over the weekend. The judges said it was the most innovative tool they'd ever seen exposed.'

Uproar. He then compounded it by asking:

'Have I missed the joke?'

Perhaps now you can understand our sense of anticipation. He did not let us down. At tea, he opted for the 'full English' – bread and butter, jam, cake and beverage. After all, he was on a good salary. It wasn't long before the silly man provided the entertainment we sought.

Our boss took the instruction to 'put it on yourself,' regarding the jam and bread, too literally. Leaning forward in a furtive attempt to sneak an illicit second slice of swiss roll, something he wouldn't dare to have done in 'Banger's' presence, he pressed up against his jam-spattered knife. This sent it spiralling into the air. The knife performed somersaults of far better quality than any British gymnast could, before coming to rest in 'April's' lap. Those of us who'd noticed–

everyone – wet ourselves but none of us dared to laugh out loud. (Things were different in those days.) There was, however, one 'olé' from an Old Boy who wouldn't have turned up to detention anyway.

The fact that 'April' was wearing beige trousers did not help. Neither did his reaction. He used the same knife to scrape off as much jam as he could from his two-legged outer garment, making even more of a mess in the process. He then spread the spoils on the extra piece of swiss roll he had palmed and muttered:

'Waste not, want not.'

Our fits of laughter were as raucous as when he cut wind in assembly in the middle of 'Jerusalem.'

'April' had never recovered from the previous year's Prize Giving when he awarded the English Prize to Michael French (whose bowling action was dodgier than Richard Nixon) and the Handwriting Prize to our middle order batsman, Ray Penn. (I wonder if Middlesex's Don Bick ever won a similar award). It was a pity there was no one at the school called IM Absent. He would have walked away with the Attendance Prize to make the Head even more confused than the Evershed player named Cakebread and the Fulham manager who had John Collins and Collins John in the same squad.

On that same night, 'April' contrived to award the 'rowing colours for swimming.' (The boat must have sunk.) His stupefaction was magnified further because, instead of all coming onto the stage from the left, as protocol demanded, five oarsmen chose the Middlesex side and three came up on the Surrey side. To misquote either Oscar or Marty Wilde:

'He didn't know whether he was having a shit or a shave.'

Alternatively, the best tea I ever tucked into at a cricket match was at Northampton in August 2003. As a late stand-in

(I wasn't dead, I was just the last resort) for Lancashire over 50s, it proved to be one of just two high spots in an otherwise depressing day.

It was a national knock out quarter final tie against Northamptonshire, who had one bloke who must have overdosed on Philosan, as he looked no older than 25. It began with a 6.00 a.m. alarm call for a 7.00 a.m. departure on a Sunday. Even the paperpersons hadn't stirred yet. No high spots up to now.

I then badly scraped my car on a garage forecourt while pulling in for petrol. This was hardly surprising as I was still asleep. Things could only get better. Having driven over 200 of the 210 miles, it persisted it down, making me fear the worst. I had visions of being asked:

'Can you come back tomorrow?'

It cleared up but I'd mistimed how long the trip would take. I was two and a half hours early. I decided to have a nap. I woke up an hour later with a stiff neck and cramp in my right calf. I'd also knocked a bottle of water over my trousers so it looked as though I'd peed my pants. I'd just about dried out and loosened up when I was told that I'd be opening. This provided me with the perfect opportunity to bat like an arse for nought, fired out lbw – front foot again – by one of the Roly Polys.

I subsequently achieved the virtually impossible; I fielded worse than I batted. Sandwiched between my two virtuoso performances, I savoured the day's high spot. We were treated to a feast. Henry VIII, Pavarotti, Billy Bunter, 'Banger' and Inzamam would have struggled to do it justice, although the fat bugger who gave me out tried his level best to clean up.

This magnificent banquet made the 420 mile round trip, garage bill and humiliating personal performance almost worthwhile. This remained so, despite getting lost on the way home, arriving back at 2.00 a.m. and not subsequently being picked for the semi-final or final.

The tea room was where I also renewed acquaintance with Gerry Shooter. (Northern for German gun.) When I was at Middleton, Gerry kept for Rochdale. We always got on well, mainly because whenever I edged one he invariably dropped it.

'Shooter, you old git,' I shouted.

This prompted team-mate, 'Rock' Hudson to chip in with:

'Marriage guidance from Saga for dealing with a nagging wife?'

Not far behind this super spread was one laid on for London Schools u19s at Beckenham in 1968. We were facing Surrey Young Cricketers again. The schedule was as for county championship matches of the period, except that we always ignored 'bad light.' 40 minutes for lunch was ample but only 20 minutes to stuff our faces at tea would be problematic.

Demolishing the mountain of grumblers and growlers (northern for various savouries) plus all the cream cakes (northern for cholesterol) seemed almost as demanding as facing Bob Willis the previous year.

We excelled ourselves by eating everything. We nearly expelled ourselves by not doing so in the allotted time. Bloated but proud, we waddled out at 4.37, only to be accosted by an angry Surrey team manager, Arthur 'Mull of Kintyre.' Arthur must have been on a diet. Either that or he'd eaten too many grumblers because he certainly moaned at us:

'You're two minutes late. Do you realise we could claim the game?'

It crossed my mind to tell him to get stuffed, as we were, and we might not have heard the last of it if we hadn't been again. Geoff Howarth, who later captained New Zealand, came in and spanked a quick 50 to win the match for Surrey.

Some clubs, north and south, operate a rota system for teas so that the same people aren't burdened with serving up salad on Saturday and Sunday afternoons to a bunch of ungrateful gannets. Whether it's cucumber sandwiches minus crusts with carrot cake and Earl Grey tea in Windsor or spam muffins and Eccles cakes in Burnley, it nearly always falls upon the ladies to do the honours. Inevitably, some are more proficient than others.

At Evershed, the rota system worked well until it came to the turn of newly-wed 'Smiler's' wife. We should have anticipated there would be a hitch due to 'Smiler's' track record. This is the five star chef who was convinced that you make cheese on toast in a toaster. His first attempt failed when the cheese would not stay in place on the bread. (Didn't he realise it needed to be placed Caerphilly?) 'Smiler' confessed he considered cellotaping the cheese on but went for a 'less fiddly' solution. He laid the toaster on its side and went for broke. Needless to say, it did.

Wisely, he kept well out of the way when his missus had the opportunity to impress with her culinary skills. Nearly all the salad on offer looked as it should – appealing to rabbits. The lettuce, however, was not happy. It couldn't have been an 'Iceberg' because it was hot.

'Oh Joy,' exclaimed 'Smiler.'

He wasn't exalting a moment's pleasure. He was summoning his wife:

'Joy. The lettuce looks like my grandad's knackers. What's the score?'

Joy replied that she didn't understand all those numbers on the board and he'd have to work it out for himself.

With the honeymoon period over, 'Smiler' felt obliged to impose his authority:

'The lettuce, you daft bint. Why has it got third degree burns?'

Joy suddenly realised she should have paid more attention in domestic science lessons at school:

'Oh, bloody hell. I thought you did lettuce the same way as cabbage.'

She'd boiled it and, like her newly permed hair had, it had curled up and dyed. She hadn't fricasseed the fennel or roasted the radish but it was too late to tell Joy not to get all steamed up.

Even that was only the tip of the iceberg. When she served up fruit salad for dessert, Joy was asked if it was fresh. Indignant, she replied:

'Of course it's fresh. I've only just opened the tin.'

'Smiler' and Joy do, I believe, eat out a lot.

Joy does have a rival when it comes to getting into hot water. Nearly as misguided, but worthy of clemency due to her tender age, was a youngster I'll call 'HP.' She was helping her mum serve up hot pies and beans on a cold April day at Boston Manor some decades ago and seemed in control.

Part way through the warming up process – the food's not ours – 'HP' ran to the tea room from the kitchen (southern for shed with a cooker) in a panic. She had a cuisinary query:

'Mum. What should I do? The labels are coming off the baked bean tins.'

Mum seemed unperturbed as she made her way to the crime scene. She soon changed from being sedate into almost having to be sedated when she saw what she saw. A string of unopened tins of beans were huddled together in a saucepan full of boiling water:

'Duck!' yelled Mum.

'Give me a chance, I haven't even batted yet,' responded her cousin, 'Greengrocer,' an ex-boxer with cauliflower ears.

'Spud,' who loves potatoes and is always thinking about his stomach, commented:

'That makes a nice change. Is there any orange sauce?'

It was left to Mum to act as bomb disposal officer and turn off the ring in the nick of time.

Most southern tea ladies did tend to play it safe and serve up similar delights. This is not to say that they couldn't adapt when necessary. 'Grace' is a pious lady with an amazing aptitude for putting her foot in it. When she heard a vegetarian declining to eat the ham on offer, she sought to resolve the dilemma thus:

'Don't you like ham, cock?' (A term of endearment in London on most occasions).

'No. I don't eat meat or fish,' replied 'Cock.'

'Oh. Are you one of those pagans? Anyway, it should be OK because it's only wafer thin ham,' coaxed the catering auxiliary.

'It's meat and I don't eat meat,' protested our 'pagan.'

'No problem, cock. We've got sausages over there. There's no meat in sausages. They're all gristle, bone and sawdust. Help yourself to a few.'

Some of the ladies do veer away from the norm. Evershed's 'Rhia' – she's dire – left us all disinfected as well as disaffected. Like most of us (and she couldn't have done), she was unaware that diluted Dettol turns white. Unable to smell a rat, or anything else, 'Rhia' mistook the jug of germ killer for milk. We decided we'd been treated to a new kind of herbal tea until the runs flowed at an unheard of rate after the interval.

The umpires, Ron and Lyd – he wasn't local – suffered more than most. Lyd acted as Mum and gave his colleague more than just a refill with a second cup:

'More, Ron?'

He must have been because he consented:

'Aye, Lyd.'

These aren't quite famous last words but they might have been (and they do work twice as well as the other way round) had Lyd not decided enough was enough:

'That'll do Ron, Ron, that'll do Ron, Ron,' putting me in mind of the Crystals' 60s hit.

Following this near death experience, our very own philosopher, Des Carter, likened the incident to the demise of the French writer, Balzac, who died of caffeine poisoning. I'd have been more impressed had he not pronounced his name 'balls ache.'

The remaining southern tea ladies tended to be unremarkable, apart from 'DIY.' She became stroppy after a comment from 'Pontoon' backfired. 'Pontoon' isn't a card sharp. He thought this was the word for the gun used to shoot whales. He got his words wrong again as 'DIY' served him his afters, a portion of ice-cream, mixed fruit and nuts:

'You can't give us this today. It's only Saturday. You're a day early.'

Our helper became less helpful from then on. Whenever anyone asked her to do anything she replied:

'Do it yourself.'

Northern cricketers are less fussy. Like the French, they will eat almost anything. Take 'Banger' and Michel Lotito, who has, to date, consumed 10 bicycles as well as a supermarket trolley. (I wonder if he got his pound back.) Consequently, barbecues are always well received. This is true even when these are advertised, somewhat ominously, at Thornham as 'Sam n' Ella's' Barbie.' This is a misnomer. Ken is nowhere to be seen and Diane, Margherita and Ella are the chefs. These ladies do a terrific job and bring in a few quid for the club, particularly as they don't restrict themselves to burgers.They regularly offer such alternatives as Steak Diane, Pizza Margherita and Pie Ella.

The trio were assisted by Gail, until she disgraced, or disgailed, herself by flirting with Bill Shannon. Despite being placed four places lower than her dog at Cruft's, she promised to give Bill a French kiss and proceded to peck him gently on both cheeks. Thereafter, any time one of the females spotted her they announced a 'Gail' warning, particularly in sea area Shannon but not in Rockall because nothing much ever happens there.

The mere presence of a few smiling ladies on the ground can do wonders for a team. Perhaps this was at the root of the Old Qs' failings. It was a male steward who prepared the teas and none of us could, by any stretch of the imagination, be deemed to be babe magnets. We were all either juvenile or senile. The younger end still played 'Cowboys and Indians' and had yet to fathom out what those things in skirts with strange lumps were. If any of us had been told we could travel across Jordan free of charge, we'd have preferred it to be the country rather than the model. We were all convinced we were induging in oral sex purely by talking about it.

The older end no longer cared. A stiff one was now a brandy and a lazy lob was how best to return the ball to the wicket-keeper. Too much excitement would have proved fatal. It was, therefore, perfectly understandable that no sane female would come anywhere near us. Consequently, we had no one to show off to, as well as nothing to show off with.

Only twice did I see anyone of the fairer sex venture to an Old Q game with a team-mate. Ron Pyke's wife made one appearance. She looked like a fish out of water and didn't make the same mistake twice. Wanda Wickens didn't either. Husband

Mo paraded her just the once. Wanda came and Wanda left, no doubt 'wanda-ring' why she gave her hubbie permission to waste his week ends with such a gang of misfits.

It wasn't quite as unhealthy at Evershed. The plethora of players walking around with thumbprints on their foreheads indicated that many were married. Of the wives, 'Loo Loo' stood out the most. This was not merely because she has no chance of hurting her face if she falls over. It was also because she is small, loud and Scottish. She is even married to a BG. (In this case, 'Big Gob.') Moreover, she has an incredibly weak bladder. She spends half her life in the toilet but did emerge long enough to do her turn at teas. They were never that good – no more than bog standard really.

Moving north, the star tea lady at Lidget Green was 'Mad' Donna. Donna hasn't adopted any children but can drink for England. Once she'd had one over the eleven vodkas she saw no reason to be diplomatic.

Alcohol can preserve most things but a secret isn't one of them. With Donna as sober as a newt, no one was safe. She caused more arguments than 'Mogadon.' Donna was under the misapprehension that alcohol is good for you. She'd read that a unit of wine every day was healthy because:

'It reduces your cholestomy.'

Silly old bag thought that one bottle equated to one unit.

At Middleton, several senior players were divorced but the daft buggers had remarried. The social scene here would have given Donna enough ammunition to invade the whole of the Far East, including Ipswich. Here again, the ladies tended to be extremely pleasant and, so, unlike those expensive condoms, aren't going to be ribbed. If you believe that...

'HRH' is better looking than Camilla Parkyer Rolls but so was Elephant Man. Like Camilla, 'HRH' aspires to the throne.

She even drove an Austin Princess and drank the same brand of gin as Princess Margaret – any. She made you feel you should curtsy or bow before addressing her. I've no doubt she fully approved of one crisp maker's decision to call its 'cheese and onion' variety 'mature cheddar and shallots' and charge three times as much for the privilege. This woman certainly isn't the one Ian Botham had in mind when he stated:

'Ashley Giles is looking for a bit of rough,' at Johannesburg in January 2005.

Then there was Pat Mycock. Who needs a nickname with a real name like that? She has one anyway – 'Sweaty Betty.' We had no choice. 'The Cat' certainly wouldn't have been able to use his favourite chat-up line on her. I know it's supposedly horses that sweat, men perspire and ladies glow. 'Betty' must have plenty of equine blood. Whenever the sun shines, she positively froths and has to change her socks four times a day. (I wouldn't like to be in her shoes.) Sweating sickness was reportedly eradicated in 1551 but 'Betty' must have missed being vaccinated.

'Betty' is married to 'Prop,' who combined playing for Middleton with a professional rugby league career. 'Prop' is built to last and has bits missing from his face, yet is both the brains and the brawn in this relationship. 'Betty' has had to take the pill throughout their marriage because that's the only way she can be sure to pack her husband's bag on a Saturday rather than a Monday.

Nevertheless, 'Betty' does have a sense of humour. When she last did the teas, she served up a chicken dish. 'Castro,' who's always on the fiddle, asked if it was 'coq au vin.' Quick as a flash (and that's another story), 'Betty' replied:

'Coq au vin.' Isn't that what we had in the back of our Transit last night, 'Prop'?'

The reference to 'flashing' is one 'Betty' can also see the funny side to. One evening, as she was on her way to pick up 'Prop' after net practice, she was treated to the sight of a lowlife exposing himself to her from his car. Despite having once declared that one of the Seven Wonders of the World was 'the hanging baskets of Basildon,' 'Betty' was smart enough to get the car's registration. The case was brought to court. She was asked if the accused had an erection. Her reply would have made even 'Botox' smile:

'I'm not very good with cars. It could have been an Erection but it might have been a Spitfire or a Triumph.'

Thornham's ladies generally serve up tip-top teas. 'Florence,' the nurse, is a gem (surname Garnett). She will do almost anything for anyone. Indeed, the only time I've heard her refuse to comply was when she whispered:

'No, I can't do that. It would be a crime, Ian.'

'Florence,' moreover, is genuinely interested in sport, has a good understanding of cricket and hates Manchester United. 'Tiddles' could have found his perfect woman.

Almost on a par, is 'Maid Marion.' This delightful woman is an 'Archers' fan and spends much of her time in the Three Arrows. She's always game for a laugh. She has to be, being married to Nel, aka 'Eskimo.' Whenever Marion asks if she can kiss Robin or one of his merry men, 'Eskimo' replies:

'Sure. It's no skin off my nose. Do whatever you want.'

'Marion' can play pool, dominoes and, of course, darts. She knows more dirty jokes than Bernard Manning and has a stronger throwing arm than 'Flicker.' All this, but she remains more feminine than Julian Clary, always feeds us chips and can name the current England Test side, give or take a Bell for a Key, a Read for a Wright, a Joyce for an Ethel, a Broad for a Long, a Swann for a Duck or a Strauss for a Bach. Sadly, her popularity has had an adverse effect on her husband. He is now easily embarrassed, elusive, stroppy and blighted by acne. He regularly goes into hiding in their French villa. He is the 'Scarlet Pimpled Nel.'

'Joan of Arc' can be relied upon to burn the steak at barbecues but she is well clued up. She knows when to say 'well played,' 'bad luck' or 'wanker.' You can't teach that. 'Joan' gets on with everyone, except her husband, 'the Rear Admiral,' an effeminate naval man. They fell out over a misunderstanding regarding 'had him over a barrel' and have yet to make up.

Although 'Rosette' wears the trousers – husband 'PT' never drinks coffee and is weak and wet – she is no feminist. She was appalled to learn that both scorers for the 2002 Test between Australia and South Africa in Sydney were women:

'If they're there all day joining up dots, who's making the husbands' tea?'

'Rosette' doesn't trust men in the kitchen and has won awards for doing the league's best teas. She did slip up once, however. She opted for plaice. Her first hiccup came when 'Pale Face' – his wife, 'Lyza,' famously rammed a bucket, which previously had no hole in it, over his head as a prize for him coming home drunk after a game – asked if there were any allergy warnings on the packet. He couldn't eat nuts yet was grateful he still had his own, given his wife's temper.

'Rosette' read the warning out loud but immediately wished she hadn't:

'Allergy warning. This product contains fish.'

'What a load of codswallop,' added PT.

'Rosette' was further confused when one ungrateful opponent complained:

'That fish was foul.'

Her reaction was to go and have a whine in the bar. She did insist on having another go a fortnight later. This time she plumped for prawn and spinach curry. This went down, and out, very well. For afters, we got our just desserts by way of some 'simply gorgeous fairy cakes.' 'Rosette's' fairy cakes had put her back on the top of the tree and she was able to retire to the bar looking as happy as Larry (whoever he is) for a proper wine.

A combination of Thornham tea ladies, a 'Florosmarjo,' sounds like an American female sprinter and would doubtless have met the approval of Bill Edrich. (He was married five times. Apparently, he just loved wedding cake.) Sadly, we've as much chance of meeting one as we have of scoring as many runs as the 'Master,' Jack Hobbs (61,000), of averaging 161.7 as V.J. Manjrekar did for Castleton Moor in the CLL in 1956 or of taking 200 wickets in eight successive seasons as 'Tich' Freeman of Kent did. (Was he really only 2ft tall?) Being realistic, the Altzheimer's Society has more chance of a night out to remember.

It must be said that cricketers do take teas for granted. Only once in nearly 2000 games have I experienced supplies not getting through. We were at Swinton in 1990. 'A breakdown in communication' (southern for stroppy wife) resulted in a bare table. Their captain, unfortunately not Captain Bird's Eye this time, went round the 13-strong crowd begging for scraps. He nearly got one when one old bloke threatened to smack him. It may have been a baker's dozen, but the spectators weren't for giving up their sandwiches.

The bar had to be raided. An alternative carvery was amassed. Beef, roast chicken and pork, of the genus crisp, crisp and scratchings made a change from lettuce. ('Salad days' really are not 'carefree periods of youth.')

Another deviation from the norm came when Terry's wife

donated some chocolates on her birthday for us to demolish at tea. Despite this being the wrong way round, they were all scoffed within seconds, with one exception. One of the chocolates 'Treacle' selected was proving inordinately stubborn. After having chomped on it for even longer than we estimate it would take him to run a three – we'll never know – he was moved (for a change) to ask:

'Did any of those chocolates have foil on them?' Not now. He then asked if they were Belgian chocolates, hoping they weren't. 'I can't stand Belgians. They speak French when they don't have to.'

Sometimes tea-breaks can be advantageous in influencing events on the field. I don't mean strategically placed extra helpings of dumplings or rock cake on the opposition's opening bowler's plate. I'm thinking more of mind games. A prime example of this occurred in 1968 in a London Schools v Buckinghamshire game at Hammersmith (something I'd been unable to do when I faced him five years earlier). It was an 11.30 start, which meant I had to get up before noon.

We had set a decent target. In reply, Bucks. had struggled to 20 odd for 4 but had rallied, thanks to a spirited knock from their number six. He looked far and away their best player, against both pace and spin. By tea, they were back in the game. During the interval I got chatting to him. I was curious to know why he wasn't batting higher:

'Why don't you bat in the top three?' I asked, half expecting him to say that it was because he didn't have his own bat.

'I'm absolutely clueless against outswing bowling,' he obligingly confessed.

Three minutes after the resumption he was caught behind nicking an outer from our part-time operator 'Merv the Swerve.'

The tea break, then, can be useful, yet it pales into insignificance compared to what goes on in the bar. With more time at your disposal, you have a golden opportunity to discover a myriad of invaluable snippets to store in your memory bank for future use. These could be for practical use in future games, for revenge, blackmail or merely embarrassment.

Tongues aren't the only things which can be loosened during post-match festivities. After college games in the 1970s, protocol dictated that, as irresponsible students, we performed pranks, congas and miscellaneous rowdy acts, such as a partial striptease. One lad from Bede, Durham, like 'Treacle' and his driving in Bury, didn't know when to stop.

This was in 1972 so he pre-empted the 'Full Monty' by 30 years. In a mixed bar (beer, spirits, wine), he left nothing to the imagination other than when was the last time he'd washed his 'Y fronts'? A few females – mostly those studying RE – pretended to be shocked and feigned to look away. The rest smiled, in the realisation that they weren't being short-changed by the locals.

The upshot of it all was that the would-be naturist had been asked for a 'bear hug' by a team-mate and had misunderstood. As a result, without so much as another cocktail to send him on his way, he was accosted by the steward and asked which college he was from. Still alert, he chose 'Luffbra' and the Loughborough cricket team got a two year ban from our bar.

His parting shot was to scrawl 'Herpes' on the ladies toilet door and 'Hispees' on the mens' in felt tip before handing out his phone number to a couple of young ladies who were convinced this wasn't a flash in the pan.

A variety of tales are routinely exchanged over a pint after games. My all-time favourite arose in May 2004. Flowery Field had just joined the LCL from the Saddleworth League. My good friend, hence no nickname, Kevin, was propping up a well-oiled spectator. Kevin had been admiring the new tearoom and bar. He enquired how the club had found the money to pay for them:

'Fund raising,' slurred Kev's drinking partner.

'What kind of fund raising?'

'I shaved me 'ead,' came the reply. (Perhaps that's why he was 'half cut.')

'Blimey,' said Kevin, genuinely impressed all of a sudden.

'And how much did that bring in?'

'40 quid,' replied the spectator proudly.

Struggling to keep a straight face, the interviewer sought to eke out more:

'Anything else?'

Upon reflection, plus a few more swigs of lager to refresh all parts, the benefactor eventually conceded there had also been 'a few other bits and pieces.'

Kevin thought about asking how they'd managed to get the Dave Clark Five involved but his pal would have been too young to understand, so he resisted. He was, however, beginning to feel like Michael Parkinson did when interviewing a very much the worse for wear George Best. Then, as an afterthought, Flowery Field's finest added:

'Oh yeah. You see those new houses? Well, Rohan Barnsley (Roland Bardsley, the builder, not a West Indian batting legend from South Yorkshire) gave us 3 and a half million quid for the land.'

'Ah,' said Kevin. 'I suppose you could say that you are both philanthropists at heart.'   '

I couldn't say that' – and in his condition he probably couldn't – 'because I don't collect stamps,' concluded Kev's mate.

Most of what goes on in the bar is harmless, but there are times when there are sinister motives afoot. Cue Royton 1980. The fixture list had pitted Middleton away to Royton in the league on a Saturday and likewise the next day in the Cup. We beat them on the Saturday so they decided to give themselves a better chance for the cup game. They targeted one of our stars, 'Proxima Centaur,' for special post-match treatment.

They knew it was pointless getting him drunk. He tended to do that without prompting anyway, with no visible ill-effect. The Royton boys thought they knew 'Proxima's' Achilles heel. As an unattached divorcee, they banked on his libido going into overdrive when they unleashed a buxom barmaid all over him.

Her brief was simple – remove his briefs and tire him out in whatever way she could. The plan backfired. Instead of turning up in no fit state to play, as intended, 'Proxima' arrived wearing a broad smile all the way down to his crutch. This smile did not wane as he blasted Royton's attack to all parts in what he boasted was his fourth top knock within a few hours.

Such perks are rare, yet socialising with team-mates and opponents can be almost as enjoyable as the game itself. In my experience, there was more mixing in the south than up here. It was certainly rare for anyone in the Bradford League to buy his wife, never mind an opponent, even half a pint. You might have got a swig from a tipsy team-mate if he'd had a good run on talent money. You might, but there was more chance of Shahid Afridi playing out a maiden against Kenya or Northamptonshire's Mark Robinson hitting a boundary. (Mark plundered a staggering three whole runs in the entire 1990 season.)

However, even the most competitive adversary can become almost human off the field. This is often so if his team has won or he has done well personally. I wonder if Percy Perrin got a round in after scoring 343 not out for Essex against Derbyshire in 1904 and ending up on the losing side. Disappointingly for us, Thornham's Mark Fallon didn't emulate his namesake, Liam, who treated 1613 people to a drink in 1987. Mark notched up 200 against East Levenshulme but only spent the equivalent of his name in the bar afterwards.

Occasionally, things go pear-shaped. After the opening game of a 'mini tour' to the Lake District with the Leeds Carnegie Overseas Students XI, 'Hardy'- he was once told not to rest on his laurels - was very much the worse for wear. A huge Fijian rugby player, he had found Guinness very much to his liking but the Guinness had failed to return the compliment. The 'tourists' were staying in a youth hostel in Keswick. 'Hardy' was assigned to the top deck of a bunk bed and the diminutive wicket-keeper, 'Stumpy,' was in the bottom half.

'Stumpy' was a quiet, shy, teetotaller. He was already sound asleep as 'Hardy' was dumped into bed above him. There was no problem until about 4.00 a.m. when the Fijian was taken short and jumped out of bed. Believing himself to be standing in front of the urinal, he relieved himself all over an unsuspecting 'Stumpy'.

Blissfully unaware of his transgression, 'Hardy' arose early and went to breakfast, leaving his victim asleep but potentially steaming in more ways than one. Once informed of his misdeed, he was suitably ashamed and went to apologise to his moist colleague. A thoroughly pissed off 'Stumpy' saw his aggressor approaching and ran off, shouting:

'Oh no, not again!' in anticipation of another unwanted warm shower.

This is just a sample of the cameraderie which prompts many to play on and on.

Food for thought:

29. Have Aussie J.Angel and Cambridge's RQC Cake ever had tea together and did J.Swiss and R.Roll ever play cricket?

30. Did Derbyshire's Bill Oates ever do porridge?

31. When Jonathan Agnew became BBC cricket correspondent, did you wonder how would Aggers do, do do?

32. Was Gloucestershire's AE Dipper a big Dipper and easily taken for a ride?

Chapter 9

EVERGREEN

When it comes to the benefits and side effects of continuing to play on until you creak, there is no north-south divide. No true cricketer in any part of the country wants to waste weekends shopping, gardening or getting vertigo going up Blackpool Tower or the London Eye. We must not give in before we qualify for an anti-flu jab. After all, bowls is only for the really old and infirm and WG snuffed it just seven years after retiring. Working on that principle, if I want to get a text from the Queen I'll need to carry on playing until I'm seven years older than the umpires who crouched in the1901 Norfolk v Suffolk Vets game. Both were 86.

We should take comfort that the passing of time didn't affect Wally, Jack or JIm that much. Wally Hammond averaged 108 for Gloucester when he was 43 and Jack Hobbs scored 98 of his 197 centuries after his 40th birthday. Middlesex's Jim Smith hit 50 in 14 balls in 1935 but three years on it only took him 11. Moreover, Bill Edrich returned to Minor Counties cricket for Norfolk aged 55, a mere 39 years after his debut, Wilfred Rhodes played for England at 52 and Raja Singh turned out in a first-class fixture for Bombay when he was 72:

'Was it a good game, Raja?' asked his jailbird brother, Singh Singh.

'Yes. It was first class.'

On a more mundane level, those of us who only take one wicket every six weeks or average five with the bat can't get much worse so we can totter on for as long as our arthritic knees and knackered spines permit without contributing any less. It doesn't matter that on the rare occasions when we dive for a ball, our team-mates run a book as to whether we'll be able to get back up or not.

No one in the south ever said anything detrimental about the rickety demeanour or lack of contribution from old Ernie, very old Jack, 'Bob Hopeless' and other members of Dad's Army in the Old Quintinians. Even if they had, the boys would have merely sucked another Werthers Original and carried on regardless.

In the north, they might have been termed 'coffin dodgers,' as I was by one pre-pubescent sprog from Glossop's seconds in 2004. Even so, I'm not as old as 'Pagey.' He's the only player in the LCL who calls me 'young man.' He's been around longer than Bruce Forsyth and is world famous. When a group of Cambodians emerged from hiding in the jungle after 25 years in December 2004, the first thing their leader asked was:

'Is Pagey still playing for Denton St. Lawrence?'

As the sterling work carried out by Help the Aged becomes ever more relevant to me, I find it most intriguing to now be at the top end of the scale. Aged 54, I finally had something in common with Denis Compton, apart from a gammy knee. As a 19 year old, he opened the batting for Middlesex with the 48 year old Patsy Hendren, giving them an average age of 34ish. In 2003, my fellow opener was the 14 year old 'Beano.' (He thinks he's a comic.) Similarly, 36 years previously, aged 18, I opened for Evershed with the evergreen, ever cheerful, ever ready, battery operated, 50 year old Tom King. (Change the 'm' for an 'n'; and you've got a big hitter.)

Tom was very much the senior citizen and, as an easy-going southerner, didn't mind being called 'grandad' and 'old git.' He did, however, take exception to being asked what it was like playing without a middle stump, as they did in the early eighteenth century.

We were all very fond of Tom and were concerned when he took a ball squarely on the thigh from a sharpish bowler. This was especially so because it was accompanied by a loud crack, a grimace and a yelp:

'Tom, are you OK?' I asked anxiously.

'I am, but my bloomin' teeth aren't,' he replied incisively.

Before going in to bat, Tom had taken out his dentures, yet had forgotten he'd put them in the front pocket of his whites. They can't have been wisdom teeth. Just imagine, if, rather than teeth, he'd left a box of matches in his pocket. Forget Tom King, it would have been Smo King and he'd have had a case for being included in the Smokers v Non-Smokers game of 1887. Unsurprisingly, it was the Smokers who collapsed, losing their last seven wickets for 54. Arthur Fagg wasn't playing but William Gunn was, in a game where the match sponsors may well have been Swann Vesta.

Most of us who are long in the tooth have encountered a variety of reasons for games being cancelled or curtailed. When I played in and around London, the threat of drizzle was usually enough. It is likely to take more in the north, unless Sam is umpiring. It took a herd of wild horses to stop one Rochdale fixture in the CLL in the mid-80s. The match was abandoned – it wasn't a colt's game – because the horses weren't for trotting off. They must have found the bowling friendly and the police had to cordon off the area until Princess Ann arrived to lead the herd away.

A committee member did suggest shooting one of the nags (not Princess Ann) in the hope this would scare the rest into leaving. When asked what should be done with it afterwards, he suggested it could be sold to a Frenchman for meat. This was rejected on the grounds that there was no point in trying to flog a dead horse.

Those of us old enough to wear cardigans tend to lose our senses, including that of direction. As such, one may end up in Scarborough. If so, the first thing you see will be a lie. It's a sign which reads 'England's first resort.' It should say 'last resort.' All I need to state to justify this is that a Yorkshire League game there in August 1951 was abandoned due to fog.

During a game at Flowery Field about 20 years ago, some youths were making a nuisance of themselves on the ground (and in the air). They had been asked to either behave or leave. They left. Not long after, they were replaced by one of the fathers...plus his shotgun. This brings a whole new meaning to the term 'good shot.' Fortunately, no one found out whether or not he was. One of the fielding side, 'Bobby,' is a policeman, a very big, brave policeman, and nobody ended up full of lead. There was, however, a need for a lengthy toilet break.

As we get closer to looking as wizened as Paul Daniels, as I've just hinted, eyesight, memory and sense of direction inevitably suffer. Cue 'Pat.' In 1989, he was playing for Lancashire over 50s in Kent. Not wanting to rush home after the game, he'd booked in at a hotel not far from the ground. He'd asked one of the Kent players for directions and was relieved to be told that this player drove home past the hotel so would lead 'Pat' to it. He'd be in a red Cortina.

True to his word, the Kent player gave 'Pat' the nod when

he was ready to leave. 'Pat' sunk his pint, collected his bag and got into his car. He noticed the Cortina pulling out of the car park. He followed it out. 'Pat' showed no concern for the first six or seven miles but became somewhat anxious after six more. After another 20 minutes, being quick on the uptake, 'Pat' decided to draw up alongside his lead man and ask how much further it was. Wrong man, wrong direction, orange Cortina.

Not as dozy as the ever-smart 'Trendy,' though. A family outing to Irlam – he was playing, his son was scoring and his wife, Mona (she often does) was being taken out to tea – was to give credence to the fading memory theory. Mona had gone in her own car so that she could make a quick getaway after the game. About an hour after she and her evergreen hubby had helped to boost the bar profits back at Thornham, Mona decided they'd all be going home. No they wouldn't. Both had omitted to bring their seemingly inconsequential son, all 6ft2 of him, back from Irlam. Not that surprising really. 'Trendy' often forgot to buy a round and even did a Bob Willis, walking out to bat without one at Wythenshawe.

North and south, most 'veterans' find it useful to establish a set of rules for survival. If we don't, we could end up like WG's brother, Fred. Fred had what could only be described as a disastrous couple of weeks in the 1880s. It started well enough with a call up to the England XI. It ended less well. He bagged a pair and dropped dead a fortnight later.

As far as I can remember (about six weeks), my rules have a common theme – sycophancy. Umpires, tea ladies, scorers, captains, fast bowlers and wicket keepers all need to be kept sweet. It's worth spending a few minutes prior to the start of games chatting to the umpires as if they are long lost grandads. It might just turn those dodgy 20-80 calls in your favour. How else do you think D.Mohanty got four lbws in five balls at Kalahandi in 2002?

A big smile and a sincere thank you to the tea ladies won't help you score more runs but who knows what perks it might bring. It could lead to extra portions…Whatever you do, don't do anything to upset your wife when she is on teas. 'Paddy,' the quick-tempered Irishman of Evershed did and it cost him dearly.

He foolishly complained to his wife Vicky that she hadn't come up to scratch. This angered her. She thought she deserved a medal for her efforts (Victoria Cross x two) so she responded by serving him his dessert down his neck.

Likewise, don't upset your scorer. The last thing you want is for him or her to 'do a Daddy' and take runs from your personal total because the book has become like a one-legged table. An impromptu visit to the score box with a refreshing soft drink for the scribe is an ideal time to explain that you actually got a bit of bat on those three sets of four leg byes signalled by that myopic umpire. Reassure your friend that, as from today, it is perfectly in order to transfer the 12 runs to the batsman, ie you, without having to get the umpire's say so. Out for 14 sounds so much better than out for two.

As you get older, your captain becomes more important to you. Never fall out with him. He's the one who sorts out the batting order, how many overs you'll bowl, and what pre- and post-match jobs you will do. More pertinently, this is the person who decides where you will field for 300 balls. If you don't get on, you could find yourself at short leg. Worse still, you could be posted in a position where you are expected to run.

Alternatively, if skip is your mate, you can persuade him first slip would be ideal. You can often go through a whole innings without touching the ball. When the opposition gets to 210 for 2 and a slip, inexplicably, is no longer required, take it upon yourself to stroll down to either third man or fine leg – whichever has another fielder closest to you who can act as your legs.

But how can us oldies ensure that the skipper remains our friend once we can no longer hope to get anywhere near emulating Aberdeenshire's West Indian pro, A.Hunt. He certainly earned his money by being instrumental in bowling out West Lothian for 48 and then scoring every run in the 49-0 reply. (Maybe KK was batting with him but it is surely a case of jug avoidance.) Those of us who are less talented can keep in our captain's good books by volunteering to do pre-match chores. It may seem to be going against the grain to offer to do extra work as a 'senior' member of the side. It's not. Skip will be grateful of the help and you can turn things to your advantage if you're smart. I always put the stumps in before we start. By that, I don't mean win the toss and insert the opposition. I'm referring to having a golden opportunity to maximise your chances as a batsman who is fading fast.

By forcing each stump down as far as it will go, using a heavy mallet to assist you, and then tapering the tops, you gain potentially vital millimetres. If confronted, plead ignorance. As far as you know, stumps should be 22 inches high and six inches wide. To give credence to this, have a pre-1931 book on the laws of cricket handy. It was only after this date that they were allowed to grow to the ludicrous size of 28 inches by nine.

Each guideline is designed to help me score runs, satisfy my stomach/loins or save energy. All of these aspects are as important to me as plastic surgery is to Cher or as having a different pair of shoes for every day of the year is to most women. The opposing team's wicket keeper also has a part to play. A well-chosen 'good stop' can turn him into an unsuspecting ally. It might make him think twice about leading the chorus designed to send you packing when the umpire mistakenly interprets the crack made by your arthritic knee for an edge and sends you on your way.

I've already touched on the necessity of not falling out with fast bowlers. This even extends to quickies in your own team. Who knows whether you or they will change clubs in the future? There's also no harm in agreeing with a hostile paceman when he calls you a 'slutchy bastard' after you have skilfully run him through the slip cordon – the opposition's least agile, heftiest, oldest member – for four. A seemingly sincere:

'Yes, I am, aren't I?' is probably less confrontational than: 'Come back when you're quick enough, Gladys.'

Granted, the latter is the more manly of the two but why risk unwanted dental work or severe bruising?

As soon as you become 'evergreen,' it is quite in order to pull rank. Use it to get pole position in the changing room. Draughts and ageing bodies don't mix well. I prefer the 'semi-detached' peg on the end, facing the window, nearest to the tea-room, the bar, the showers and the car park. If some young whippersnapper arrives before you and pinches your spot (rather than one of his own), you have every right to recycle his gear into the showers, out of the window or up the flagpole.

Once you've acquired old stager status, don't abuse it. There are far too many cantankerous old toss-pots shuffling around already. Pyrford's opening bat did when the Old Quintinans played them in 1960 something. He and his junior partner were going along handsomely until a mix-up resulted in them becoming conjoined. There was no question that it was the old war-horse who should walk off. Not so. With two team-mates as umpires, he instructed the youngster to leave, justifying his actions thus:

'You go. You batted longer than me yesterday.'

Some might protest that's not cricket. True, but it's not as offside as this next piece of skulduggery. I knew Superman look-alike, 'Clark' from our London Schools days. He was a fine player and, despite being only 19, was threatening to take over as his club's leading run-getter. This didn't sit well with the long-faced, 'Shergar,' the veteran number four, who was accustomed to topping the averages. He was sufficiently peeved by the threat to his dominance to have no hesitation in emitting a dreaded 'wait, yes, no, yes, sorry!' call to run out 'Clark.' Bad enough in itself, but made worse because misery-guts had only just come in and 'Clark' was on 99. Even more despicably, the guilty party made it crystal clear he was top dog, or top nag, when straight from the horse's mouth, he neighed:

'I'm the only one who scores centuries in this team.'

I'm glad to report that 'Clark' had the last laugh. He toppled 'Shergar,' who didn't end up in a meat pie but did eat so many of them that he nearly burst. He became too slow to run anyone but himself out and was put out to pasture. He retired from his job at Samaritans to become a capital letter D wherever one was needed for display purposes in the Home Counties. He then turned schizophrenic and was reduced to appearing in adverts for Double Diamond beer.

Most old stagers will have picked up a few quirks and superstitions along the way. The great Majid Khan of Glamorgan and Pakistan, a combination I equate with a footballer turning out for Cowdenbeath and Brazil, did. Whenever Majid was out for less that one he blamed his bat. He ceremoniously sawed the offending blade into pieces.

As he was so talented, this didn't often occur but imagine if it was someone less gifted. If either of New Zealand's legendary number elevens, Chris Martin or Daffy/Danny Morrison had been of the same persuasion, it would have been the end of the Brazilian Rain Forest. Between them they've seen more ducks than Bill Oddie and David Attenborough combined. As for me, if I'd have followed suit I'd be bankrupt. Today's new-fangled, full size, triple spring contraptions cost a bit more than half a crown.

Some cricketers I've played with, particularly in London, are superstitious about other clubs. 'Tastless,' a Spurs supporter, refused to play at Gunnersbury, the illiterate, 'Picture Book,' wouldn't play at Reading, whilst 'Quirky' would not come to Aylesbury in case he got a duck.

In the north, it's less idiocyncratic and is based more on fact. No one in their right mind would play for Tottington in the North Manchester League. Not only do they hold the league record for the lowest score, three all out, but a town of the same name was given over to the Army during World War One and never given back. The name is obviously cursed.

My own customs tend to be trite. I used to strap the right pad on before the left. (An exception to this was at primary school where, as you'll recall, it was Hobson's choice.) I stopped doing this when my memory became so unreliable that I constantly forgot which leg I was supposed to put the first pad on.

One foible which did prove effective was a fashion statement I made in the 80s. Before trenchfoot set in and I was sprightly enough to be in Thornham's 1stXI, I frequently sported a pair of tasteful, flesh coloured 'Y' fronts on match days. Amazingly, the donning of this high-class garment regularly coincided with me getting a relatively decent score.

This just about made it worth the abuse I received for wearing them.

When these designer briefs fell to pieces, I soon became a Hank Marvin of my former self and was relegated to the seconds in 1996. A new era cried out for a new pair of grundies. I opted for a classy shade of burgundy. They worked wonders until I lost them in 2001. I have my suspicions that Trevor Picken of Longsight nicked them because it was then that he suddenly started to score runs for fun.

Nowadays, rather than drum up another pair of wonder undies, I'm at the stage where I have to consider whether buying new kit is worth the 'domestic' it is sure to cause. A new bat means one less new dress for 'her indoors' but at least I don't have to negotiate the purchase of a helmet.

In July 2004, I had my pearly whites rearranged against Woodbank. This prompted an ultimatum:

'Wear a helmet, or else!'

Worried that the 'or else' could be a threat of physical harm involving scissors, I complied. Now, as the owner of expensive protective headgear, I either have to keep going for a few more years, take up fencing or buy a motorbike. (Full circle back to the cubs.)

Over the years, we are all bound to experience our fair share of highs and lows. There is a saying that you make your own luck. Leslie Baines didn't subscribe to this school of thought (or to any other school come to that). He missed out on the only organised game of cricket he was ever likely to feature in – for St.Mary's Primary School – as a consequence of falling out of an apple tree whilst scrumping and breaking both arms. As it turned out, he might as well have played because he wouldn't have done any worse than the rest of us.

Perhaps the notion of what constitutes luck does vary

north of the M25. As a youngster, I remember wishing Middlesex's Clive Radley 'all the best' before he batted on a flier at Lords. He modestly conceded that he would need it. Compare that to a morose ex-Yorkshire and England opener. When wished 'good luck' before going out to bat in a Test Match, he turned to his well-wisher and asserted that luck didn't enter into it. It was all down to skill. Was he, therefore, consoled with a 'bad skill' upon his dismissal?

I bet he'd have changed his opinion if he'd been in F.Morton's shoes in 1926. He was a member of the Victoria side which posted a world record score of 1107 versus New South Wales. Morton's contribution? Run out 0. Alternatively, Australia's T.Andrews surely stepped in something nasty before batting against Middlesex in 1926. He made 164 not out, but not before being caught three times from no balls. I must say I've never been 'out' from a no ball. Nor have I ever scored 164.

Sometimes being unusual brings you good fortune. The owner of a Swiss yellow tre skilling stamp got £1.4 million for it purely because it was the wrong colour. Sometimes it doesn't. Evershed's 'Get a move on' (Luke Sharp), was different in that he would often change from bowling right-handed to doing so left-handed in the same over. It made little difference. He was as useless as a solar-powered torch either way round, although it could be said that he didn't start as he meant to go on.

I must admit I'm glad that I didn't either. My various debuts haven't been on a par with, say, Majid the bat sawer. As a 15 or 16 year old, it hardly matters, he hit an unbeaten 111 and took 6 for 67 on his first-class debut in Pakistan. My first secondary school innings saw me amass 0 not out, batting at 11. I didn't bowl. Whilst RE Foster smashed 287 in his first Test Match in 1903, my introduction to club cricket, as mentioned, was less impressive in that the bails saw more action than I did.

Of course, by the time I made my school 1stXI debut, I'd made great strides. I wasn't far from emulating Frank Worrell. Aged 19, he made 308 not out for Barbados. Aged 14, I got the 8 not out without breaking sweat and thought I was the next Ted Dexter.

Old age hasn't helped. Australian Roy Park got a duck in his first/last Test innings in 1920. 80 odd years later, I followed half suit on debut for Lancashire over 50s against Yorkshire, just as I was fancying beating David Hookes' feat of a ton from 34 balls.

As luck, rather than skill, would have it, I did do a Wilfred Rhodes by working my way up from number 11 to opening. Like me, Wilfred also played on until he reached the doddery stage. Unlike me, he achieved the double twice as many times as WG Grace and took 100 wickets in a season 13 times more often than Grace did – 23 times more than I have.

That apart, how lucky have I been? As a 'soft southern rent boy,' I was extremely fortunate to have survived the Bradford League. Alternatively, we, the Old Quintinians, had no luck, ever. If we had, we'd have crossed swords with Chacombe from Northamptonshire. They managed to get bowled out for three in a game in 2002 and all three runs were extras.

I've also been cursed with less than perfect eyesight, giving me more in common with Jamaica's A.Binns than South African A.Seymore. Unlike Binns, I haven't had the misfortune to be given out for hitting the ball twice. This is simply because I have enough difficulty hitting it just the once. Binns made a spectacle of himself by doing so in 1956 against British Guiana. Perhaps it was a case of double vision.

I tend to take the 'winging' southerner's ground, rather than the northerner's more pragmatic approach to good fortune. I'm convinced there are a good number of lucky so-and-so's playing cricket but can easily persuade myself I'm not one. What other explanation could there be for being run out despite following the golden rule of getting my body between the ball and the wicket I was running to, only for the throw to go through my legs? (OK, I'm bandy.)

Would a lucky person be run out by his own runner going for a suicidal single at Castleton Moor in 1980? I tweaked something and couldn't run any faster than Douglas Bader. That meant I'd have to either deal solely in boundaries or call for a runner. 'Marzipan' (hardly anyone likes him), volunteered. This constituted the kiss of death. We didn't get on. It took two balls. I pushed one straight back to the bowler, who answered to 'Curly,' even though he had straight hair. Like an open wound, 'Marzipan' started running. Another day ruined.

He hadn't finished. At Milnrow, we found ourselves hugging one another at the same end after a difference of opinion, which, naturally, wasn't my fault:

'Sod it,' we both simultaneously decided.

I did so because I was on 49 with a collection looming, probably big enough to buy my wife enough bottles of cider to keep her sweet for a whole season. He did so because I wasn't his flavour of any month. We both began to 'sprint' to the other end in search of salvation. 'Marzipan's' voodoo curse must have worked. I slipped. Inexplicably, my team-mate didn't stop to pick me up. I departed, penniless. He stayed, only to be castled by the very next ball for a well-deserved blob. We lost.

I'm now becoming Polaroid. We were at one of my favourite grounds, Prestwich. The weather was glorious. The pitch was an absolute belter. Prestwich had a weakened attack. (Southern for crap.) 'Marzipan' wasn't there to run me out. I was in such a confident mood that I was fantasising about emulating David Whatmore. (He clubbed 210 from 61 balls for Alderney in 1983.) I'd even worked out where I'd hit a full toss if I got one first ball up.

'Douglas,' who hails from the Isle of Man, despite having only two legs, obliged. I somehow contrived to place the ball roughly where I wanted to:

'Four runs,' I thought.

My partner, it seemed, also foresaw a boundary. 'Mystic' Greg shouted:

'Shot!'

I didn't realise he meant he had been. Prestwich's best fielder, 'Twizzle,' who subsequently ran me out three years in a row – I'm a slow learner – scuppered my plan. The poser dived full length and parried the ball away to his right. It wouldn't now be four. Nevertheless, 'Twizzle' was lying prostrate on the turf and is left-handed, so there was an easy single to see me on my way. I called 'yes,' and set off for a leisurely run. It wasn't until I got to the point of no return (the first, not the third stroke, in this instance) that I twigged all was not well. Greg was doing a Walt Disney. He was in a state of frozen animation.

I was running. Greg wasn't. He was leaning casually on his bat, gazing at the horizontal fielder. I expect he was thinking that on this wicket, with this bowling, he'd fill his boots. Mine felt as if they were already full...of bloody concrete, as I tried to go back from whence I came.

It was a lost cause but there was too much at stake to go meekly. Was it worth a headlong dive or belly flop, as it turned out, on ground as hard as Norman Hunter? It wasn't. Out first ball, covered in shite with third degree grass burns. Still, on the bright side, I could watch Greg plunder the attack, there were only 99.5 overs to go and it was bound to be salad for tea again.

At least there was the next day's game at Denton to look forward to. Greg wouldn't be playing. You can't expect to pass a fitness test when you've been struck repeatedly over the head with a now full-size bat. 'Marshy' would be opening with me. He isn't from Hackney. He's just a bit soft and rather wet. He was, however, a good judge of a run.

Being no more superstitious than your average neurotic sportsman, I asked him to take the first ball. He agreed. There was no way I could now be out after five seconds for the second time in one weekend. 'Marshy' smarted the opening delivery to cover. He called 'yes,' presumably because he'd middled it and thought he deserved something, if only for novelty value. He was out of the blocks like a greyhound on heat. I set off in hope rather than expectancy. The odds on getting in were similar to those on George Best or Oliver Reed opting for cocoa as a nightcap. Holding back the tears, I blubbered:

'Carl Lewis might have made it.'

'Not with pads on,' replied the fielder, 'Truculent,' who owns a lorry hire firm.

He added that even Donald Campbell in Bluebird would have struggled. To complete an unwanted hat-trick, I then ran out of petrol on the way home.

In case bemoaning my lot makes me sound like Ellen MacArthur, I must point out that, like my sexist comments, it's all tongue-in-cheek. For nearly all seasoned campaigners, things tend to even themselves out. I know many cricketers who have fared far worse than I have. Unlike several team-mates, I avoided having my features rearranged by a conveyor belt of fast and furious bowlers. It may look as though they are, but I was born ruggedly disproportioned. It does, however, pain me to admit that I have now been nailed... twice.

Woodbank's Barry ('MFI') Kitchen, who's only marginally quicker than Shane Warne, bounced one off my bonce in 2002. For me, Barry Kitchen is now a household name. Two years later, against the same opposition, I top edged one from another medium-pacer, 'Braveheart,' (he taught my daughter to drive) and chipped three teeth.

Despite looking like Dracula, I came through the trauma, thanks mainly to some comforting words from my mother-in-law. On hearing the news, she sympathised, as only mother-in-laws can:

'What a pity. Your teeth were your best feature.'

My son was equally consoling. Adopting a more pragmatic approach (he was born in Manchester), he asked me if I'd carried on batting after the sound of leather on enamel. When I confessed I hadn't, he called me 'lazy.'

To cap it all, the dental receptionist, 'Floss,' also got in on the act. After no less than six visits to the dentist over the next eight weeks, I presented the cheque as payment for my treatment, only to be told:

'You're due for your six monthly check-up. Is tomorrow convenient?'

I politely advised her to complete this well known saying:

'Shove your check up and my cheque up…'

'Luckily,' any pain I've suffered has been due to my own inadequacies. The top edge was from a long-hop which I should have dispatched into Kevin's garden. Barry's bouncer only hit me because I got my summer and winter sports muddled up. Instead of ducking, I rose like a salmon (tinned) and headed the ball into the top corner. Senility.

It was no different as a youth. Playing at West Park for the Old Qs, I cut the two of diamonds and had to keep wicket. It was just as well, since on that day I was the only one who could bend down and have a realistic chance of being able to stand up again. How times change.

I decided to pretend to know what I was doing. The London Schools' keeper got a fair number of stumpings standing up to medium pacers. He would arrange for them to bowl a full length delivery down the leg side, say on the fifth ball of the over. He'd be ready to skip across and 'Bob, c'est ton oncle,' as they say in the Orange adverts.

Nothing to it, I thought. Once I'd got used to fielding in armour, I outlined my plan to our most accurate bowler, the well blessed 'Nobby.' We settled on the fourth ball of his next over. It almost worked. 'Nobby' played his part. He was spot on. The batsman played ball, too. Well, he did and he didn't because he missed it. He lost his balance and was out of his ground. Even I was where I was supposed to be, down the leg side ready and waiting like a youthful Wally Grout. The umpire was awake. Bingo.

One minor detail foiled us - my lack of skill. Too much of a Wally and not enough of a Grout, I failed to catch the ball. I did gather it but right in my meat and two veg. instead of in my mitts. Rather than it being whipping the bails off, it was almost a case of whipping my balls off and I sounded more like Alan Ball than Helen Shapiro for the next fortnight.

Mulling over all the ups and downs, I can't think of anything I've experienced to match the euphoria and the despair felt by South Africa's Geoff Griffin at Lords in 1960. He achieved a hat-trick and was no-balled 11 times for throwing in the same match. He must have begun by feeling like Gloucester's WH Brain did in 1893. The aptly named wicket-keeper used his grey matter to coax three Somerset batsmen out of their ground for three stumpings in three balls. This then subsided into rivalling the despair felt by Bangladesh's number one, Javed Omar in 2007.

He was out to the first ball of the first innings against Sri Lanka, only to do no better in the second innings.

Nor can I recall any innings I've played which was quite as lucky as the one Andy Roberts enjoyed for Littleborough at Middleton in 1981. Andy was in a hurry. He decided to opt for the aerial route. Nearly every ball he connected with either went high over the ropes or even higher straight up and up into the stratosphere.

'Adam' was the first to sin. He dropped the initial chance, claiming he got a stiff neck waiting for the ball to come down. The second offering bisected Mark and Spencer, neither of whom moved a muscle. They cut their losses and got ready for a re-launch. Unperturbed, Andy hit a few more sixes, swung and missed several times, then clouted a steepler which went up into the clouds five metres from 'Adam' and 25 metres from me. It was probably less, but I don't want to come out of this too badly. Twice shy, 'Adam' belatedly called:

'Yours.'

I misheard. I swear he shouted something very similar, such as:

'It's mine, Jim. Don't worry, leave it to me.'

I did.

The fourth opportunity also did a Big Issue seller and went begging. The ball went so high that it nearly bounced off the police helicopter keeping an eye on 'Brian the Bus.' Ten of us called:

'Keeper's.'

The only one who didn't was the keeper, 'Teflon.' Having 'volunteered,' he had to make an attempt. He spilled it, claiming he'd come unstuck because it slipped out of his gloves due to the ice it now had on it.

We were in danger of rivalling Bertram Mills for the title of best circus in town, particularly since Andy did not stint on his generosity. His fifth gift descended suffering from altitude sickness. I'd decided to run in the wrong direction and blame an imaginary swirling wind. 'Simple' Simon hadn't. He yelled:

'Mine,' upon which a gang of eastern Europeans in the crowd immediately dived for cover.

Somehow, Simon clung on but reverted to type by throwing the ball up in celebration and dropping it as it came down again. No matter. Andy's luck had finally run out but our fallibility did not go unnoticed. One astute spectator was heard to comment:

'I bet they don't spill their beer that easily.'

His mate concurred:

'I bet they don't. Well, not at these prices anyway.'

Even this wasn't the luckiest innings I've witnessed. That honour belongs to 'Rugrat.' 'They' – whoever 'they' are – say there's no such thing as a bad hundred. There is. Despite it being as long ago as 1985, it still crops up intermittently in conversation. Each year, it's made to sound even more dire. We now refer to it as 'doing a Nasser.' It really did bring a new meaning to the term:

'He's edging his way towards a hundred.'

To make things worse, we endured the ordeal through steady drizzle, with 'Rugrat's' partner playing a 'proper' innings at the other end. The name of Dibble certainly didn't get Thornham any free wickets that afternoon.

The one bright spot was that the rain drenched 'Rugrat's' poorly fitting Brillo pad of a hairpiece – hence the nickname. It gave him the look of an ageing Davy Crockett. He didn't even have to look far for the Red Indians because the other batsman was named Savage.

If you play for a long time, you're bound to come across

players who push their luck, or in this case, punch it. In 1981, Heywood had an Aussie overseas amateur called Wayne. If I add that he had a perm, you now have enough information to draw your own conclusions. He wore out more mirrors that 'Vidal.' After every shot he played he would hold the pose, presumably to give the kiss he'd just blown himself enough time to rebound back off the bowler.

Wayne lost any chance of becoming more popular than Robert Mugabe when he put his fist through the hardboard wall, which obviously wasn't very hardboard, in Crompton's changing room. This was his way of showing displeasure at having just been bowled, posing down the wrong line.

He must have made up his mind this was to be his calling card. The next week, at Radcliffe, possibly irked at the lack of photographers, he again went for the right hook after being dismissed. This time, it proved to be harder board. Radcliffe's changing room walls are made of brick. Wayne lost on points and was awarded a broken hand. With a girlfriend named Judy, there are no prizes for working out his nickname.

To round off this section on good and bad fortune, I'll describe the three unluckiest incidents I can remember.

The first was partially down to me. It was the last game of the 1986 season at Thornham. There was little at stake other than my opening partner, 'Blunderbuss' reaching 500 runs for the season, something he'd never done before, even though he'd been playing for longer than Kim Barnett.

He came into the game on 499, so the odds were heavily in his favour. Fate wasn't. Only marginally quicker between the wickets than 'Speedy Gonzales,' he compensated for his slow movement – I've seen milk turn quicker – by backing up excessively. (MA Wahind, from chapter seven, wouldn't have been able to contain himself.)

'Blunderbuss' will never be able to learn the quick step, canoe on rapids or contract athlete's foot, so run outs were always a good bet for the man whose nickname is a consequence of him repeatedly getting on the wrong bus home after post-match over-indulgencies.

Early in our innings, I sliced a ball straight back up the track. 'Bb.' had done what 'Bb.' did. The bowler got the faintest touch on the ball. It kissed the stumps and dislodged the bail, even though I'd put on the heavy ones. Out went 'Bb.' He retired the following year to become a coach, albeit a 'slow' coach, never having reached the magic 500. Sorry mate.

You can't mention bad luck without thinking of 'Party.' If you recall, he was jinxed in his dealings with pacemen. It will, therefore, come as no surprise that he got 'stitched up' by Joel Garner. Ironically, he wasn't hit by the legendary Test bowler. Well, he was, but he was fielding in the slips at the time. Joel was batting. He edged one and 'Party' went for the head high catch. The ball sped through his hands and he got a big bird's eye view of it - five stitches worth. There was enough blood to paddle in.

The poor bloke was just as unfortunate off the field. After having retired from playing, he moved to Blackpool. Four years after the move, he went on holiday to Scotland and paid to go on a 'Mystery tour.' It took him to Blackpool.

My prize for the biggest hard luck tale is reserved for Montague. Montague was a cricketing fanatic. He was at Liverpool University in the early 1980s. His burning ambition was to play for the university, but was 'not the best.' Week after week he was overlooked, yet this did not deter him from coming to watch every home game. Then came the day when there were a number of cry offs and with half an hour before the start, still one place to fill.

Montague got the nod. He was overjoyed but dissatisfied with the state of his kit. There was just enough time to rush into town to update it all. He bought brand new everything. It cost him a packet. Still, it would be worth it. As a reward for his enthusiasm and extravagance, the skipper batted him at six rather than the nine places lower his ability suggested.

Needless to say, he was padded up, ready and waiting, way before numbers four and five were. When his time came, he was out there quicker than the most premature ejaculation. This was it. His dream had come true.

The wicket had fallen on the sixth ball of the over. Perfect. Montague didn't have to face. This provided him with the opportunity to play himself in from the non-striker's end. He could settle himself. He could assess the bowler, the light and the pace and bounce of the pitch. He was nearly 67% of ready, willing and able.

The bowler bowled, as they do. The delivery passed harmlessly through to the keeper, who took it comfortably. Inexplicably, Montague began running. His partner, 'Paul,' frantically sang 'Get back,' followed by other Beatles numbers including 'Help.' It was to prove futile. The world's keenest non-cricketing cricketer was run out, without facing a single ball.

'I feel fine' couldn't have been further from the truth. It was too much for Montague to take. After letting out a cry of anguish, he walked off, wailing as he went. He did leave his mark with the bat before he departed - a great big one, right on a length. He won't have been the first or the last to throw his bat, or even his gloves on the turf. Montague didn't, however, stop there. Off came his brand new sweater, cap and shirt. It could have become the 'Full Monty' but for the restraining order (southern for full Nelson) put on him by the captain.

Montague was far too distraught to take the field after tea. Sadly, his career was over before it had started. No one saw him anywhere near the cricket ground again. Anybody want some slightly old-fashioned but unused kit? Contact Liverpool University Student's Union on 01 …

For those of more tender years who aspire to obtaining evergreen status, a healthy diet is inconsequential. Follow the example of Jacques Kallis. I'm sure that if he was in a market and was asked if he needed any fruit or veg., he'd answer in the negative by way of:

'No. I've got plenty of potatoes for chips, thanks.'

The only stretching Jacques reputedly does is for a pint. Although walking fast uses up eight times as many calories as writing a letter, there is no need to walk fast. Write eight letters instead of one. Jogging is only required when last orders are called.

If, on the other hand, you don't want to self-combust, you may want to watch what you eat and drink. Otherwise, you might miss your mouth. 'Treacle,' now, paradoxically, fast approaching the stalwart stage, always has gammon and chips, as well as a sticky pudding, before a game. It doesn't slow him down. If it did, he'd be running backwards. 'Andre Previn' bowled speedily for years, fuelled principally by swiss roll and plane crisps. (They're the quickest.) 'Lloyd' (see chapter eleven) kept going until he was 45 on liquid breakfasts and lunches, while a dentureless old Tom performed admirably on soup, scrambled eggs and jelly until he set fire to himself.

Be advised that there is no need to go anywhere near a salad during the week. As my father-in-law maintains:

'Cucumber is poison.'

And look what pasta does. It makes you short, fat and hysterical. Fruit and fibre give you the wrong sort of runs, muesli is only of use as sawdust and vegetables are for vegetarians. Sir Donald loved a steak, Mike Gatting has yet to find an unappealling pie and Ian Botham didn't get that hefty on quorn burgers. There's more protein in insects than in beetroot, so sprinkle some ants on your bacon buttie / sandwich and munch away.

Being green has nothing to do with basil or cabbage. It's about conserving energy. Never sprint unless you're being chased. Get a runner whenever you can if you're batting on a hot day. Never mind the chaos that can bring. You can't be seen to be gasping for breath. An ugly person might run on and give you the kiss of life. Worse still, you might be offered a 'health drink' to resuscitate you. You can now call for a three and not risk a collapsed lung as it won't be you who is running 66 yards.

Longevity depends on being prepared. You don't need enough degrees to make up your own pop group or have an IQ twice the size of Bradman's batting average, as Mike Brearley has. Should some insensitive sod call into question your poor run of form, reinforce the thoughts of that famous person named after a county. It was either Devon Malcolm, David Essex, Clark Kent, Lester Piggott, the Duke of Gloucester, Bertie Wooster, Somerset Maugham, Susan Hampshire, Bucks Fizz or the Avon Lady who said:

'Only a mediocre person is always at his best.'

That should shut him up. With a little imagination, even a score as low as six can be made to sound impressive. I expect Surrey's Graham Clinton was proud of the half-dozen he made for his county when they were dismissed for 14 against Essex in 1983. I must say, however, that I'm glad I wasn't there to witness it. If 'Clint the Splint' batted in the same vein as he used to for London Schools, it probably took him all day.

If I had to pass on one piece of advice to any cricketer, aside from don't play in plimsoles, it would be don't pack up too soon. You're retired for a long time. Even when the time comes that you are so enfeebled with age and infirmity that you feel the need to call it a day, it doesn't have to be the end. Make it known that you would be willing to turn out any time the club is desperately short. This might get you as many as a dozen games a season. You simply have to get full wear out of your newest piece of equipment.

You start off as a youngster with delusions of grandeur:

'Herbert Sutcliffe scored over 50,000 runs and Bill Ponsford amassed 903 runs in just five innings in 1926, so why can't I?' (Because they had talent.) Arthur Mailey once took 4 for 362. I could do that. Patsy Hendren began and ended his Middlesex career with ducks. I could certainly do that. Australian Warwick Armstrong weighed 22 stone by the time he finished playing. No problem.

You end up grateful for a phone call five minutes before the start on a freezing cold day, asking you to make up the numbers and bat at 11 without the chance of a bowl. You don't hesitate. It's still better than trolling around C and P or B and Q, whatever it's called.

As I become ever more decrepit, all I now hope is that my final game will contain an incident as hilarious as one in my first. It was 1958. We, St. Mary's Primary School, were playing (one pad each) St. Paul's. We only needed St. Peter's to turn up and we'd have had an American folk trio. They didn't, so there was no music. There was, however, a 'what happened next?'

Minus Leslie Baines, we plundered our way to 16 all out, with nine players registering ducks. Although mildly disappointed, we took heart that this was one more than Hampshire accumulated against Warwickshire in 1922. The fact that they went on to scrape their way to 521 in the second innings, winning by 155 was irrelevant. Ours was a one innings match.

We took the field confident that all was not lost. We had a demon bowler of our own in 'Lobster' (a shellfish child but speedy for a 10 year old, despite the wingnut ears which hindered his run up). Two balls changed everything. Both went over our wicket keeper, Malcolm Bryning for four byes apiece.

With the target halved within 30 seconds, our teacher, manager, coach, fitness trainer, physio/sports psychologist, Mr. Glassup (cheers!) sensed defeat. It might have all been over after five balls if he hadn't put his finger on the problem:

'Malcolm. For goodness sake, think about it. Use your head, boy.'

This confused me. As far as I knew, we didn't have a school captain to utilise. It didn't confuse Malcolm. When the next ball came through, he did as he was told. He headed it. He really did. In the post-match postmortem, and it could have been if he hadn't had such a hard head, all became clear. When quizzed by Sir, Malcolm revealed why he stopped the ball in such an unorthodoxly effective fashion:

'You told me to, Sir.'

Despite this being years before you could claim a small fortune by blaming someone else for your own clumsiness, Mr. Glassup sought to clear his good name: (It is a good name, don't you think?)

'If I told you to run head first as fast as you can into that piano, what would you do?'

Ask a silly question…Believing action to speak louder than words, Malcolm went for it. The world record for demolishing a piano is 97 seconds. This would have been broken but for a last ditch rugby tackle from the piano-loving Mr Glassup which saved both Malcolm and the instrument from needing to be retuned. Thereafter, no more fixtures were arranged and Malcolm was head-hunted by Middlesex as a potential successor to John Murray.

Little did I know then, that, as Mr. Glassup approaches his 130th birthday, I'd still be as excited as a five year old on Christmas Eve every match day. We may think we're over the hill but, take WG (please). He was on the field for every ball of Gloucester's three day game against Kent in 1895, aged 47. He was unable to move for months afterwards but he did it.

More impressively, Charles Absolom, a club cricketer from London, bagged 100 wickets in a season at the age of 80. Imagine that. 100 people had to confess that someone much older than Cliff Richard got them out. Charles answered to the pet name of 'Fido' and often got:

'There's life in the old dog yet.'

In 2006, I had the pleasure of playing in the same Lancashire over 50s side as the 72 year old OPENING bowler, Cec Wright. Cec bowled his nine overs for a mere 18 runs and is so trim that I've seen more meat on half a rasher of streaky bacon.

Even if I'm fortunate enough to play for another 20 years, I'm aware that we never stop learning. A little knowledge is a dangerous thing, as, I believe, 'Dopey' warned George W. I've managed to build up a stockpile of cricketing misconceptions throughout my life. The first of these occurred during my early teens when I virtually lived at Lords. I thought I'd noticed a correlation between wearing caps and going bald.

Colin Cowdrey, John Murray, Maurice Hallam, Geoff Boycott, Raman Subba Row, Cyril Poole, Martin Horton and Max ('Olga' of the Old Quintinians) were, I'd decided, thin on top because they wore their cricket caps all the time they were on the field. It undoubtedly stunted the growth of their barnets. (Southern for struggling football team.) Only several years later did it dawn on me that I'd got it totally the wrong way round. They wore caps because they were bald.

Latterly, like most cricket fans, up to our 2005 Ashes triumph, I was convinced that the Aussies ruled. Fortunately, there is one area of the game where they lag miles behind us and probably always will. England are the undisputed top dogs of the cricket world when it comes to ... the Smiths. Casting aside the morose pop group, we've had 14 represent our country. Australia are stuttering way behind with a paltry two. They are even lower in the league table than South Africa, West Indies and New Zealand. In fact, they're only two ahead of Bangladesh.

I was also convinced that it was only me who was so insecure about being dropped when you become too old to cut your own toenails. Wrong again. The great Wilfred Rhodes must have been of the same persuasion. Why else would he not miss a game for 32 years? Wilfred clocked up a staggering 762 consecutive appearances between 1898 and 1930. After that, I expect that's how he ended up...staggering. Similarly, fellow Yorky, Jimmy Binks did not miss a single county game between making his debut in 1955 and his retirement in 1969. This was not because he was injury-free but more that, as a Tyke, he was too tight to lend his wicket-keeping gloves to his understudy.

Some of my misconceptions are more understandable. Most connoisseurs would follow me in putting Michael Atherton at number one and Bishan Bedi at number 11 if they turned out for Woodhouses together and I'm sure I'm not the only one who believed that India's CG Borde came very close to qualifying to play for Pakistan. If I now let it be known that both Mike and Bish each managed to register 20 Test ducks, maybe a re-think is required.

What's more, my allusion to Dunlop Green Flash footwear being inconsequential when up against such madmen as AJ Suffling, 'Smithy,' 'Sonny' Liston and the like does make them sound naff. I was certain they were until I was persuaded they are, in fact, the height of fashion nowadays. I spotted my son's girlfriend wearing a pair in July 2007. I was tempted to tread on her foot to ascertain how much protection they now offered but refrained in case she responded by kicking me in the nuts with one.

Then there's Chris Gayle. Why wouldn't any of us associate him and Durham's Gareth Breese with the Windward Islands? After all, my gullibility, if you cast your mind back, did permit Steve Orrell to run me out in 1987, 1988 and 1989. I was duped into thinking that he is a nice man. I should have heeded my dad's warning about people named after small towns in the north-west. As long ago as 1954, he advised me not to play with Billy Burnley, Stanley Accrington or Charlie Chorley because it would all end in tears. And he most certainly wouldn't let me listen to George Formby, Bing Crosby, Jimmy Clitheroe or Tony Blackburn on the radio. You know best, Dad.

What about Geoff Boycott? I'd never doubted that he is a heterosexual average basher. Half of that assessment is borne out by the fact that he contrived, as an opener, to be not out as many as 23 times in 193 Test innings. Compare that to Graham Gooch's six in 215 innings or the brilliant middle order batsman (where you'd think red inkers are easier to come by) Seymour Nurse's tally of one in 54. Imagine my surprise, therefore, to hear Geoff utter these immortal words at the aptly termed 'climax' of the third Ashes Test at Old Trafford in August 2005. As England pushed desperately to claim the final Australian wicket, Tony Greig's pal confessed to the nation:

'I must say, I fancy Flintoff, I really do.'

It's not just me. I'll wager that when Worcester's T.Straw was given out obstructing the field against Warwickshire in 1899, he felt this would be the only time that would happen to him. Dozy bugger! Two years later the same fate befell him against the same opposition. I bet that really broke the camel's back.

I'm also not the only one confused by collections. In the south, you don't, or didn't, get them. In the north you do on some grounds, but not on others. At Rochdale, it's possible to get one for one less than 50. (Talk about elephants never forgetting, an ex-Rochdale player, 'Pantomime,' so called because he thinks the bloke with the magic lamp is 'Anadin,' reminded me of this fully 26 years after the event.)

The wife of Thornham's President, Roy Lomas, whom I'll call plain Mrs. as I don't know her Christian name, was equally misguided 50 plus years ago. She and Roy had gone to a Test Match at Headingley. When Denis Compton reached his 50 (probably with a sweep), Mrs. turned to Roy and asked him for some change. Thinking it was probably for the chocolate machine, hubbie, generous to a fault, blew the dust off two sixpenny pieces without any semblance of a struggle. He asked her to get him a bar too, only to be corrected:

'No silly. I don't want any fruit and nut. It's for Compton's collection so he can buy the boys a drink afterwards.'

Others' misinterpretation regarding my screwed-up accent is, as I've confessed, commonplace, which aptly describes where I used to live. I started out with a south-eastern twang similar to ex-Middlesex man, Keith Dutch. Then, due to northern influences, my golden tones became mistaken for fellow countrymen of Aussie leg spinner Bob Holland. This combination has deluded many. Put the two together and it becomes a little clearer why people can't understand me. They think I'm speaking double Dutch.

Sometimes we are misled into believing things will be fine but it turns out to be a mistaken belief. My home groundsmen have frequently told me that the pitch they'd prepared was full of runs... I also genuinely heard a disgruntled senior citizen complain about his treatment in the Manchester Eye Hospital with these ever so apt words:

'It's like the blind leading the blind here.'

Returning to the statement I made earlier, a little (medical) knowledge is a dangerous thing. At Thornham in 2004, the appropriately named Jim Burke and I both tried to give the impression we were going for a high catch. The ever-helpful Ben (undoubtedly short for Benevolent) called:

'Jim's.'

This proved as much help as 'Treacle's' Driver Improvement Scheme. In keeping with this, we collided. We both bit the dust. My specs and I parted company. I got up and put them back on. I was immediately overcome by a head spinning, can't focus sensation:

'Shit, I've got concussion,' I concluded.

On the point of seeking medical attention (southern for sympathy) from the female contingent to my right, I was brought back down to earth for the second time in a minute by 'Kestrel.' (He's not eagle-eyed. He simply drinks cheap lager or 'larger' as it was advertised outside our local. Over-sized pint pots?)

'Your specs are knackered, Jim,' he informed me, bringing to bear all his experience as an optician's receptionist.

No wonder I felt as if I'd drunk three pints of 'pain.' They were as bent as Quentin Crisp and were almost triangular, making it per rather than con–cussion.

Age has also enabled me to differentiate between theory and practice. No player under 21 at Thornham takes a shower nowadays. Theoretically, this is because, like Louis XIV, each one has a petrifying fear of water, ie rabies. In practice, they have all clocked the 3rdXI captain who is named after the multi-purpose cutter, 'the Ultimate Chopper.' They must feel unable to compete. Or it could be that under-arm deodorant is no longer considered iffy.

Just as one would expect an admiral to be a good sailor, one would also assume that if you were a much better wicket-keeper and batsman than your geriatric rival, you'd get the nod. Not so. Nelson suffered from sea-sickness and Chris Read got Nixoned.

I now realise that theory and practice can be one of the same thing. During an Old Qs game, a huge black cloud decided not to leave us out. Our ever-smiling geography teacher, 'Happy Valley,' calculated:

'It might rain soon,' reassuring us that all those years of study hadn't been wasted.

Similarly, Charles Colvile covered both posts in July 2006 with:

'I've got it all wrong,' when he got in a muddle over the 20/20 qualifiers, failing only to add 'yet again.'

I, too, got it wrong when I heard a Bangladeshi commentator say:

'There's nothing in the wee.'

I assumed he was referring to a negative drugs test whereas he was actually pointing out that Ashraful's wagon wheel showed his preference for shots square of the wicket.

Stretching the same point somewhat, 'Rentokill,' a registered child minder, related his latest bowling stint to the barmaid, who was on duty and so couldn't walk off, in these contrived terms:

'I had 0 for 35 from five overs but that included three sixes. If you exclude those, I had 0 for 17, which isn't bad.'

By the same token, if you take out each of the six sixes Garfield Sobers smashed off Malcolm Nash at Swansea many moons ago, it's a maiden. Malcolm, incidentally, is carrying on the good work. He is developing the game in the United States.

As I get older, I am comforted that old batsmen never die. We just lose our grip. Old bowlers, on the other hand, lose their appeal. Still, at least I'm not as old as Joan Collins. She's even older than Donald Duck. What's more, unlike Irlam's 'Rowdy' Yates, I don't quite go back as far as playing in top hats, bow ties and braces. 'Pagey' says it made him bowl like a clown. His excuse these days is poor eyesight.

I can, though, readily recall playing in a drip-dry white shirt which I also wore for school. This was subtly set off by a thick woollen jumper, lovingly hand-knitted by my dear mother. It was big and loose enough to fit Warwick Armstrong twice over. Back then, brand names were limited to such dainty items as carbolic soap, hair remover for womens' legs and a disgusting chocolate bar designed to cure constipation. But what's in a name?

Food for thought:

33. After Gloucester's Sid Kitcat bowled a poor over, was he told to have a break?

34. Could Yorkshire's A.Dolphin bowl a flipper?

35. Did Gloucester's Tom Pugh ever have a stinker?

36. Was Aussie William Woof related to Essex's Gordon Barker?

Chapter 10

WHAT'S IN A NAME?

As well as differing attitudes to winning cricket matches, northerners and southerners can have different interpretations on names. Nob End is an insult in the Home Counties. In Bolton, it's a cricket team near Darcy Lever. In Yorkshire, Nicky Boje is a tailer-ender who can bowl a bit. Down in Northampton, he's a star number four batsman.

For Londoners, Nelson conjures up a picture of an admiral or the number 111. Say the name to a Lancastrian and he is liable to relate it to anyone with their own sizeable column or a small town as welcoming as anthrax. Nevertheless, this chapter is designed to bring the north and south closer together by having some fun with cricketing names.

My own puerile sense of humour was aroused while waiting to get stitched up after a mis-timed hook at Woodhouses. A Chinese man stood up in the hospital waiting room to acknowledge the nurse call out:

'Sik Wun?'

David Lloyd seems to be of the same persuasion. I was full of admiration for his observation in 2006 about the Sri Lankan bowler:

'Maharoof's on fire,' was a winner.

David did, however, miss out in the series against Pakistan. He could have said Gul was flying round the boundary, although this would have worked better had his initial been C. rather than U. I wonder what Lloydy makes of Surrey's TC O'Brien. I expect he thinks he was TC O'Brien. Not necessarily. In the 1890s, O'Brien also called himself JE Johnston. Was it so that he could bowl simultaneouslyfrom both ends?

In the same vein, throughout this book I have illustrated my obsession via the 'food for thought' sections and my predilection for nicknames. Even cricketers as charismatic as Danny Baker or Gyles Brandreth, who can't measure up as 'characters,' don't escape.

'Rob' is a negligible cricketer. He is as talented as Peter Brough. For the non-senior citizens amongst you, Peter was, nominally, a ventriloquist. He had a dummy named Archie Andrews. To be a successful performer it's taken as read that you have a dummy and can speak without moving your lips. Peter had, or maybe was, the dummy but his lips wouldn't cooperate. What did he do? He became a ventriloquist on the radio. Why not call road sweepers neighbourhood environmental action team officers or Tim Ambrose a Test-class number six?

Being equally gifted, 'Rob' made his name at Evershed, not as the mediocre stumper that he was, but by pinching other players' kit. He wasn't proud. Anything he found lying around after a game became 'finders keepers.' Even out-of-date chocolate was acceptable, particularly if it had a coconut filling; 'Rob' was a bounty hunter. He had a more discerning rival. 'Nick' wouldn't touch anything sweaty and left empty-handed on most occasions. This caused him to take a season out to go on a 'Gap Year,' during which he worked in a clothing chain store for 12 months.

'Jimmy Saville' is an obvious choice for Lidget Green's left armer D.Jay, especially as he set a Bradford League record after moving to Manningham Mills. He conceded the most runs in a single over, more than my aggregate for the whole season. However many it was, it made the batsman say:

'How's about that, then?'

Less evident is 'Model,' or 'Gucci,' for Rick of Denton. Rick is a whole-hearted all-rounder, in every sense. During our game in 2004, his team-mate Terry ('Chocolate Orange'), called him 'Model,' and later 'Gucci.' I thought the former might be due to his penchant for making Airfix kits. Perhaps he also bought fancy clothes or helped Napoleon design the Italian flag.

I was like the exit... way out:

'He's an ugly boy, isn't he?' explained Terry, who has only a passing resemblance to Dawn French.

I showed my appreciation by getting out next ball. As I passed Terry, I commented that Rick was 'doing a Darren Gough' and pulling funny faces as he ran up to bowl. Terry put me straight:

'No. It's the only one he's got.'

'Psycho' played at Leeds Carnegie. His nickname isn't due to a demented style of batting. In fact, he was more like Trevor Bailey (whose three most notable Test innings saw him plod his way to an aggregate of 102 runs in nearly 14 hours) than Chris Cairns (87 sixes in 62 tests). 'Psycho' owes his sobriquet to the Hitchcock thriller of the same name.

Along with three other members of the college 2ndXI, 'Pixie,' 'Dixie' and 'Trixie' (one was named Dixon. The rest merely fell into place, like 'Rugrat's toupee), Pete, as he was known until now, was engrossed in the film at their digs. He must have shown signs of weakness because shortly before the climax, 'Pixie' left the room, ostensibly to sand down his bat.

Once the film ended, Pete sheepishly made his way to his room, having decided not to take a shower. No sooner had he settled down in bed with the light off than 'Pixie' jumped out of the wardrobe (he only jumped off the top of it on Saturday nights) and gave off a blood-curdling shriek. Pete screamed even louder, leapt out of bed, ran downstairs, switched the light on and stayed put on the sofa all night. Hence, 'Psycho.'

Some names are too long, like Nigel Llong and Colin Ingleby-Mackenzie. As my ex-maths teacher decreed:

'One surname's enough for anyone.'

Some names are too short, e.g. Charl Langeveldt. How can you expect the poor sod to bowl properly with only half a name? No wonder, when he was pro for Colne, near Nelson and almost a column, in the Lancashire League in 2002, that they only finished mid-table.

Some names give you the wrong impression. When I was with the Old Qs, I could never understand why John Clouting couldn't hit the ball off the square. I did, however, work out why Ted McDonald continually farmed the bowling. As for Stewart Opelberry Sweeney, he was, naturally, always in need of assistance and was born on May Day.

Moving up several notches, neither Surrey's Alec Bedser nor Jack Crapp of Nottinghamshire actually played for the Old Qs. Nevertheless, this did not prevent them from going on an England overseas tour together in the 1950s. As they checked into the hotel, the receptionist, a netball fan, seemingly got the stars muddled up. (As a muddler myself, I can sympathise. Last Christmas I bought my wife some saucy underwear. It was designed to make her laugh but when she saw it she cringed. I'd got Ann Summers and Shelley Winters muddled up.) As for the receptionist, addressing Jack, she enquired:

'Bed, sir?' only to be corrected:

'No. Crapp.'

'Second door on the right, sir.'

It might not have been that different if Jack had booked in alongside another Surrey bowler, Peter Loader. In reply to the request for their names, she could have heard:

'Loader, Crapp,' leaving her to request:

'Give it a chance before you condemn it, gentlemen.'

Being a cricket fanatic, if I'm not playing, I love to watch. I've been fortunate enough to have lived near Lords, Headingley and Old Trafford. During intervals, I make lists. These are drawn from both professional and amateur circles. They include such thought-provoking categories as 'dual-internationals,' e.g. anyone who might represent their country at both cricket and ice-skating. There could be more contenders than you think since cricket on ice has been played in England since 1838. That said, Robin Cousins did come closer to selection than the 18 stone Colin Milburn.

During breaks in play, throughout staff meetings at school or whenever I'm dragged out to look at furniture etc., I mentally update my Father and Son XI. If only Don Bradman had a cricketing son of any standing. Age wouldn't be a problem here. In around 1990, Don was asked how many runs he thought he'd average if he was playing in a Test series against the current England XI. He modestly estimated:

'Oh, about 70, I suppose.'

An astonished reporter came back with:

'Is that all?'

A smiling knight replied:

'I am 82 years old, you know.'

Since, unlike a few of the '3rd' XI's in the North Manchester league, I'm not including ringers, Bradman's place goes to the

Butchers, not the one who gave David Steele all that meat for getting double figures against the Windies, but Mark and Alan. This is on the strength of Alan's bowling performance for Surrey Young Cricketers against London Schools in about 1968 (even though he looked 35). He took seven for and then saw Surrey home in spite of the efforts of John Emburey, who turned it square, rectangularly and trapeziumly.

If I include Jeff and Simon Jones, will they form a choir with Tony Lewis and his dad, Jerry Lee? Finally, can I justify including my son, James and I on the strength of a slutchy 50 run partnership against Rochdale 3rds in September 2005. Most of the runs were scored off an incredibly slow off-spinner who would have struggled to keep New Zealand's Geoff Allot quiet when he smashed 0 in 101 minutes against South Africa in 1998.

An Over-rated XI can take hours to select. It can also be as contentious as my campaign to have the lbw law altered so that right-handed batsmen over the age of 55 can never be given out thus.

It goes without saying that WG Grace had plenty of highs, (including 400 for an All-England XI against XXII of Grimsby!) but can someone with a batting average of 39 (32 in Tests) be that special? After all, my mates Walshy (north) and Juster(y) (south) consistently averaged higher than that for Thornham and Evershed and neither one had any gates at Lords named after them.

Then there's Sir Learie Constantine. He averaged under 20 in Tests and was hailed a great all-rounder. His figures pale into insignificance compared to Middleton's Roger Clarkson and Evershed's Roger Cook, but I don't see Liz rushing to do any rogering and tap them on both shoulders with a sword.

It's as much a mystery to me that Liam Plunkett became an

England player as it is that the Welsh football team, Caersws is pronounced 'Karessooss.' Likewise, I consider Vince Wells's selection as surprising as a driving school offering crash courses.

I've got more chance of understanding Duckworth-Lewis than of comprehending how Mark Lathwell ever played for his country or why Thornham's Paul Duckworth preferred to be called 'Ducky' rather than Paul. There again, there's hope for us all. If Sven can somehow manage to bed a bevy of beauties and Ian Blackwell was seen as our answer to Darren Lehmann, anything is possible.

. You've got to hand it to Sven, though. He really set things off with that Faria Alam and, as they say, there's no smoke without Faria.

Alternatively, it grieves me that some players who merit being household names, not, in this case Barry or Merv Kitchen, Matt or Tony Windows or Joe Dawes, aren't as famous as they deserve to be. In an attempt to redress this, I proudly announce my team of unsung heroes who'd compete well on northern puddings or southern shirt fronts:

1. Clarrie Grimmett, the Australian leg spinner. He wasn't selected for a Test until he was 34 yet still picked up 216 wickets at 24 in only 37 Tests. Perhaps he sounded too much like a bottle of wine. He'd still (or sparkling) have got a game for the Old Qs every week.

2. Martin Donnelly of New Zealand only played in seven Tests during his short career, averaging 52. He scored 206 against England and was regarded as the best left-hander of his time. Even Bruce Edgar's 'mate' at Thornham would have approved.

3. George Lohmann of Surrey was a medium pacer who took

1805 wickets at 13. In 18 Tests he got 112 victims at just 10.7. With such talent Thornham would give him at least a fiver a game.

4. Dudley Nourse, of South Africa, averaged 54 in his 34 Tests. He hit 208 with a broken thumb (and a bat) off England in 1951. That's an excuse 'Popeye' would have been proud of.

5. Kent's 'Tich' Freeman bagged more wickets than anyone except Wilfred Rhodes. He took 3776 at 18 apiece with his leggers. This earned him only 12 Tests and 66 wickets at 25. It smacks of sizeism to me. 'Pee-Wee' suffered similar bias.

6. Joe Hardstaff Jnr. of Notts. might have played more than 23 Tests but for World War Two. He averaged 46 and was far too talented to be unheard of by most of the world's population, just like Mo Wickens.

7. Charles Kortright (which is more than Malcolm Bryning of St Mary's ever did) of Essex was considered to be the 'fastest bowler that ever lived,' a hundred years ago. How would 'Party' have dealt with him?

8. Philip Mead of Hampshire made 153 first class centuries, averaging 49 in his ridiculously low total of 17 Tests. He did tour Australia twice within 17 years. Just how slow was the 'Queen Mary'? Only marginally up on 'Treacle?'

9. William Clarke, 'the one-eyed wonder,' of Notts. from 1835-1855 was the founder and captain of the all-England side from 1846-1856. He died, having taken a wicket with the last ball he bowled, when he was 58. Definitely a bit of a character, his team talks went:

'I have summed them up and they are worth bugger all,' making him ideal for the Bradford League.

10. Was Surrey's Bobby Abel? 'Pagey' says he was. Aged 41, he carried his bat for 357 in 1898 and scored 247 when he was 44. Abel must have been 'knocking on the door' of the Test XI even at that age and would have enjoyed batting at Boston Manor.

11. Ernest Tyldesley of Lancashire put behind him an unlucky start to his Test career. He was bowled off his cheekbone, knocked out and then left out. (Pole-axed and axed in one go.) He came back to average 55 in 14 Tests but has anyone apart from 'Migraine' ever heard of him?

My 12th man is Spencer Chorlton of Yoxford (Suffolk). In 2002 this man proved that Sobers has got nothing on him. Forget six sixes in an over. Spencer had no trouble in emulating the great Sir Garfield and then went one better by also hitting a no ball over the ropes, too.

I know we can do whatever we want with figures – just look at Cher and our MP's, who claimed no less than £87 million for 'expenses' in 2006 – but why are people like the Hamiltons and George Gallopaway more famous than these talented individuals? As Aussie, J.Wiener probably says (assuming he lives up to his name):

'It's not fair.'

On an only slightly more mundane level, I have to admit to regularly weighing up who should be in my Fat XI, skippered by Warwick Armstrong. My Ugly XI is not a pretty sight and my Prats XI is apt to change as often as the Pakistani national side changes its coach. The ultimate accolade is to make it into all three teams simultaneously. 'Model' of Denton isn't a prat so he only makes it into two and there aren't many cricketing overweight, ugly tossers other than 'Ribena Man.' Most of those who fit all three categories are too busy appearing on 'Wife Swap' and 'Big Brother.'

For the record, my current 'Prats XI' of amateurs is composed of these little gems, six northern, five southern.

1. The old bugger who would never run a three unless it was for himself.

2. The captain who reduced a youngster making his debut to tears by telling him:

'You'll never make a player as long as I've got a hole in my arse.'

3. 'Captain Marvel.' When questioned as to why he refused an easy single off the sixth ball when he was on nought and his partner was racing away on 60, replied:

'If I had, you'd be facing now and I wouldn't.'

4. Yet another 'leader.' This one strained his side while bowling. It prevented him from having his customary 25 overs so he instructed the specialist wicket keeper to hand over the gloves and go to first slip so that he – 'Captain Fantastic' - could 'still be fully involved in the game.'

5. The 'multi-talented' all-rounder who never lifts a finger – he'd make a great umpire – before a game. It interrupts his mental preparation. He can't help out afterwards either. He's too mentally exhausted. Mental arsehole.

6. The captain of an under 18 XI who refused to declare

during a 20 over game against a team of 13 and 14 year olds. He got a double hundred as his side made over 300. The opposition scraped to 60 for 8 before it rained. Two points each. Ha!

7. 'Rip Van Winkle,' the captain who declared prematurely when I was 96 not out at Slough in 1969. He said he'd had no idea how many I had, despite a bloody huge scorebox. Did Michael Atherton spin a similar yarn when he let Graeme Hick get to 98 at Sydney in 1995 before pulling the plug?

8. Steve Orrell, of Prestwich. Steve's the sod who ran me out three years in succession. Of course I bear grudges.

9. Denton's Mike Batty. Not for inventing the Wombles, but for only ever bowling me one full toss in 20 seasons of combat. Predictably, I failed to cash in and Mike cheered me up by telling me I wouldn't be getting another. I might, but I'll be older than Raja Singh from chapter nine when he finished playing for Bombay.

10. 'Woody' of Dukinfield for a truly outrageous lbw appeal – upheld, naturally – in 2004. He justified it by telling me that he 'had to.' He needed one more wicket to qualify for the averages. Being from Lancashire, he did buy me a pint afterwards. Being from London, I did pour it over his head.

11. The team-mate who lovingly smeared my box with Fiery Jack the week after I'd had a vasectomy. I can think of better ways of putting the heat back into your love life.

Names can be misleading. I'm told that scorer Jo King isn't funny, while sister, Vi, hasn't got horns growing out of her head. As for places, I bought some batting gloves in Ripon. Ripoff, more like. I also played a game in Settle but really wasn't comfortable. As for Redcar, most people there seemed to be driving blue ones. Bearing all this in mind, don't read too much into this team of professionals to be steered clear of at all costs wherever you are, north or south. NB: Not a Burke or a Pratt in sight.

A.Dick (New Zealand)
E.Nutter (Lancashire)
J.Ricketts (Kent)
A.Din (Warwickshire)
A.Wellard (Somerset)
A.Mold (Lancashire)
E.Bastard (Somerset)
D.Steyn (South Africa)
M.Burden (Hampshire)
A.Payne (Northants)
M.Bore (Yorkshire)
12th man: R.Daft (Notts.)

Daft couldn't quite break into the side. He let himself down by not living up to his name. As the pioneer of protective headgear, Mr. not so Daft wrapped towels around his noggin to bat in a county game in 1870. ('Gilly' would have still pinned him, though.)

David Graveney squeezes into my hefty squad but isn't as daft as some of his selections made him appear. This southerner must have inherited some Geordie common sense when playing for Durham in the 1990s. During Brian Lara's epic 501 out of 810 for 4, chunky Dave contrived to bowl only 7 overs (0 for 34). Compare that to Messrs. Cox, Brown and Bainbridge (0 for 163, 1 for 164 and 1 for 169) and you have to concede that he got it right, for once.

Food for thought:

37. Has Somerset's Keith Parsons kept his nose clean?

38. How good a player was Indian Palwankar Baloo?

39. Did the Rennie brothers provide any relief for Zimbabwe?

40. Was Hampshire's Cardigan Connor happy bowling in a sweater?

Chapter 11

BEST AND WORST

As a self-appointed pundit, here are my Oscars (Old Sod's Cricket Awards, Rochdale to Southend). I'll begin with grounds, possibly for both divorce and cricket. Being ancient, I can list over 300 that I've tried to play on. This number has necessarily been restricted by coming north to compete in the leagues where fixtures vary little each season. In the south, of the 200 plus grounds, the best playing surface was Elliot's, Blackheath. The strip was like glass. Anybody who could breathe unaided could score runs with a stick of rhubarb on it. No bowler, including good wrist spinners, could get the ball to grip. Even Sydney Barnes, hailed as the greatest bowler in all cricket history by the esteemed writer HS Altham, would have struggled to perform on that. Syd combined a Test career spanning 12 years (189 wickets at 16 apiece) with a 39 year career in league cricket. This included spells in the Bradford and Central Lancashire Leagues. As a club cricketer, he took 3741 wickets at a ludicrous cost of 6.6 each. Nevertheless, if he'd been condemned to bowl at Blackheath every other game he'd be no more famous than 'Mucker' Barnes from chapter two and would have fared little better than resident leg spinner, 'Glossy' Pamphlett. (We could all read him like a book.)

The worst southern wicket I ever trod in was Gilteck's in Surrey. The track was like the proverbial minefield. If the ball hit the seam, it struck coal or oil. You needed a tennis racquet rather than a cricket bat. Kent's William Fairservice might have managed. He was an ace batsman, I believe. Nobody from Evershed or Gilteck could cope. I think we won about 5-3. Even the outfield was treacherous. Mowers were first utilised on grounds in the 1850s. Judging by the state of Gilteck's surface, they employed the original cutter. (Man and machine.)

Moving north, the best facilities are undoubtedly Northern's in Cheshire, unless it's recently been moved. It's palatial. They could give it stately home status and charge for guided tours. A cousin of mine used to be a member. When we played there I enquired as to his whereabouts. He must have committed a serious misdemeanour because I was told:

'He's been dismembered.'

The strip at Northern is excellent too, but not quite as true as Newton Heath's in their Lancashire and Cheshire League days. It was like Sally Gunnell as a teenager – flat, white and even-paced. I get a lazy lob on just reminiscing about it (the strip, not Sally). Their groundsman always greeted us with these heavenly words:

'I've prepared a good 'un for you today.'

As reasonably as I did there, I could hardly claim to have been as successful as the Don was at Headingley – 914 runs in 4 innings.

'Beat that,' as Fanny Craddock said to Johnny after throwing him either a whip or a whisk, depending on her mood.

Back to Newton Heath (but mind your wallet). Even when it was wet, the strip had one up on Mr.Dyer. It could be trusted. The less-than-honest Aussie stumper allowed an edge to go to ground against the Kiwis in 1987. My physics teacher wasn't standing at slip to question him, so he scooped the ball back into his gloves and got his man. Anyway, we were due to play an inter-league fixture against the North Lancashire League in 1986 or 7, or even 8. (As I confessed earlier, I'm dateless.) A heavy downpour rendered the wicket unplayable. The groundsman promptly cut a new strip. With only 10 minutes rolling, it played infinitely better than Gilteck's.

What's more, it made for a cracking game. North Lancs. needed two to win off the final over from Graham Howard of Denton St. Lawrence. Not even Hansie Cronje would have put money on us. The six balls went like this. Swing and miss. Swing and miss, followed by a quiet word between the batsmen. Push and run...run out. Push and run...run out, followed by more frantic words. Swing and bowled, followed by prayers. Push and run...run out. Six balls, four wickets, no runs. We won by one run. Graham had been so tight he could have doubled as a duck's backside, not the first time the likeness has been made.

I need look no further than Bollington for my least favourite northern surface. I was as effective as a sniffer dog with catarrh there. My first innings was like Stuart Law's Test career – short-lived. Thornham cruised to 320 for 5. I scooped a full toss to mid-on in the first over. Out for nought. Determined to compensate, a year later I fell to a cunning long-hop. Gone for zip. The next season, I spooned a half-volley gently back to the bowler. Dispatched for a blob. Three innings no runs. They were subsequently relegated to the second division of the Lancashire and Cheshire League to save me further embarrassment.

Now for fielders. 'Lucky' was an RAF man (Really Awful Fielder) and was also awarded the CBE. (Can't Bat Either.) The only thing lucky about him was that he played for the Old

Quintinians. This meant his ineptitude went almost unnoticed. I'm convinced his dire displays were because he was scared of the ball. There were other little details. He was as agile as James Ormond, only marginally more interested in cricket than my wife and so nervous that he once copied William Hamilton's howler from the 1882 varsity match by running the wrong way when going for a single.

Being proud, 'Lucky' stood up for himself, ie without a zimmer frame. He vigorously maintained that if it wasn't for bad luck, he'd have no luck at all. In his opinion, he would have been able to drown in the Dead Sea.

We were lumbered with a fielder who had more characteristics of Zandra, rather than Jonty Rhodes. (He wore strange dresses and didn't dive around like a maniac.) Every week, 'Lucky' could be relied upon to make more fumbles than Henry Blofield. To be honest, as OJ once said, he did get more than his fair share of bad bounces, skiers into the sun (not literally) and knee-cappers.

At least he was consistent. He never dealt with any of them with his palms. His shins, on the other hand, had so many bruises that they looked like a weather map forecasting torrential rain.

It has to be said that 'Lucky' was as competent as a Scottish goalkeeper. (This excludes English-Scottish ones like Bob McWilson and Neil McSullivan.) He was also injury prone. He dislocated a finger when, without thinking, he did use his hands to try to take a catch. His impersonation of a crocodile left him in tears.

Fully recovered, but not for long, a few weeks later he had a lucky escape. He was set to take a skier – that's a catch, not Jean-Claude Killy – by trapping it on his thigh but misjudged it. All four of his eyes were focused on the descending ball.

'Lucky' did a Malcolm Bryning. He nutted it. The impact snapped his specs in two and left a seam mark in the middle of his forehead. All that was missing, apart from a catch, were the words 'tear along the dotted line to open,' underneath it.

Renowned for his insensitivity and inquisitiveness, 'Nosy' Parker (who has a chatty wife, 'Noisy') immediately wanted to know, not if 'Lucky' was now blind but why he'd dropped the catch. Without considering his choice of words, 'Lucky' answered that he had no idea. White smoke could be seen coming out of a nearby chimney.

Parker got right up 'Lucky's' nose some weeks later at Kodak. (Rôle reversal.) 'Lucky' needed a pre-match tinkle and asked the skipper if he had time to go. He was told that he had but to make it snappy. He asked for directions and was informed that the loo was straight ahead. Skip added, innocently:

'You can't miss it,' to which 'Nosy' replied:

'I bet he does!'

'Lucky' was so incensed that he threatened to 'do some plastic surgery' on 'Nosy.' Consequently, 'Lucky' became 'Camel' because he got the hump when anyone alluded to the fact that he fielded like a donkey.

As well as bemoaning his misfortune, 'Lucky' also often complained about his health. This infuriated 'Nosy,' who eventually informed his ailing team-mate that he was suffering from hypochondria. 'Lucky's reaction was to say:

'Oh no! Not that as well.'

One thing 'Lucky' didn't suffered from was malaria. He'd never been able to catch it. On the ecological scale, he's sandwiched in between 'Dopey' and plankton. At the end of the 1967 season, he grabbed a list of the batting and bowling averages from my hand as I was perusing it.

'These are no good,' he exclaimed.

'Why not?' was my automatic, defensive response (which is a bit like my batting).

I fully expected 'Lucky' to indicate that no batsman averaged over nine and our chief wicket taker was 'run outs.' Instead, in all seriousness, he explained:

'It's written upside down.'

At the top end, the best fielder I ever competed against was either Steve Orrell or Andy Goram. As Steve ran me out every time he saw me, I've no hesitation in plumping for Andy. This was, of course, in his Oldham Athletic days when he was one of those.

I played against Andy in the Lancashire and Cheshire League in the 1980s and with him in the League side against the Ribblesdale League XI in 1984. He caught anything that moved. When he emigrated to Scotland, however, the deep-fried Mars Bars began to take their toll. He now caught anything so long as he didn't have to move.

I exaggerate and Andy wasn't merely a great fielder. He was a gifted cricketer and something of an icon. Most cricket buffs are aware that the last man to represent England at both football and cricket was Arthur Milton of Gloucester and Arsenal. A smaller number will know that Andy Goram is the Scottish equivalent. The chances are that Andy will remain the last dual tartan international unless Duncan Ferguson works harder on his leg breaks or Paul Dickov polishes up his ice-dance routine.

Moving on to bowling, the worst performance I've witnessed was also the shortest. While it doesn't quite rank up there with Khan Mohammad's 0 for 259 for Pakistan versus the West Indies in 1958 when Sobers made 365, it is noteworthy and possibly unique. Thornham's 'Samson' was a big, strong lad with aspirations of being a quick bowler but rarely got the chance in a game because he was erratic. (He'd have preferred to be erotic but with a face like a slapped backside, his chances were minimal.)

On the eve of a big cup game, 'Samson' made the mistake of having his hair cut. This caused him to lose much of his strength and was, ultimately responsible for ending his bowling career. His figures of 0.1 overs 0 for 8 do do him justice. With the opposition requiring seven for victory, 'Samson' was thrown the ball and told to do his worst. He took this too literally. As an 'hors d'oeuvre,' he served up four wides (which only counted as four in those days, not five). He followed this up with a juicy full toss for main course. The batsman didn't make a meal of it. He smashed it for four. This meant that there was no dessert, although 'Borussia' did call 'Samson' a pudding.

The best bowling performance may be controversial. It doesn't involve any of the big names mentioned previously. I did briefly consider the spell of Captain Nigel Knott. We faced him on an Old Qs tour to Somerset in 1965ish. Knott was then the opening bowler for the Combined Services. He was very tidy but not that quick, more of a military medium. He didn't get many wickets but he did tie down one end.

I soon dismissed this spell as infinitely inferior to the one I'm about to pontificate about. Casting modesty aside, I have no worries (well only one or two) about nominating myself for this award. I can do so because my bowling is no better than Samson's. At best, it is as accurate as the BBC's five day weather forecast and as lethal as the drink Prince Charles had when he visited the set of Coronation Street – a pint of 'alcohol-free shandy' (southern royalty for brown lemonade).

Nowadays, I'm not even allowed to bowl in the nets. My

arm is so low that it gets caught in the middle net as it swings forward from my hip. If I attempted to bowl in a game I'd concuss the smaller umpires and neuter the taller ones. My action is as dodgy as Elton John's hair (according to Boy George).

Nevertheless, I did, once, wreak havoc. It was during that London Schools versus the West Indies game. All seven bowlers I'd used were pretty shell-shocked by the time the tourists had racked up 329 for 6. Even the great John Emburey (who went on to be one of only 10 Englishmen to have achieved the 1000 run/100 wicket double in Tests at the time of writing) was getting tapped. Not wanting me to feel left out, our strike bowler, 'Arthur Scargill,' encouraged me to lead by example.

Before marking out my run up, I checked that we had a few spare balls. Above all else, I had to maintain my dignity. This wasn't easy when you are wearing a London Schools 1stXI cap. It was a red and white hooped affair with a bright red peak. (Is this where the word 'madcap' originates from?)

Back then, I did feign to bowl a form of off spin for school and club in emergencies. This was not an option. We had the best off-spinner for his age in the country and he was being spanked all over. Not being a masochist, I decided to bowl in a style rarely found in coaching manuals – widish, mediumish tripe, à la Graham Gooch.

Syd Matthews was facing. He was playing a shot a ball. I set my field with Keith Miller's words:

'OK fellas. Scatter.'

Amazingly, my first delivery met my criteria. Syd stretched for it and got a below par two runs:

'Not wide enough,' I decided.

My next attempt was even wider than the flares I wore in the 70s. Syd has long arms. He reached out as far as he could and got the toe-end of the bat on it. Since Syd is built like Lennox Lewis, this was enough to send the ball spiralling towards the boundary. Howard Masters called for the catch. Howard Masters then fell over in a heap.

'Tit,' I thought, but remembering the occasion, was set to shout:

'Tough luck, Howie. Never mind. Chin up. They'll declare when they reach 500 in 20 minutes, anyway.'

This all changed when Howard stuck out his right hand in the form of a beg, while still lying on his back. The ball nestled sweetly in his cupped palm. Syd had succumbed.

Obviously terrified by what he had just witnessed, the West Indies' captain declared on the spot at 331 for 7. Amidst bowling figures of 0 for 81, 1 for 75 and 2 for 108, Carnegie 0.2 overs 1 for 2. Read them and weep. Watch out Tich Freeman and Wilfred Rhodes. If only I'd come on earlier. If we had let all 15 of their party bat and they hadn't panicked into declaring, I was all set to do a Pat Pocock and take 7 wickets in 11 balls.

Moving on to my biggest disappointments, from a team perspective, this is the British Colleges National Knockout Cup Final of 1974 versus Bede at Durham. Bede may sound like a team of hippies but they had a strong line-up, including Gehan Mendis, who went on to play for Lancashire and Sussex. We had Mark Wallington, who went on to play for Leicester (at football). They needed 70 from the final seven overs and got them in six. We had, as they say, snatched defeat from the jaws of victory. I assume Surrey bowled equally well at the death in 1946 when India went from 205 for 9 to 454 all out.

After that, even Mark couldn't make me laugh for about a month. He didn't like losing either and later, in a rare serious moment, told me he was unable to sleep on the night of our defeat. Admittedly, this was probably due to the dreaded whirlpools. Mark asked if I'd also had trouble. I said I'd slept like a baby. He appeared surprised until I added:

'I woke up every hour, screaming.'

Our team-mate, 'Fish and chips,' is more into angling and computers than cricket so he slept like a log. He woke up in the fireplace. Such apparent indifference offended us until 'Fish' explained that it's easy to take things the wrong way:

'After all, Baden Powell's first book was called 'Scouting for boys' and Buffalo Bill hunted bison.'

When considering disappointments from a purely individual standpoint, three stick out. I still cringe at my dismissal in the London versus Middlesex u19 fixture somewhere in the south of England in 1967. We were in trouble – not, in this case, for eating our tea too slowly – when I went in. This was mainly down to a fine spell of spin bowling from a slow left-armer called either Noel or Phil Edmonds. It was only my third county game. It was a great opportunity to get noticed. Consequently, I put on my red and white hooped cap and went out to join John 'Pilau' Rice, later of Hampshire fame.

We were going along quite nicely – he scored plenty as I watched and clapped – until I lapsed. Alistair Campbell's protégé served me up an inviting full toss. My instinct was to smack it over mid-wicket for six. (I'd seen Peter Parfitt do that may times at Lords.) I got into position but then my feminine side took over. I changed my mind. That bloody voice in your head – or is that just me? – warned me:

'You can't do that. You can't play across the line. You're not playing for the Old Qs now. Purists are watching. You must play straight.'

The voice reminded me of my girlfriend so I sought to obey it automatically. I was too slow, again. By the time I'd wrestled with my (club's) bat in a vain attempt to bring it down from the horizontal to the perpendicular, I'd been stuffed like one of Nigella Lawson's artichokes. Bowled by a pie (in the sky.) I felt as humiliated as when I asked a soon not to be friend:

'Who's that old slapper over there?'

It was his mother. Oops!

My next 'downer' lasted longer then disappeared more readily. It was the Wood Cup Final of 1977, Middleton versus Werneth. These are big games in Lancashire, attracting two or three thousand spectators. As ever, the local press predicted a 'bumper crowd.' This prompted visions of spectators bombarding us with short-pitched deliveries during the warm-up. It would be a small price to pay.

This was going to be the biggest day of my sporting life. It would even surpass the day I was presented with my pre-metric ten yards swimming certificate from the 'Hampstead Schools Athletic Association' ('Swimming Branch') by Mr. Glassup in July 1961.

It would to be more thrilling than when I won the school 100 yards hurdles. I began in lane one and finished in lane six, taking down hurdles in a different lane each time yet somehow escaped disqualification. I was more excited than when I was told I'd be representing my school in the national tennis championships at Wimbledon in 1966. It turned out to be on a shale court and never mind sets or games, I only won about three points in total and two of those were from double faults.

The scene was set. It couldn't have been better. We were at home. The weather was glorious. For once, the opposition didn't have a crazed, head-hunting fast bowler as their professional. Werneth's paid man was an English seamer, John Helmstalk. He was a real handful on soft wickets but this pitch was a belter. He'd be as effective as a eunuch in a harem. It would be a run fest.

A couple of close mates from Evershed had made the 450 mile round trip to lend support. My wife, parents-in-law, other friends, neighbours, colleagues and pupils from school would all be there. Three or four (well-paid) pupils had even made banners extolling fictional virtues.

All I now needed was for us to win the toss and get first use of this perfect strip. We did. I was at number four on the scorecard. This was confirmed by our captain, 'Basil.' The whole place was buzzing. (Northern for really good.) If I could get 50, the collection would amount to a bit more than half a crown from 'Neddy' this time.

Being innumerate, I lost count of the number of people who wished me good luck (unlike Geoffrey, I needed it) beforehand. I was as excited as Cameron Diaz's husband on a promise. (Herein, I'm on a par with mosquitoes.They also prefer biting blondes.) I padded up (two pads) and sat outside to get used to the light, a tip I'd heard on t.v.

If all went well, we'd get a good start and I'd go in as their 'step and fetch' bowlers came on. Our openers put on 80 in reasonable time. I was getting a bit stiff – sitting around plus a touch of fantasising made that inevitable – but I was feeling happy.

Then a wicket fell and 'Happy' had to go in to bat. One more wicket and it would be my turn. I'd be positive and pre-empt Steve Wundke. (50 off 12 balls for Stockport against Rochdale in 1990.)

Another long partnership ensued. 'Basil' came over. I thought he was either going to give me some penicillin for my dose of pad rash or ask me if I liked his latest hairstyle. I was wrong on both counts. (Innumeracy once more.)

'Jim,' he whispered menacingly, 'the overs are running out. Drop down to five. I'm putting 'Slogger' in for a slog.'

At first, I thought he'd said 'snog.'

'That's a bit cheap,' I said to myself, knowing no one else would listen. 'If you kiss the skipper, he'll put you up the order.'

I was adamant I wouldn't swap spit with him, not even for such a prize. It was a matter of principle and, anyway, 'Basil' had a cold sore.

I was disappointed to be demoted even though it made sense. My chance would come soon enough. It appeared to have done when 'Slogger' soon mis-slogged. I jumped to my feet as if the Queen had just arrived. I imagined where I was going to place the first delivery to get off the mark, happy in the knowledge that Steve Orrell wasn't fielding.

Before I could re-adjust my box on the way down the steps, as you do, 'Basil' was at it again:

'Hang on, Jim. Change of plan. 'Basher's going in for a bash.'

I could just about see where he was coming from but, still on the snogging theme, couldn't help thinking:

'Kiss my arse, 'Basil'.'

This incisive tactical move also failed. With time running out, my game plan altered to one of getting bat on ball and pushing ones to give 'Bambi', our youngest player, the lion's share of the strike. There did prove to be one obstacle, 'Whacker.'

'Basil' sidled up to me, gave me a mint and announced that he was sending him in before me for a 'quick whack.' It was an After Eight mint.

When he failed, other agriculturists such as 'Mower' and 'Scyther' were given a go. Even 'Banger' was set to precede me. I now found myself at number 11. I'd had my pads on for the whole of the bleeding innings. We finished on eight down so I didn't even get to walk out to the middle. I know it's essentially a team game but I was devastated. I felt even more upset than when I buried our hibernating tortoise, believing it to be dead.

At tea, I couldn't eat. (It was rubbish.) I tossed my salad (out of the window) and contemplated becoming a slogger. I gave my swiss roll to 'Banger' before he took it from me. I'd collected eight match programmes to keep as souvenirs (in case I lost seven) but tore them up. (In 'Franglais,' this constituted 'shredded huit'.) I'd have been even more reckless but had to prevent my father-in-law from throttling 'Basil.' It's only a game.

In the field, my bottom lip dropped further when I spilled a catch. Then we won the game thanks to some superb bowling from our senior pro 'Methusela.' I lightened up (no tea) and helped 'Bambi' spend his collection. I told 'my supporters' I had a slight injury which I'd aggravated while knocking up and had requested to go in last. I think the 'special needs' kids believed me.

My third individual letdown was that I missed playing against my all-time hero, Garfield Sobers, by just one season. Many enthusiasts consider Viv Richards to be the greatest ever West Indian batsman yet Sobers made two more Test tons in 28 less innings. I first played in the CLL in 1976. Sobers' last season there was in 1975. It would have been a dream come true, especially if he'd nipped one back into 'Basil's' knackers.

Alternatively, the biggest team high was reaching the semi-final of the London Senior Schools Cup sponsored by the Cricketer magazine in 1968 with a team of no-hopers. We were only accepted into this elitist competition because our master-in-charge, the incomparably fantastic Mr. Cordiner, was on every schools sports committee imaginable. We were more out of place than Ian Salisbury standing next to Shane Warne, Rochdale College on University Challenge or the old boy I was sitting next at the Manchester Eye Hospital. He missed his turn and offered this excuse to the nurse:

'I didn't hear you call my name. I'm deaf.'

Our team consisted of representatives from such cricketing hot-spots as Poland, Spain, Madagascar and Bedfordshire. Only three of us played club cricket and that was for the Old Qs. I had to bully a few hockey players into making up the numbers. Unbelievably, we kept knocking out vastly superior teams. Hardly any of us could play but we did look the part. You can fool some of the people some of the time, as Nasser did a few years after. He was considered to be the best young leg spinner in England in 1983.

Our opening bowler, 'Sitting Bull' was no cowboy, however. He claimed a succession of notable scalps, inspired by the support of his timid girlfriend, 'Shy Ann.' It soon became apparent that he was a potential match winner. As I said to our keeper, Maurice:

'Mo, he can bowl. I bet we'll soon have scouts here looking out for him.' (This didn't happen, although I did notice several girl guides with his sister, Sue, at the quarter-final.)

Modelling himself on Northamptonshire's George Tribe, 'Sitting Bull's' brave efforts were backed, fronted and sided up by some largely unorthodox, yet highly effective fielding. All parts of the anatomy were used to form the 'long barrier.'

The team's batting philosophy was basic. We eliminated all frills. Tip and run or swing and hope were our main weapons. It upset a few game plans. Opposing captains were incapable of setting fields as the ball was sliced to all parts.

Like Martin Peters, we were 10 years ahead of our time. If we'd reached the final, Lords would not have known what to make of us. Every win was a bonus but, just as I nearly did on School Sports Day, we fell at the last hurdle.

William Ellis had a proper team. No hockey or rounders players, nobody from mainland Europe or tiny exotic islands. They weren't conned by our clean look or our green and red caps. Even with 'Sitting Bull' on the warpath, they scored too many for us. Tip and swing as we did, as the peseta always seemed to, we fell short of the mark. The Long Room was safe. We wouldn't be taking the short trip on the 159 to HQ. We'd ruffled a few feathers on the way. Mr. Cordiner was proud of us. We played throughout the competition with smiles on our faces despite the bruises and brought a new meaning to the term:

'That just isn't cricket.'

Cricketers' most nerve-wracking moments usually involve debuts or finals. Looking beyond that, my most apprehensive cricket-related experience lasted a lot longer than a few moments. It came after, not during, a game.

It was 1972. I'd travelled up from London to Birmingham with Evershed to face a strong Britannic Assurance side. The game itself didn't cause me any palpitations but it did contain a 'champagne,' or more precisely, 'several beer moments.' These involved 'Lloyd,' a banker. 'Lloyd' was the 3rdXI vice-captain and doubled as the Os Clark of beer. 'Five-a-day' had nothing to do with apples, oranges or sprouts for him.

'Lloyd' wanted to visit the Midlands to sample the local ale. He is living proof as to why some beers are called 'stout.' A late cry-off resulted in 'Lloyd's' intended session being punctured by having to play cricket as well. One would imagine that this might have had an adverse affect on his personal crusade to increase the national hourly consumption rate from 58,000 litres up to a more rounded – as he is – 1000 per minute. It didn't.

When we arrived at the ground, 'Lloyd' was informed he'd be opening the batting with me. Either to make up for lost time or to calm his nerves, he quaffed a pint before getting changed. As soon as he discovered that the opposition's opening bowler was a regular for Warwickshire's 2ndXI, he needed a second and a third. I then let it slip that the other opener was actually the better of the two. He supped two more pints.

Apart from drinking before a game for most of us being as taboo as admitting to liking Bananarama, what was most noteworthy was that the beer tasted like bizz. It did look cold and frothy. This was because it was a cross between washing-up liquid and anti-freeze. To down over half a gallon of the stuff in 40 minutes without hurling was nearly as impressive as the great FR Spofforth's achievement in 1881. The Australian fast bowler rode 400 miles to play in a 'minor' match. He took all 20 wickets, all clean bowled, and then failed a breathaliser test on his way home. (It's that one out of two again.)

Perhaps I shouldn't have been surprised. 'Lloyd's' previous claim to fame was that on a club tour three years earlier – and way before Tommy Cooper thought of it – he shocked the civilized world by pouring a bottle of Guinness on his Cornflakes at breakfast. He'd obviously gone for the 'full Irish.' His party piece was to down a yard of ale in less time than it took umpire 'Sam' to decide it was raining and say:

'Fill her up,' and go again.

So it was with some apprehension that I walked out to the middle with a partner who was more well-oiled than his bat. My first concern was whether or not he'd be able to walk in a straight line. Would he be 'a little bit all over the place?' a phrase coined to describe the AC Milan defence by Andy Townsend when they were under pressure against Liverpool in May 2005.

My second dilemma was could I distinguish between a Garneresque slurred yes, no and wait. My third, major, worry was that 'Lloyd' might get injured. If he saw three balls coming at him, would he know which two were imposters? Would he care?

I needn't have worried. We made it to the wicket like synchronised swimmers. He didn't call at any stage of his innings. He found his own way of not getting hurt. (Giant pads.) He also clouted the first ball he received straight back over the bowler's head for four. This proved to be his zenith. I said:

'Great shot, 'Lloyd'.'

'Lloyd' said:

'I shouldn't have done that. He'll be angry and bowl even faster. I need a drink.'

He was physically shaking but I didn't know if it was fear or the 'DTs.' As the bowler ran in again, 'Lloyd' opted for the safety of square leg. We were in Birmingham but his backside (considerable as it was) had almost been sent to Coventry. I certainly wasn't going to talk to it.

Mercifully, 'Lloyd' was caught at third man. He then proceeded to drown enough sorrows for both teams but still managed to take the field after tea. Needless to say, he came back for more after the game. I can still picture him propping up the bar in his favourite tee-shirt which had 'beer is food' printed on it. He didn't go hungry.

'Lloyd' sometimes drank in another tee-shirt which also appealed to me, though not as loudly as the umpire from Bingley College. This one warned that 'floggings will continue until morale improves.'

We socialised in the bar afterwards. No one was as sociable as 'Lloyd' but we tried hard enough for me to miss the last tube home. I'd been dropped off at Hammersmith (or was it Leatherdale?) station too late for the last train or bus. A taxi, even the chocolate biscuit, was too expensive. I could have taken a leaf out of 'KP's' book, but he was nuts. He knew the tube timetable off by heart. If he'd just missed a train, he set off walking down the thin ledges alongside the tracks to his destination. That was as attractive as thumbing a lift, which was tantamount to volunteering to be a suicide bomber. All I could do, since we were a car-less family, which explains why some friends call me 'Negie,' was to walk the 10 miles home.

It was already midnight. It would be a two and a half hour walk. I tried to ignore the fact that someone in Britain is mugged every 90 seconds, making it possible for me to be set upon exactly 100 times. My chances of getting home unscathed were on a par with Custer's at Little Big Horn or Bangladesh's of scoring quickly against England at Durham in May 2005 with Michael Atherton and Geoffrey Boycott commentating in tandem.

I set off as happy as if I was about to have a Brazilian wax performed by Stevie Wonder with a heavy cold. I could think only of Oates's words on Scott's fateful expedition to the Arctic:

'It's bloody cold for August!'

I was grateful that coffins for carrying gear had yet to be invented but fearful I might end up in one. By the time I'd reached Shepherd's Bush, which is far less attractive than Kate and put me in mind of that Brazilian wax again, it was late enough for all respectable people to be indoors. This was mildly reassuring. I had no cause to be judgmental. I could mistrust everyone I saw.

I'd safely cleared the threat of Hammersmith and was thankful I didn't have to encounter Gerard's Cross, in case he was. Even so, I remained as apprehensive as Mrs. Parkin used to be every time her husband told her he fancied a bowl. Cec Parkin, as you will soon discover, was no fan of Johnny Douglas, the England captain and none too bothered about equal rights for women either. Although he was born 20 yards outside the county boundary, Cec did buck the trend and played one game for Yorkshire around the time electricity had filtered up beyond Bedfordshire. This followed spells in the Yorkshire League and the Central Lancashire League with Rochdale.

Parkin couldn't have had any mates because he perfected his offers and leggers on his wife. He constantly used her as a dummy batswoman and often reduced her to tears due to her getting bruised fingers. If he'd got one to bounce and hit her on the temple, it could have been a case of No Parkin, without the need for double yellow lines.

Shepherd's Bush threw up a few drunks, and vice versa. They were no problem; they kept falling over in the style of a Portuguese winger. This meant there was no beating about the bush this time. I continued to take the corners wide as I approached Westbourne Park. I resisted indulging in my perennial habit of playing mock straight drives in case it was misinterpreted as being something more effeminate.

I must have looked in need of sustenance because one kind chap threw me a carton of curry and rice whilst his mate chucked me a bottle of something to wash it down (or off). I've never walked so quickly in my life. It must have been the equivalent of writing about 60 letters. In what felt like only a matter of weeks, I eventually made it to my estate (council, not country) without hitting anyone's fist with my face.

Paddington had provided two scary moments. I noticed a woman walking around with no shoes on. I was worried it might be Sandie Shaw. Worried, in case she begun singing 'Puppet on a String.' It wasn't, so there was no need to fret about being approached by someone with a criminal record this time.

I must confess to being more concerned when I passed a big house with an outdoor swimming pool. I had visions of a game-show host of dubious sexuality inviting me to drown my sorrows. My 10 yards swimming certificate would have counted for nothing.

Once I'd passed the 'Bird in the Hand' I'd be safe, so long as there weren't two in the bush. As I got to within vomiting distance, a huge drunken Irishman surrounded me. Did he want me to partner him in the River Dance? He didn't but I would have flatly refused anyway.

He was a financial advisor. He advised me to give him a quid for a cup of tea. I wanted to ask him to show me the tea first so I could ascertain whether or not it was a good swap. I didn't. I panicked. Flustered (southern for blobbing it), I answered:

'That's funny. I was going to ask you the same thing.'

To the relief of my underpants, 'O'Goliath' was in no state for bartering or battering. He was completely nonplussed. (French for useless at adding up.) He uttered a bemused 'oh,' and zigzagged off in several directions, in a bit of a paddy. He must have been as confused as Princess Ann was at the 2008 Olympics when she watched badminton with two blokes whacking a dead budgie over a net without any trace of showjumping.

Against all the odds, I had arrived home unsoiled and unjumped. I even saw two friendly faces, or rather backsides, before I locked myself in my bedroom for the remainder of the morning. Jack Noon and his 'squeeze' Jean Light were performing oral gymnastics near the dustbins. I greeted them both in the customary manner:

'Hi, Jack, hi, Jean.'

Coincidentally, this works just as badly with their surnames.

On a more positive note, my nod for the most satisfying change for the better goes to the significantly higher scoring rates in Test Matches since the turn of the century. Gone seem to be the days when an off-spinner can take 8 for 38 from 53 overs, as Lance Gibbs did against India in 1962. (Why wasn't Lancelot knighted for that?) Thank goodness figures of 116 overs 78 maidens 127 runs 7 wickets achieved at Lords in 1950 by Alf Valentine are a thing of the past. (Or am I romancing?)

Nowadays, there's less chance of falling asleep in front of the television set (I do, but put that down to hormones), being bored to death by the likes of Mudussar, Boycott, Bailey Tavaré and Ramesh.(He plundered 126 in a mere 10 hours 26 minutes at Chennai in 2002.) As an added bonus, if you tune to Radio 4, with so much more happening, there's less opportunity for 'Bloers' to babble inanely on about insignificant rubbish and more likelihood of him getting the score muddled. He may call Graeme Thorpe, Jeremy or mistake Gus Logie for Joel Garner. Just like Australian table tennis player, Miao Miao, Henry is in the wrong job. She should be a model, ie on the cat walk. Henry should be pumping up hot air balloons. That said, he is prophetic. When reflecting on the length of the stand between De Villiers and Prince at Edgbaston in 2008, he called it 'a lot of balls' and immediately went on to prove it. 'The dear old thing' turned a South African wicket keeper into an English batsman by having Anderson coming in to bowl at Mark Butcher. He then had the keeper keeping and batting simultaneously with:

'Broad bowls and it's well taken by Boucher,' having

already called Flintoff, Botham and then giving a Test debut to Arnie 'Sidefoot.'

Welcome as the trend for quicker runs is, it could have been even more exciting if my award for the greatest player of all-time, Don Bradman, was playing now. To go past 200 three or four times in a career, as Boycott and Atherton did, is a decent effort. Sir Donald did so 43 times. Compton can be justifiably proud of being the second quickest man to reach 100 hundreds. It took him just 552 innings. It took Bradman a mere 295. (A hundred in every 2.89 innings cf Viv Richards 6.75 and 'Hard Nut' 1752.00.)

This genius is also at the hub of my favourite tale. Bill Tallon, the less famous brother of Aussie keeper Don, was having a good start for New South Wales against South Australia before even 'Pagey' was born. A perfect outswinger accounted for the opener. 1 for 0. (The Aussies are backward and put wickets before runs). Enter number three. Another jaffa and he's caught behind. 2 for 0. Cue Bradman. Tallon bowls another beauty. Bradman is also caught behind. 3 for 320.

Returning to changes for the better, I'm opting for ready to use bats. We've come a long way since the days of my size six Gradidge. If the ball didn't hit its middle, it sent a shudder right through you, shaking out your fillings and shifting the wax from your ears. It also gave me splinters every time I used it. Happily, I don't get any these days...touch wood.

The current crop of bats, which don't require oiling, can save you a fortune. Well, they can if you're as clumsy as I am. I was illicitly putting linseed oil on a new bat indoors, as opposed to in the garden, as ordered. I inadvertently – I was unguarded – knocked the bottle over our new beige carpet. Unlike the 0898 phone calls to the weather centre, I couldn't blame my son because he was out shopping with my wife.

(Somebody has to do it.) Nor could I blame any pets. We only had goldfish. I did think about it, though:

'It was amazing. It leapt out of the pond with such force that it knocked the bottle out of my hand all the way to the lounge. I didn't know we had any flying fish.'

Instead, I came clean. It's a pity the carpet didn't. I used enough '1001' to add up to a million as well as sufficient elbow grease to give me a severe case of 'scrubber's elbow' before the rest of the carpet became sufficiently dirty for the stain to blend in.

These new blades also eliminate the need to spend a life sentence smacking them with an old cricket ball (or match ball as we called it at the Old Qs) pushed into a sock until dizziness and cramp ensue. That could be put forward as an alternative to Borstal.

Changes for the worse are, for an old dog, easier to come up with. Cricketers playing in sunglasses, how poncey is that? Save them for the beach. Roy Orbison would turn in his grave. We constantly moan about playing in bad weather in the north or not playing in nearly bad weather in the south, yet when it's sunny these 'cool dudes' want to hide from it.

Shades are nearly as bad as those softies who wear padding on their padding. They look more like Michelin men than batsmen. You wouldn't have seen Middlesex and Kent big-hitter, Charles Thornton (he once lost seven balls in an innings) with any body-armour. In fact, he never used to wear pads and seldom wore gloves (cf French footballers).

Then there's this sliding about in the field. It's unnecessary. Leave that for baseball. What's wrong with keeping your whites clean for the following day by staying upright as God intended and sticking out a trusty size 10 every now and again? 'Daz,' an amateur and paid man for Thornham, who had a 'mental health' problem, was of this persuasion. He remained whiter than white from ball one to ball 300 every week.

Club cricket used to be so serene. Then Ian Chappell came along. It has become what Maurice Wickens would term 'clamorous.':

'Come on boys, make some noise. I can't hear you. It's too quiet.'

No, it isn't. We're not at Anfield.

Such absurd comments as:

'Work hard, lads,' should result in five runs being awarded to the other team.

Work hard? How? Do press-ups between deliveries? Paint the boundary boards at the fall of each wicket? It's play, not work. Enjoy yourselves.

'Encourage the bowler.'

What should we say?

'Nice long-hop, Francis. Don't worry. We'll use the spare ball.'

As for the most volatile match I've ever played in, there's no contest. In Lancashire, there is an annual inter-league cup competition 'fought out' by eight of the county's top leagues. In 1985, we reached the final, as did the Saddleworth League. We'd been told to expect a fiery encounter. Anything goes over there.

Most of their grounds are near the Yorkshire Moors. It's rumoured that too much inter-breeding goes on and there are plenty of worried-looking sheep and 'high sixes.' (One extra finger.)

We batted first. Every ball was preceded by advice from fielders. Their dwarf-like wicket-keeper seemed keen for each of us to get back to the warmth of the pavilion as soon as possible. He even tried to put us at ease by singing just as the bowler was running up.

First slip really shouldn't have been playing. He had an awful cough which only subsided in between overs. But he can't have been in as much discomfort as square leg. He groaned constantly. He must have also been very frustrated. He kept calling for sexual favours which brought no takers.

Saddleworth's captain, 'Schizo,' was forever in two minds, which he changed at the last moment, usually in the middle of the bowler's run up. It was uncanny how often he had to surreptitiously remind fielders where they should be fielding. To his credit, he did move them without the batsmen noticing so we wouldn't be put off.

Short leg, the ugly one, 'Hapsburg,' was blessed with receding chin and forehead. He was the strong, silent type but had no manners. He stared at the batsmen throughout and grunted intermittently. His wife/cousin would not have approved.

Extra cover was the exception. He seemed to want us to win. After each shot, he proffered advice, coaxing us to analyse our faults:

'What the f**k was that?'

He was even thoughtful enough to provide us with alternatives for the future:

'You'd be better of playing bleedin' badminton.' (Not a form of the game I'm familiar with.)

Surprisingly, they seemed unsure of certain rules. Several were convinced that you could be given out leg before if you hit the ball or adjudged caught behind if you didn't. Short leg got really confused. He believed you could be caught even if the ball had rolled after being hit. Their wicket keeper had a nervous habit of flicking off the bails just prior to catching the ball and was adamant this should go down as clean bowled. It was the Bradford League revisited.

Then, after tea, the whole atmosphere altered. They were now all decidedly taciturn, yet still misguided. Their captain must have been present at the Rochdale versus Middleton game when Hartley Alleyne didn't know if he was coming or going. He was clean bowled and reacted by picking up the bails, replacing them on the stumps and retaking his stance. We almost had to get a JCB to remove him, or a JVC as 'Acronym' called it.

There was one incident after tea which reminded me of the tea – it was unsavoury. Saddleworth's number 10, 'Colditz' (initials POW) was in such a hurry to leave he must have had a train to catch. Near the end of the skirmish, he was run out by a distance. The bowler, 'Tim,' had a reputation for always knowing precisely what the time was. On this occasion, it was time to get out of the way. The batsman's breaks failed. He deliberately ran right into 'Tim,' who fortunately isn't tiny. Pleasantries were exchanged before 'Tim' got to his feet and brandished an imaginary red card.

The opposition's erstwhile affable keeper then imitated our female middle distance runners. He came in last. He was now more like a noise abatement officer. The slightest murmur offended him and he certainly didn't have a train to catch judging by his comment:

'I can wait all night.'

He didn't have to. He hit one to short leg which didn't bounce and the title was ours. (I think it was recognised by all of the boxing boards of control.)

The shenanigans didn't end there. Our opening bowler, big Dave, had endured an inordinate amount of stick from Saddleworth's diminutive, periphrastic stumper throughout the day. I should point out that 'big' Dave is really a misnomer. He is really, 'enormous' Dave. He is the archetypal gentle giant but his patience had been severely tested by a man 18 inches shorter than him. Despite endless provocation, Dave had kept his cool. Until now.

We were celebrating in the bar. They were moaning about anything and everything. They were unlucky. The umpires were bent. (They did booth stoop a bit, but no more than that.) They'd hammer us next time. ('Tim' said he thought they had this time.) In the midst of all this, I spotted Dave following his tormentor-in-chief to the toilet. I sensed a scene so I brought up the rear. With strides twice as large as his number one fan, Dave soon caught him up. Dave picked him up by his shirtfront. He effortlessly lifted him up high enough off the ground so they were face to face. Politely, albeit with a 'soupçon' of menace, he enquired:

'Have you got anything else to say to me, Brigitte?'

Possibly feeling similar to Radio Caroline in 1980 when it sank, 'Brigitte' struggled for breath. All he could do was shake his head. Dave let go. Action had spoken louder than words and I'd just witnessed our very own Action Man in action.

The evening ended in high drama with a fire in the tea room. Joy wasn't on teas but we were all asked to 'ejaculate the building without delay,' presumably because there was insufficient water to extinguish the blaze.

Man of the Match awards can be straightforward or random. I expect 'the Demon' Spofforth fancied his chances when he took 6 for 4 in the first innings of Australia's very first game at Lord's against MCC.

'Top that,' he may have said to his fellow opening bowler, Boyle.

'If you insist,' Boyle may have thought, as he took 6 for 3 in the scond innings.

My choice for the most mystifying adjudication isn't

contentious. When Lancashire won the Gillette Cup some time back in the last century, their captain, John Abrahams got the nod. Why? Did he take five for? No, he didn't bowl. Did he take six stunning catches? No, none. Did he score a ton or steer his side home with some lusty hitting under pressure at the death? No, he was out for a duck. Was his dad, Cec, the adjudicator? No. It can, therefore, only be because John is a really nice bloke.

Australia's Ken Mackay may, or may not have been, but I doubt if anyone would have begrudged him the award in 1939. He scored 367 not out for Virginia High School and then weighed in with 10 for 53:

'Let's think about this. Shall we give it to Ken or to that lad who almost caught him three days ago?'

I'll conclude my 'Oscars' by nominating the best and worst captains I've played under. From my first meaningful school game, ie post St. Mary's, to the present day, I've been subjected to 30-odd captains, spanning six decades. A few have been just that. Some have been unremarkable, others inspirational. I've noticed that the best skippers tend not to be the best players, and vice versa. Indeed, the two worst, one southern and one northern, were top performers with the bat but couldn't organise an orgy in a brothel.

Anomalous they were and anonymous they shall remain. Their principal fault was that they only saw things from a personal perspective. I'll call the northerner 'Alter Ego,' not for being a regular churchgoer but because he was his own best friend. He had eight of us padded up simultaneously at Radcliffe because he couldn't decide which number to bat himself. During his one, long season in charge – he had as much chance of being re-appointed as Mike Gatting had with that Shane Warne delivery – he would bat anywhere from three to eight, depending on the quality of the bowling. Not exactly leading from the front, the weaker the attack the higher he'd bat. (There's no 'i' in team but there is an 'm' and an 'e'.)

At Stockport, he surprised us all. Without warning for either the bowler or the bloke who thought he would be bowling, he threw the ball to 'Hush' (initials RIP) at the start of their innings. He said:

'Here, 'Hush.' Keep them quiet by pulling a few strings with the new ball.'

Unprepared and not having bowled all season, the only strings 'Hush' pulled were of the ham variety.

Similarly, a fortnight later he gave me fully five minutes notice that I'd be opening – I'd been at four for the previous 20 games – against Franklyn Stephenson. His instructions were succinct:

'Go out there and tame him.'

I might have done if I'd had enough time to find a chair and a whip. He was equally self-obsessed when we were in the field, having more in common with Johnny Douglas than Mike Brearley. The latter could be said to have under-bowled himself. In the whole of 1976, nobody was able to score a run off him. (1.1.0.0.) Johnny was a touch more selfish and oblivious to the tap he was getting from the Aussies in the 20s. He kept himself on for so long that a colleague felt moved to advise him to change ends so that he could see his figures more clearly on the giant scoreboard. Not one to heed advice or be put off by being as effective as Ian Salisbury (Test bowling average 76.0), Douglas later received a further reminder from colleague, Cec Parkin:

'Here's McCartney coming in to bat, Sir. You go on for an hour and bowl him in, then I'll come on and bowl him out.'

The southerner sharing this dubious honour is 'Moody Blue.' He didn't play in the varsity match but most of us wished he would 'Go now.' No one knew what to expect from game to game. He could be pleasant, exuberant and logical for a week or two. Then, just as we'd been lulled into believing he wasn't a total arse, he'd prove he was.

'Moody' could sulk as well as any teenage girl who has been grounded at the wrong time of the month. He really had it on him at Teddington some decades ago. His wife, 'Carol', a singer, must have upset him since he certainly wasn't on-song that day. Out of the blue, he decided to base the batting order on arrival at the changing room, but hadn't told anyone beforehand. It wasn't as if anyone was late. The last to arrive, 'Nick,' crossed the threshold just in time to avoid the statutory fine but found himself batting at 11 rather than his usual number three spot.

Crazy as this was, this idea may have been adopted by South Africa in 1924 against England. It would explain why they were dismissed for 30 in their first innings, with the 11 extras as top scorer.

If things didn't go according to plan, 'Moody' would post himself at mid-off, arms folded in the style of a teapot with an expression similar to that of a five year-old who has had his or her jelly babies pinched. As a batsman, 'Moody' was up there with the best around. As a captain, he was down there with the skipper of the Titanic and the Mary Rose. When he sulked, he was the 'spitting' image of El-Hadj Diouf.

Moving upwards, my southern selection for top man is 'Warren.' (He keeps rabbits.) He had more enthusiasm than Richie Benaud and it was infectious. On the field, he always encouraged everyone, praising us when we deserved it and issuing constructive criticism for the other 98% of the time. He smiled a lot so it could never be said of him that he was not a happy bunny.

Off the field, he continued to lead by example. As a pioneer, he could usually be relied upon to make an admirable attempt to implement the notion of 24 hour drinking long before the government thought of it. His maxim was simple:

'So much beer and so little time.'

He slurred a lot and was an early victim of the Breathalyser in 1967.

His northern counterpart is 'JP'. 'JP' is a fair-minded man and he, too, plays with a smile on his face. He commands respect by being objective rather than objectionable and by buying a round to celebrate victories. After all, it's attention to detail which separates the men from the boys.

Another factor in JP's success is that he is not a selfish cricketer. He would have been appalled by what WG Grace got up to before he starred in 'Are you being served.' Upon mis-hitting a shot, the ZZ Top look-alike was dismayed to see the ball fly high but not very far. The self, rather than soft, centred doctor hastily declared the innings closed before any chance of a catch took place.

Imagine if that was still possible nowadays:

'Don't bother consulting the third umpire, Shep. (Fancy having a dog as an umpire.) Innings closed. I'll take the red-inker.

'JP' can also go one better than most English slow bowlers; he can put a positive spin on things. Upon his return from down under in 2007, he was inventive enough to give our lads some credit for the whitewash. Citing the fact that 23% of Australia's population is foreign, it goes without saying that the majority of that number is of British stock. Therefore, whatever 12 the Aussies select, three are down to us.

My final award is, for me, the most significant of all. It goes to my father. Not an avid cricket follower himself, he nonetheless introduced me to the game by taking me to Lords to watch Middlesex in 1956. Denis Compton was playing and

Dad was sufficiently clued-up to know that Compton's batting was infinitely superior to his calling. He told me that Denis had even run out his brother, Leslie, in Leslie's benefit match. He explained that Denis was so bad at judging a run he often added 'good luck' after calling 'yes.' Take note, 'Mystic' Greg.

He also ensured I never got too big for my boots/plimsoles/pumps. When I boasted I'd hit a six, he asked how far the ball had travelled. Clueless, I tried to impress by saying it must have been a good 50 yards. He kept my footwear firmly on the ground by saying that William Ford hit one 143 yards in 1890 something. (Like me, he is as dateless as Ian Ward, who described the 2007 Friends Provident semi-final as 'a repeat of the 2005 final back in 2005.')

From that day on, I was hooked and have been ever since. All of the happy times I've had, all of the friends I've made through cricket are ultimately down to my old man. Cheers, Dad. Thank goodness we didn't live near Richmond Ice Rink, Mount Eiger or Middleton Gymnastics Club.

Food for thought:

41. Who is the better looking: Chanderpaul, Prettipaul or 'Model' of Denton?

42. Is anyone surprised that Saffron Walden's captain in the 2002 National Club Final, S.Plumb was out lbw? Was the umpire D.Trigger of Kent?

43. Was Peter Sleep a walker? (That's rhetorical. He's Australian.) Was Glamorgan's Peter Walker a sleeper?

44. Were Arthur Alloo (New Zealand) and his two brothers in the police force?

45. Could Yorkshire's Geoff Cope?